Legal Issues in Information Technology

Thomson Reuters (Professional) Australia Limited
19 Harris Street Pyrmont NSW 2009
care.ANZ@thomsonreuters.com
http://legal.thomsonreuters.com.au/
For all customer inquiries please ring 1300 304 195
(for calls within Australia only)

INTERNATIONAL AGENTS & DISTRIBUTORS

NORTH AMERICA
Thomson Reuters
Eagan
United States of America

ASIA PACIFIC
Thomson Reuters
Sydney
Australia

LATIN AMERICA
Thomson Reuters
São Paulo
Brazil

EUROPE
Thomson Reuters
London
United Kingdom

Legal Issues in Information Technology

MARK PERRY
Professor of Law
School of Law, University of New England

ALPANA ROY
Dean of Law
Te Piringa Faculty of Law, University of Waikato

MELISSA DE ZWART
Professor (Digital Technology, Security & Governance)
Jeff Bleich Centre for
the US Alliance in Digital Technology, Security &
Governance, Flinders
University

MICHAEL ADAMS
Head of School
School of Law, University of New England

NILOUFER SELVADURAI
Program Director
Legal and Ethics of Cyber, Optus Macquarie Cyber Security
Hub, Macquarie University

HEATHER FORREST
Associate Professor
School of Law, University of Tasmania

MONIQUE CORMIER
Senior Lecturer
School of Law, University of New England

SIMON MCKENZIE
Research Fellow
TC Beirne School of Law,
University of Queensland

LAWBOOK CO. 2022

Published in Sydney by
Thomson Reuters (Professional) Australia Limited ABN 64 058 914 668
19 Harris Street, Pyrmont, NSW 2009

ISBN: 9780455245140

NATIONAL LIBRARY OF AUSTRALIA

A catalogue record for this book is available from the National Library of Australia

Product Developer: Stephen Rennie

Edited and typeset by Newgen KnowledgeWorks

Printed by Ligare Pty Ltd, Riverwood, NSW

PEFC™
PEFC/21-31-17

The book has been printed on paper certified by the Programme for the Endorsement of Forest Certification (PEFC). PEFC is committed to sustainable forest management through third party forest certification of responsibly managed forests.

for Melanie and William

Preface

This book is a collection of essays designed to provoke both thought and discussion. It is aimed at reaching those interested in how governments, corporations and civil society are managing the regulation of data in a technology-based society. This probably means every thinking person, as who could not be interested in how our information- and technology-focused society is developing? And data regulation has become even more prominent over the last two years as the world deals with pandemic conditions, with a need for disseminating the means of disease control. Readers who have looked at a cell phone or computer in the last year should be aware of the developing issues that are driving intervention in the acquisition or provision of information. The editor asks readers to contemplate this work as a whole, and to see how the authors spotlight key issues in the heterogeneous mixture of areas that are linked by their operation within a framework built on information technology.

It should be noted that this is a group of essays that have been written by internationally acknowledged leaders in their fields. They include: Professor Michael Adams, a specialist in corporate law, governance and e-learning; Dr Monique Cormier, with a broad experience in international criminal law including work at the International Criminal Court UN Liaison Office; Associate Professor Heather Forrest, President of Intellectual Property Interests Constituency of the Generic Names Supporting Organisation of ICANN; Professor Alpana Roy, whose research focuses around international intellectual property rights in the online realm; Professor Niloufer Selvadurai, Program Director, Legal and Ethics of Cyber, Optus Macquarie Cyber Security Hub at Macquarie University; and Professor Melissa de Zwart, Professor of Digital Technology, Security and Governance, at the Jeff Bleich Centre for the US Alliance in Digital Technology, Security and Governance. This influential group of authors not only includes six current or former deans and associate deans of law, but most importantly scholars with an informed passion for their subject matter. Most are located in Australia, but all have a great level of international experience – key as the context of this book, the issues raised and the solutions considered, are all of a global nature.

Readers will be well-aware of the daily challenges to living in the second decade of the 21st century. We have faced daily requirements that would have been unthought of just a few years ago: having to share your location with the New South Wales government when buying a piece of cheese, a move to permanent hybrid working models, pressure to have vaccinations, school and higher education learning at home, and, for many, the inability to see loved ones for years except in a video frame. Some would say that the technology that we have been pursuing and developing over the last 50 years to enable the easier sharing of information has become a burden, with constant intrusions into our physical lives. Of course, the design parameters for information technology systems did not usually include the inclusion of social impact considerations at the outset, and there has been a drift from tool purpose to types of uncontemplated tool use.

Any work at any time requires the support of unsung heroes, without whom no projects would ever be completed. The past two years has seen global upheaval with an emerging recognition of the effects of climate on the planet through direct experience of disaster, increasing intrusion into the personal lives of citizens through technology deployed by the state, and an ever-increasing feeling of despair for the future among many. Universities across Australia have not been immune. Indeed, they have been given more to do with less resources. Where I sit, in regional Australia, there have been particular challenges: drought, firestorms, flooding, pestilence and minimal services. Individuals give support directly to a project, obviously colleagues and the management of the university, or loved ones who provide succour, whether at home or from a distance, and those that continue to provide essential services in health, food supply and other amenities are all part of the story. Thomson Reuters have played their part, especially Stephen Rennie, not least in understanding the cracked lives that we now live. My research assistant, Cristina Avallone, was great help. My family not only put up with the malaises common to all editors, but actively encouraged progress. Each author would have many such comments, indeed pages of names to acknowledge and many appreciations to give: let me offer mine to all of you who have helped the completion of this work.

The paramount consideration is for this book to stimulate discussion around information technology and its current and future regulation, as well as topics not yet considered in this volume. Recent events have forced rapid reactions but hopefully in the coming year we shall all have time for contemplation, reflection, and even purposeful design that negates the drift into a technocracy. Let us hope it brings also systems that support sustainable and meaningful lifestyles.

Mark Perry

October 2021

Armidale, New South Wales

Australia

Table of Contents

Chapter 1

Options for the Future: The Regulation of Information Technology

Mark Perry*

Introduction

[1.10] The last few years have seen a resurgence of interest in the application of information technology and its regulation. We have been forced to face a new reality where much greater reliance is placed on computer and internet distributed information and direct and reliable information from state "endorsed" sources (such as the Australian Broadcasting Corporation), or reputable independent reports are threatened by political or economic stresses. The ability to meet in-person with family, friends, colleagues, business associates or customers has been severely restrained. Leaving the Australian federation has looked like a dream as inter-state borders are regularly closed, and children and higher education students have been denied access to a physical classroom where they can engage with their peers. The alternatives have seemed less appealing to many, with every aspect of life "going online", whether virtual lectures, exams, meetings, mediations, court appearances[1] or job interviews. Although many of these changes have been in response to the COVID-19 pandemic, it is likely that many will stay at least partially in place for years to come and become the norm. The hybrid will be usual. A memo to Westpac employees noted that "We expect that post-COVID most people will still work remotely at least a couple of days a week, but also be based on site

---

* Professor of Law, University of New England, Armidale, New South Wales. The author thanks Cristina Avallone for her research assistance.

1 For example, in the state of Victoria: <https://www.countycourt.vic.gov.au/going-court/virtual-hearings-and-trials>.

Cybercrimes

[1.50] This chapter brings together Drs Monique Cormier and Simon McKenzie in "Cyber-Dependent and Cyber-Enabled Crime: Legal Responses and Challenges" where they delve into the shadowy area of criminality facilitated by networked computers. Again, this is an area that has demanded a great deal more attention over the last two years. The risk has probably risen with state driven demands for network use even for the simplest activity, such as entering your local cheese shop. Most people are now using networks and computing power on their phones to assist their compliance with public health orders to check in when visiting a business.[8] There has been a growth industry of ransomware attacks which the authors discuss as a prime example of malevolent actors using networks, computers and trust to extract financial rewards illegally. Another area of attention is the use of computer networks to perpetrate family violence in the form of harassment and threats. Although using computers for nefarious activities has been criminalised for many years in most jurisdictions, the range and type of offences continues to grow.

Privacy and Data Collection

[1.60] In the 18th century, Lord Camden, Chief Justice in England, pronounced "We can safely say there is no law in this country to justify the defendants in what they have done; if there was, it would destroy all the comforts of society, for papers are often the dearest property any man can have."[9] In "Protecting Data Privacy in an Evolving Technological Environment", Professor Niloufer Selvadurai gives the overview of Australia's principles based approach to privacy laws, and the need to understand the basic concepts, such as "personal information", "information about an individual" and other key terms. She lays out the current status of the *Privacy Act 1988* (Cth),[10] as well as other pertinent legislation. It is clear that into the future it would bode well for states to address this issue by ensuring that all new systems include as a fundamental part of their development framework the concepts around "privacy by design".[11]

---

8 For example, the *Public Health (COVID-19 General) Order 2021* (NSW) made under the *Public Health Act 2010* (NSW), s 7.

9 *Entick v Carrington* [1558–1774] All ER Rep 45.

10 *Privacy Act 1988* (Cth).

11 See in the educational context, for example, S Warburton and M Perry, "Design for Balance: Addressing Challenges of Safety, Privacy and Identity Management in Online and Hybridised Learning and Teaching Spaces" in E Gil et al (eds), *Hybrid Learning Spaces* (Springer, 2021).

Social Media

[1.70] Professor Melissa de Zwart's "Social Media and Social Influences" brings a spotlight onto the platforms that are used by billions daily. Most now know Facebook, Snapchat, Instagram, WhatsApp and TikTok as networked tools for sharing often trivial ("how are my eyebrows looking today") to deadly serious ("bush fire view out my window") information. The key to understanding such sites is that there is very little to ensure that the content is the truth, and much opportunity for those who wish to mislead others. The chapter points us to the possibilities of regulation, but there is also a lacuna of legislation that can be effective in these environments without killing their potential for benefit. She highlights the need for deep discussions and thought over the role of social media which is perhaps the most influential communications medium today.

Technologies and the Future

[1.80] The final chapter of this volume brings together Professors Heather Forrest and Mark Perry to address how "Technologies and the Future" may fare post pandemic. The practise of law has changed to its core, with wide acceptance of the virtual appearance, the use of digital everything from signatures to artificial intelligence (AI) computing resources. In this final chapter, the authors cover a range of topics, including proposals for the future of computer addressing from China, the replacement of much lawyer work by AI, blockchain and tamper resident distributed ledgers and the future.

For the Future

[1.90] In this book, there are many issues touched upon that require deep thought, discussion, debate and policy direction. There are social aspects, such as information overload for individual, sustainable aspects, such as how much energy is being used to send or save useless or redundant information. Platform and software biases, where the construction of software, even games, may be tilted towards the world view of the creators, and many other topics. Whether these will be addressed within legal systems, or whether they will affect the way law is used online, remains to be seen, but this is a space that needs constant review and refresh.

This book aims to inform, to generate discussion and to raise questions and debate as to the management and control of our dominant means of communication and sources of information as controlled or managed by a legal framework that in the main has not been designed to meet these needs. Suggestions for other topics in a new volume are most welcome.

actually keep directors of public and private companies, and particularly those listed on a stock exchange, awake at night.

Some of the reasons for concern are that the legal penalties for breaching the *Corporations Act 2001* (Cth), as well as other legislation, are criminal, with up to 15 years imprisonment and multi-million dollar fines, civil financial penalties and traditional civil remedies, such as unlimited damages and injunction.

Also, in the light of the COVID-19 global pandemic, all organisations have had to be agile and change their "business as usual" (BAU) approaches. No one is alive in business or professional practice when the Spanish Flu hit the world in 1919. As such this current pandemic is a moving feast and everyone is learning quickly about "pivoting" and doing things differently. Governments, State/Territory and Federal have all had to do things very differently to the previous history of health regulations, economics stimulus and law enforcement.

Within the technology space, who would have thought that the humble "QR code" would become a major tool for checking into venues and the need to show primarily digital "vaccine passports" and other contemporary requirements under Public Health Orders (PHO) is becoming a new norm. The issues relating to cybersecurity have become the number one topic and trend for directors to understand in 2021 and beyond. This is discussed later in the chapter.[1]

Has the Role of Social Media Changed Legal Landscapes?

[2.30] Before delving into the constructs of corporate governance and the overlay of information governance. The example of the growth in social media and its links to legal manageable risks is an excellent illustration of how boards of directors must contend with a changing playing field and why BAU is a challenge. Australia was one of the first countries to deal with the issue of where a statement was made for the purposes of the tort of defamation, by a final court of appeal. The case *Dow Jones & Co Inc v Gutnick* [2002] HCA 56; (2002) 210 CLR 575 involved a Melbourne based trader who alleged he was defamed on paper and online in the *Barron's magazine* (part of the *Wall Street Journal* and Dow Jones group). Dow Jones wanted the matter heard in New York, where they are based or where the computer servers were located. Mr Gutnick wanted the case heard in Victoria, Australia, as that is where the damaged to his reputation had occurred. The High Court followed traditional reasoning in defamation cases that it should be the injury had occurred, that

1 See [2.230].

is, Melbourne. The case was then referred to the Victorian Supreme Court for determination.

In September 2021, the High Court of Australia (HCA) has had a second opportunity to visit this issue in the *Fairfax Media Publications Pty Ltd; Nationalwide News Pty Ltd and Australian News Channel Pty Ltd v Dylan Voller* [2021] HCA 2. The Voller appeal related to a youth in Northern Territory detention, which led to a Royal Commission of enquiry. All the media outlets published articles on Mr Voller on Facebook (and similar social media channels) and derogatory comments were made online. Mr Voller sued the various outlets as publishers for defamation by its readers, for their comments. Justice Rothman in the NSW Supreme Court found that the media organisations were a publisher for this purpose.

All the media companies appealed as a matter of principle to the NSW Court of Appeal, which also held up that they were in fact publishers. So as a matter of national interest the HCA agreed to hear the case. In a majority judgment, the High Court with Kiefel CJ, Keane and Gleeson JJ rejected the arguments of the media outlets and followed the principles in *Webb v Bloch* [1928] HCA 50; (1928) 41 CLR 331 that they had been instrumental in the publication of the defamatory matter is a publisher. Gageler and Gordon JJ agreed with the finds for slightly different reasons. There was dissent from Edelman and Steward JJ and all justices agreed that there could a successful defence of innocent dissemination of the statements.

The case has been referred back to the NSW Supreme Court now that the media outlets are deemed publishers. It is also noted that the media organisations did delete the Facebook comments and now the technology has been altered so publishers can prevent such comments being made public before being checked for defamatory purposes.

Defamation laws are being amended across Australia and this is sure to feed into that review. But until the law is clarified or amended, many organisations should be very careful of having open access or public forums, where anyone can make a defamatory statement and the owner of the Facebook or other social media software could be deemed a publisher for these purposes.[2]

---

2 K Lynch and M Nunan, "The Voller Appeal: High Court Confirms Liability for Third Party Facebook Comments", *Insights* (September 2021) <https://jws.com.au/en/insights/articles/2021-articles/the-voller-appeal-high-court-confirms-liability>; E Byrne, "High Court Finds Media Outlets Are Responsible for Facebook Comments in Dylan Voller Defamation Case", *ABC News* (8 September 2021) <https://www.abc.net.au/news/2021-09-08/high-court-rules-on-media-responsibility-over-facebook-comments/100442626>.

So what is the Corporate Governance Framework?

[2.40] It is truism that corporate governance has been a hot topic of debate for at least 25 years and it is a wide concept, which covers many different disciplines from accounting, finance, management, risk, strategy and law. This chapter has a clear legal focus and deals with the tensions arising from an aspect of corporate governance, in the form of CSR and ESG. To help place the issues that arise in CSR (which is closely linked to "stakeholder theory" and in the United Kingdom the ideal of the "enlightened shareholder"[3]) and the paradigm of investors (particularly institutional investors, such as superannuation funds) for the application of ESG.

To help explain and centre these ideas, back in 2003, Professor Adams wrote an article entitled "The Three Pillars of Good Corporate Governance".[4] This article linked the central concepts of linking corporate governance with due diligence and compliance. In 2018, these ideas and concepts were reimaged to expand the *Three Pillars of Corporate Governance*[5] to include the impacts of international corporate governance, information governance, CSR, ESG and update the various developments in due diligence and compliance.

To additional aid directors and officers of listed boards to keep a keen focus on strategy and risks, the acronym #SEMTEX, was used to identify the 2018 top six issues that boards face. In 2020 and beyond, these same acronyms are true, but with a greater focus on "T" technology.

#SEMTEX stands for: "S" is for strategy, a key role with corporate governance and the role and function of a board. "E" is for evaluation of risk, in a systematic approach, such as a risk register and relevant traffic light reports from senior management.[6] "M" is for multi-generational, reflecting aspects of the diversity debate[7] beyond gender to age, ethnicity and technology. "T" is for technology, in a period of history where disruption and cybercrime and vulnerability are huge. "E" is for the environment and a major concern for the current generations, particularly around climate change and CSR. The final "X" is the reflection of

3 *Companies Act 2006* (UK), s 172.

4 M Adams, "The Three Pillars of Good Corporate Governance" (2004) *Risk Management* 8.

5 M Adams, "Three Pillars of Corporate Governance" (2018) 70(6) *Governance Directions* 268.

6 A risk register is a method for bringing known risks into a single reporting mechanism and a calculation of high risk matters in red; medium likelihood of occurring and level of damage (usually expressed in dollars) in amber and low risk being shown as green. The commentary against known risks usually has mitigation and actions taken to reduce any such identified risks by management.

7 M Adams, "Board Diversity: More than a Gender Issue?" (2015) 20(1) *Deakin Law Review* 279.

toxic culture in various industries and corporations that are publicly reported via social media and traditional mainstream media. Unpacking the concepts of CSR and ESG are central to the concern of #SEMTEX.[8]

So what is Corporate Governance?

[2.50] Corporate governance is not a new concept. Time and again bad governance seemed to be complicit in corporate failures, creating much fanfare and misconception about this issue. Along with the emergence of competing theories various disciplines have all together saturated and obscure the debate as to the real meaning of governance. As the business world globalises, organisational life becomes more complex and the demands on governance undertakings seem to multiply. Corporate directors confront both structural and relational factors in governing a large modern corporation. Globalisation of markets, the role of the World Trade Organisation and bilateral and multinational treaties, with easy communication, via the internet, have changed perceptions on corporate governance. Thus, for a small number of global companies, there are concepts of international corporate governance.

So what is the Meaning of International Corporate Governance?

[2.60] There is no formal definition of "international corporate governance". However, as corporations around the world have grown, many operate in a size and complexity that impact as if they were sovereign states (the same as a country). This has meant that the corporation must comply with laws and regulation in many languages, countries, currencies and other controls. It is easy to imagine a UK incorporated company that is listed on the New York Stock Exchange, securities exchange, with a Brazilian based board of directors, that manufacturers product in China, through a joint venture, but also imports components from its German subsidiary and then ends up with a consumer whom resides in Australia, opens many legal challenges.

A real example of this type of corporation, in the Australian context, is the company BHP. As of September 2021, BHP (Australia's largest resources company and second largest on the Australian Securities Exchange (ASX) by market capitalisation) is worth A$106.2 billion at a share price of A$33.08. BHP

---

8 M Adams, "Effective Governance in a Changing Corporate Culture" (Presented at Governance Institute of Australia NSW Governance and Risk Forum, Sydney, NSW, 7 June 2018). Reported by J Doraisamy, "Counsel Must Play Role in Evolving Governance Structure", *Lawyers Weekly: Corporate Counsel* (12 June 2018) <https://www.lawyersweekly.com.au/corporate-counsel/23430-counsel-must-play-role-in-evolving-governance-structure>.

(known previously as BHP Billiton or colloquially as "the big Australian") has been required to produce a number of annual reports and simultaneous disclosures to the United Kingdom, United States and Australian regulators, as well as various stock exchanges. BHP is required under the different legal systems and regulations to produce financials in different currencies, of the UK pound sterling, US dollars and in Australian dollars. Complying with the many countries it mines in and sells resources is a big challenge for the governance unit and board of directors, as well as regional executives and employees. This has led to the BHP management team examining moving to a single share market in 2021.

The meaning of corporate governance is critical to not-for-profit companies (charities), for government entities (particularly governed businesses, such as Australia Post) and for private,[9] as well as public listed companies on the ASX.

Domestic Corporate Governance

[2.70] So what do we actually mean by "corporate governance"? Many have used this term like a label for many things about corporations and how they are run. Like trendy topics it becomes the "blame" and hence the "solution" for many corporate ills leading collapses and under performance.

At a board level governance is concern with both structural and relational issues. Structural concerns can be further divided into organisational configuration, board structure and processes. Relational dimensions are dynamic and ever changing. Broadly relational considerations categorised into leadership issues, corporate culture and corporate social responsibilities. These two facets encapsulate the responsibilities of the board.

In September 2006, the Corporations and Markets Advisory Committee (CAMAC) produced a report on "Personal Liability for Corporate Fault". The report expresses concern about two major issues. First, "[i]ndividuals should not be penalised for misconduct by a company except where it can be shown that they have personally assisted or been privy to that misconduct, that is, where they were accessories".[10] Second, "[a] need for a more consistent, as well as a more principled, approach to personal liability across Commonwealth, State and Territory jurisdictions".

---

9 In Australia, private companies are known as proprietary limited companies (usually abbreviated "Pty Ltd").

10 Corporations and Markets Advisory Committee, *Report on Personal Liability for Corporate Fault* (26 September 2006) 9.

Professor Farrar in 1998 commented that corporate governance is a fashionable concept that is "remarkably imprecise".[11] The many influences in the emergence of corporate governance as a new field of study can make it difficult to develop analytical tools. To make matters worse the ever-increasing number of publications by economists, organisational theorists, lawyers, sociologists, accountants, criminologists and even political scientists laying claim to its meaning, interpretation and applications can often confuse and at times altogether obscure the topic altogether.

Over the last couple of decades there have been several theories about governance emerging. These theories range from agency, contractual, managerial hegemony, stewardship, resource dependency and life cycle to institutional.[12]

These theories are often the product from an array of disciplines. Each discipline draws from a bounded set of assumptions and methodology to derive at a normative set of prescriptions from predisposed hypothesis shaped by contextual considerations. Nevertheless, whichever theory one examines, the key element is the importance of the board of directors confronting an ever-growing list of demands and duties they ought to perform and be accountable to. The theories also attest to the complexities in governing a corporation, which denotes there is no definitive or "one size fits all" model.

Professor Pettigrew in 1992 wrote corporate governance lacks coherence in either empirically, methodologically or theoretically, and many researchers seemed to be piecemeal endeavours to try to understand and explain how the modern corporation is run.[13] Reality might well mean that there are intermix of theories integrating into a multifaceted paradigm. Effective governance would therefore warrant the participation of the key internal and external stakeholders, and shaped by other influences like market expectations (see Figure 2.1).

Consequently, corporate governance is a multidimensional issues, which could help explain why many governance measures are articulated as principles rather than manuals.

---

11 J Farrar, "Opinion: Corporate Governance" (1998) 10(2) *Bond Law Review, Special Issue: Corporate Governance* 141.

12 For an overview of corporate governance theories, see T Clarke (ed), *Theories of Corporate Governance: The Philosophical Foundations of Corporate Governance* (2004).

13 A Pettigrew, "On Studying Managerial Elites" (1992) 13(1) *Strategic Management Journal* 163.

Figure 2.1: Modern corporations are disciplined by internal and external factors

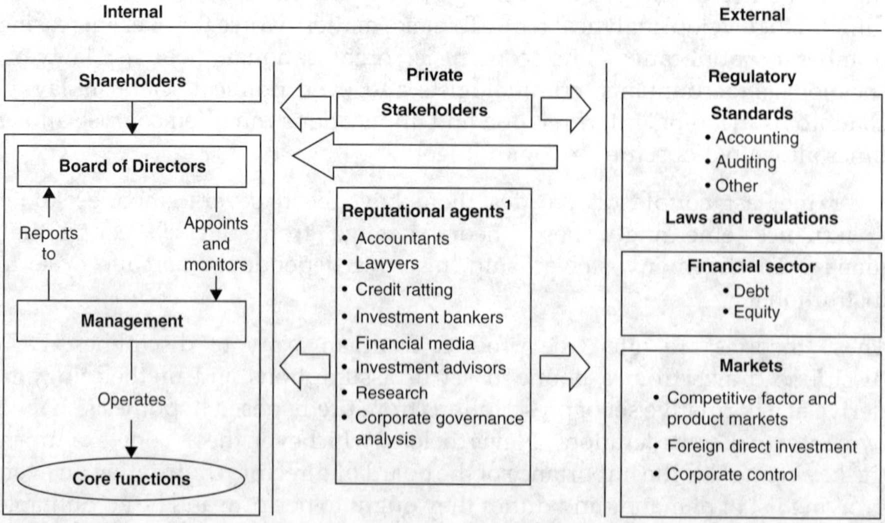

[1]*Reputational agents* refer to the private sector agents, self-regulating bodies, the media, and civic society that reduce information asymmetry, improve the monitoring of firms, and shed light on opportunistic behavior.
Source: Adapted from Muir and Saba 1995.

Source: Magdi Iskander and Nadereh Chamlou (2000).

Yet principles may suffer from misinterpretation and even be misrepresented. Even if theories can be extracted and adapted into a series of legislations, much of the expectations lie with the stakeholders' willingness to take action. Corporations, regulators and other stakeholders must be willing to act against bad governance practices.[14]

Another important point to note, while the board of directors are pivotal in governance, one can easily be confused with the roles of the board is governance. The roles of the board like strategic planning and risk management is part of decision-making and leadership from a governance perspective. These operational issues would not be discussed in this paper. More important, governance at a board level requires both structural and relational issues.

14 See OECD, *OECD Principles of Corporate Governance* (1999); I Millstein et al, *Corporate Governance: Improving Competitiveness and Access to Capital in Global Markets* (OECD Report, 1998); M Iskander and N Chamlou, *Corporate Governance: A Framework for Implementation* (2000).

The law, via case law, statutes and enforceable rules (such as the ASX Guidelines and Listing Rules) provide blunt instruments to change wrong-doing and corporate behaviour rather than to change how companies are actually to be directed and steered. Thus, there is a clear distinction between the management or business philosophy on governance and the legal requirements to avoid wrong-doing.

There are some accepted views on corporate governance which can be simply stated as follows:

- Governance refers to how companies are governed and directed emanating from interaction between key stakeholders where individual psyche and group behaviour would impact on decisions.
- Both domestic and international economic development also impacts on how corporations are governed since corporations have to adapt to new economic challenges.
- Governance tends to receive much more attention in the aftermath of corporate failures, which can prompt legislatures to overreact by introducing new laws because of economic and social consequences.
- The interdisciplinary nature of governance creates a multitude of influences, which has to be taken into account.
- Corporate governance is shaped by a number of factors both within and outside the corporation, like organisational growth, accounting rules, legislation, politics, economic policies, ethics, technology and social norms.
- A key source of governance is the board of directors. At the board level governance concerns both structural elements to ensure there is proper process and relational issues that emerges from the interaction between key stakeholders.

In 1992, the now world-famous *Cadbury Report* took a simple approach, proposing that corporate governance is "the system by which companies are directed and controlled". A broader definition is found in Cochran and Wartick's 1988 publication *Corporate Governance: A Review of the Literature*, which suggest that corporate governance is "an umbrella term that includes specific issues arising from interactions amount senior management, shareholders, boards of directors and other corporate stakeholders".

In 1997, the Australian Commonwealth Treasury went a little further in the context of the *Corporate Law Economic Reform Program Paper (CLERP) No 3, Directors' Duties and Corporate Governance*, defining corporate governance as "the term used to describe the rules and practices put in place within a company to manage information and economic incentive problems inherent in the separation of ownership from control in large enterprises. It deals with how, and to what extent, the interests of various agents involved in the company are reconciled and what checks and incentives are put in place to ensure that managers maximise the value of the investment made by shareholders".

In 2003, the Australian Stock (now, Securities) Exchange (ASX) released its original *Principles of Good Corporate Governance and Best Practice Recommendations*, which contained the following definition: "Corporate governance is the system by which companies are directed and managed. It influences how the objectives of the company are set and achieved, how risk is monitored and assessed, and how performance is optimised. Good corporate governance structures encourage companies to create value (through entrepreneurism, innovation, development and exploration) and provide accountability and control systems commensurate with the risks involved." This has been revised four times, with the current fourth edition in 2019.[15]

While this debate of semantics is provocative in an academic sense, it does little to develop clarity for the commercial world. Seeking to define corporate governance is, perhaps, akin to searching for the Holy Grail that does not exist. Justice Neville Owen, the Royal Commissioner, in his final report arising from the HIH Royal Commission, hints at the futility of the search simply stating "corporate governance is not a term of art".[16]

His Honour's guidance is worth remember: "I think that any attempt to impose governance systems or structures that are overly prescriptive or specific is fraught with danger. By its very nature corporate governance is not something where 'one size fits all'. Even with companies within a class, such as publicly listed companies, their capital base, risk profile, corporate history, business activity and management and personnel arrangements will be varied. It would be impracticable and undesirable to attempt to place them all within a single straitjacket of structures and processes. A degree of flexibility and an acceptance that systems can and should be modified to suit the particular attributes and needs of each company is necessary if the objectives of improved corporate governance are to be achieved."

Once there is a general agreement on what constitute corporate governance practices, the bigger challenge is to demonstrate that good corporate governance

15 See <https://www.asx.com.au/documents/regulation/cgc-principles-and-recommendations-fourth-edn.pdf>.

16 The HIH Royal Commission, "The Failure of HIH Insurance – Final Report" (Canberra, 2003).

produces actual benefits.[17] There is overwhelming corroborative and empirical evidence of the impact of sustainability in governance.[18] There are numerous studies as to the benefits of corporate governance for global entities, whether they be the transnational corporations or the more traditional multinational companies. Around the globe, by far the majority of business entities are privately owned (and/or family businesses) with a small percentage being quoted on a local stock exchange, in a single legal jurisdiction.[19]

Impressive data was produced by Claessens and Yurtoglu[20] who examined the corporate governance literature from the fields of economics, finance, management and legal scholarship in many countries and jurisdictions over the last decade. The authors' detailed survey of the literature provides evidence of the importance of corporate governance at a number of economic points.

These extensive studies provide clear evidence of a link between economic development and corporate governance. The extensive cross-country research demonstrates that corporate governance is central to financial development. Weak corporate governance can be seen to prevail in financial markets that tend to function poorly by global standards.

Poor governance increases market volatility and lack of transparency, creating unfair markets. Countries and companies that adopt best practices in corporate governance are not guaranteed success, but provide evidence that good corporate governance improves sustainability and lays the groundwork for long-term success.

Corporate governance has many elements, including risk management, due diligence and compliance. It is necessary to highlight the fact that these oft-quoted terms are not merely synonyms for one another, rather, they are three distinct, yet inextricably fused elements of corporate governance. A business

17 M Head, S Mann and S Kozlina, *Transnational Governance: Emerging Models of Global Legal Regulation* (Ashgate Publishing, 2012); A Armstrong, "Corporate Governance Standards: Intangibles and Their Intangible Value" (2004) 17(1) *Australian Journal of Corporate Law* 97 cited in M Adams, "Global Trends in Corporate Governance" (2012) 64(9) *Keeping Good Companies* 516.

18 A Klettner, T Clarke and M Adams, "Corporate Governance Reform: An Empirical Study of the Changing Roles and Responsibilities of Australian Boards and Directors" (2010) 4(2) *Australian Journal of Corporate Law* 148; a report on the implementation of the ASX Corporate Governance Principles between 2003 and 2007.

19 M Adams, "Global Trends in Corporate Governance" (2012) 64(9) *Keeping Good Companies* 516, 518.

20 S Claessens and B Yurtoglu, *Corporate Governance and Development – An Update* (Global Corporate Governance Forum, 2012) <https://www.ifc.org/wps/wcm/connect/topics_ext_content/ifc_external_corporate_site/ifc+cg/resources/focus_case+studies/focus+10+corporate+governance+and+development+-+an+update>.

may formulate a compliance program as part of internal due diligence, which, in turn, may have been undertaken because of the company's commitment to sound corporate governance.

As well as the legal duties imposed on officers of the company (of which directors make up 99%), corporate governance will also include other stakeholder interests. This has become known in the literature, as well as by the public as the CSR element.

There is an expectation that company will be a "good corporate citizen" and will not be unnecessarily hard on its workers (employees and contractors) or its suppliers, nor the local community and broader environment or its customers. Investors also have concerned and they will express them as ESG. Both ESG and CSR are less well understood than corporate governance, but are growing in significant importance.

An example maybe an investment company that does not hold shares in a company that manufacturers or sells alcohol or tobacco products. Many Australian universities will not hold shares of companies that produce fossil fuels (just as coal and gas). Ethical superannuation funds (pension funds) worth over two trillion Australian dollars have been created to avoid investment in such products or services, which may breach ESG or CSR policies and guiding principles. This has come under further scrutiny with the Australian Prudential Regulation Authority (APRA) prudential report on Commonwealth Bank of Australia (CBA)[21] and the Hayne's Royal Commission.[22]

So what is Due Diligence?

[2.80] One generally associates the expression "due diligence" with the American securities law defence of due diligence provided by the American *Securities Act of 1933* (Federal, United States) to those charged with the task of investigating prospectuses issued during takeover machinations or fundraising through debt or equities (shares).

In Australia, a similar defence is available in relation to misleading or deceptive statements made in a prospectus under s 731 of the *Corporations Act 2001* (Cth), but, curiously, there is no such specific defence for misleading or deceptive conduct under s 18 of the *Australian Consumer Law*[23] (previously known as

21 See <https://www.apra.gov.au/media-centre/media-releases/apra-releases-cba-prudential-inquiry-final-report-accepts-eu>.

22 See <https://financialservices.royalcommission.gov.au/>.

23 The *Australian Consumer Law* is a schedule to the *Competition and Consumer Act 2010* (Cth), which replaced the former *Trade Practices Act 1974* (Cth).

s 52 of the *Trade Practices Act 1974* (Cth)). The *Corporations Act 2001* (Cth) also provides officers with a *quasi* due diligence defence under s 180(2) (known as the "business judgment rule") and s 189 (reliance on others). A general due diligence defence to criminal actions is also available under Pt 2.5 of Div 12 of the *Criminal Code Act 1995* (Cth).

However, due diligence has evolved beyond its original role as a defence. Much of the confusion relating to due diligence results from its treatment under different statutes or in different contexts as if each use is completely unrelated. It is now a moniker for the process of evaluating everything from a prospectus to the assets of a potential takeover target, and more recently a corporation's internal legal audit process. Thus, it is no longer merely a concept relevant to a corporation's external transactional activities (such as investigating the veracity of prospectuses during fundraising) the additional meaning of an internal processes (eg, legal compliance).

It is when considering due diligence within a corporation's internal operations that the link between, and, indeed, the confusion relating to, due diligence and compliance programs becomes apparent. The use of the expression "due diligence" in common parlance to describe the system implemented within a corporation of checking day-to-day legal statutory compliance (such as intellectual property, trade practices, consumer laws, employment/industrial relations, environmental, corporate and privacy law) is somewhat disingenuous. Due diligence and compliance are related but not to be treated as one and the same. It may be that a corporation, in carrying out its internal due diligence, will conduct a legal risk audit, from which compliance plans will be developed in order to manage and minimise legal risk.

However, merely determining a compliance program will not amount to due diligence per se.

Simplified internal due diligence risk model:

Step 1 = Legal risk audit

Step 2 = Compliance planning

Step 3 = Implementation compliance plan

Step 4 = Review of compliance program

Step 5 = Adapt compliance plan for due diligence reports to board

Step 6 = After one to two years a new audit of risk commenced (Step 1 repeated)

It is accurate, therefore, to say that a compliance plan may come within the broad concept of internal due diligence. However, it is inaccurate to suggest the two are synonymous. The UK case of *Tesco Supermarkets Ltd v Nattrass* [1972] AC 156 illustrates the difference between due diligence and compliance, and how the satisfaction of the former will not necessarily result in the same for the latter. Tesco was prosecuted when a discount sign was left on display after the discounted stock was exhausted, and a shop assistant refused to sell at the discounted price. Tesco had put in place a genuine management system to prevent breaches of the law. The court was impressed by the board's involvement, the good management selection and training process, the regular supervision of stores by four levels of visiting executives, the regular communications designed to secure compliance, and operating procedures right down to ones designed to ensure shop assistants complied with the law. The court found that Tesco's due diligence was sound; it could not reasonably have done more. However, notwithstanding its sound due diligence, Tesco failed to secure compliance with the legal requirements of the law.

Within the Australian context, the Federal Court of Australia has ordered companies to implement or review an existing trade practices compliance program. A sound example is found in *Australian Competition and Consumer Commission (ACCC) v Target Australia Pty Ltd* [2001] FCA 1326, where, having found Target to have breached the former s 52 of the *Trade Practices Act 1974* (now s 18 of the *Australian Consumer Law*) the court ordered Target to broadcast a corrective advertisement nationally on 88 television stations and to publish correct notices in 37 newspapers across metropolitan, regional and rural Australia. The court also issued injunctions restraining Target from advertising in the same way for four years, ordered Target to review its trade practices compliance program and ordered Target to pay Commission costs of A$65,000.

A key aspect of the internal due diligence system, is that management and employees, have a clear set of compliance programs, linked to their risk register and known corporate risks. This will vary from industry to industry/profession.

So what are Compliance Programs?

[2.90] It is to state the obvious to observe that the commercial environment has become increasingly regulated in recent years. Compliance is demanded with a greater number of statutes, regulations, industry standards and principles than ever before. What is more, society is becoming more litigious,[24]

24 Particularly, with the growth in class actions by shareholders and customers/clients and litigation funding businesses. There is a review of class actions underway in 2018 by the Australian Law Reform Commission: *Inquiry into Class Action Proceedings and Third-Party*

and regulators are having their arsenal bolstered by greater powers and a greater range of penalties.

An example was where the corporate (general) counsel and company secretary of the James Hardie Industries litigation was held to be in breach of his officers' duties under s 180(1) of the *Corporations Act 2001* (Cth) by the HCA in *Shafron v ASIC* [2012] HCA 18. The roles of the c-suite (most senior executive roles start with the letter "c", such as CEO, CFO, CIO, COO,[25] corporate counsel and company secretary) are generally legal defined as officers of a corporation (even if they are not legally directors) and thus bound by common law and statutory legal duties.

So what does CSR Mean?

[2.100] Before, jumping into the background to CSR, it is important to remember that most common law countries apply a "shareholder primacy principle". That is, the directors owe their legal duties under common law and equity (as well as under legislation), to the company as a whole (represented by the shareholders).

The United Kingdom in 2006 developed a principle that is wider than mere shareholders, which has become known as the "enlightened shareholder principle" and enables the directors to take a wider range of stakeholders. This has been expressed in s 172 of the *Companies Act 2006* (UK). Thus, understanding the basic corporate law duties of directors and the tension with considering other stakeholders.

In Australia, it is worth remembering that there are approximately 2.5 million registered companies, and each must have at least one director. Each year, the Australian Securities and Investments Commission (ASIC), through the Commonwealth Director of Public Prosecutions, successfully prosecuted about 25 directors per annum. There are additionally increasingly important issues relating to diversity within the boardroom, which hold the potential to add value to the corporation. The diversity might relate to gender, culture, ethnicity and even technology!

Litigation Funders (Discussion Paper 85, 2018) <https://www.alrc.gov.au/inquiry-categories/class-action-proceedings-and-third-party-litigation-funders>.

25 CEO: chief executive officer; CFO: chief financial officer; CIO: chief information officer; and COO: chief operations officers all form the c-suite of executives in large public companies.

So who is an Officer?

[2.110] It is worth noting that the legal term is "officer" (broader than just "director") and is defined in the statutory dictionary, in s 9 of the *Corporations Act 2001* (Cth) as:

(a) a director or secretary of the corporation; or
(b) a person:

(i) who makes, or participates in making, decisions that affect the whole, or a substantial part, of the business of the corporation; or
(ii) who has the capacity to affect significantly the corporation's financial standing.

The majority of officers of a corporation are the directors, but this does include the CEO, possibly the CFO and other senior executives, depending upon the size and structure of the corporation. In a small corporation, there is likely to be only one director, who is also the CEO. The 2003 Royal Commission into the collapse of HIH Insurance recommended the change of terminology from "executives to the more functional approach of 'officer'".[26]

The *Corporations Act* also provides a definition of "director", which is found in s 9, as:

(a) a person who:

(i) is appointed to the position of a director; or
(ii) is appointed to the position of an alternate director and is acting in that capacity;

regardless of the name that is given to their position; and

(b) unless the contrary intention appears, a person who is not validly appointed as a director if:

(i) they act in the position of a director; or
(ii) the directors of the company or body are accustomed to act in accordance with the person's instructions or wishes.

In the vast majority of circumstances (probably over 99% of cases), it is absolutely crystal clear who is an officer of a company, as it automatically includes every director and the company secretary (if appointed). Even if they are not a registered director, they would be deemed to be an officer of the company and thus bound by the same laws.

26 The HIH Royal Commission, "The Failure of HIH Insurance – Final Report" (Canberra, 2003).

Officers of a company have very well-defined legal obligations and there is a clear link to the role of corporate governance in all entities.[27] Over the last decades,[28] corporate governance, and in particular the role of officers' duties, has come under the microscope of the Australian courts, in all jurisdictions.[29] The HIH Insurance Royal Commissioner re-stated the need for a commitment to education on the fiduciary principle and for greater professionalism in governance.

The former Federal Minister, responsible for developments in this area of law, has noted that a review into the Safe Harbour Rule (known as the Business Judgment Rule[30]) in the *Reviews of Sanctions in Corporate Law*[31] paper, did not expect any quick changes. This is a very true statement, as there has been no change to this officers' defence and few directors have ever been able to successfully rely upon it as a defence.

The courts do not remain static in the developments of corporate law and directors' duties. In large part due to the wonders of the common law system of precedent. A broader meaning of the term "officer" was given in the Victorian Supreme Court case of *Hodgson v Amcor*,[32] where a senior manager was deemed to be an officer for the purposes of the *Corporations Act*. Similarly, the more complex issue of *de facto* directors occurred in *Grimaldi v Chameleon Mining NL (No 2)*[33] stressed the need to look beyond the formal appointment procedures to determine whether a person owes a fiduciary duty. The HCA reexamined this issue in *ASIC v King* [2020] HCA 4.

---

27 A Klettner, T Clarke and M Adams, "Balancing Act – The Tightrope of Corporate Governance Reform" (2007) 59(10) *Keeping Good Companies* 648.

28 M Adams, "Are All Directors Created Equal? Reassessing the Role of the Chair in the Light of ASIC v Rich" (2003) 55 *Keeping Good Companies* 204; M Adams, "Officers' Duties – Are We Keeping Up with the Changes?" (2008) 60(8) *Keeping Good Companies* 344.

29 A Klettner, T Clarke and M Adams, "Corporate Governance Reform: An Empirical Study of the Changing Role and Responsibilities of Australian Boards and Directors" (2010) 24 *Australian Journal of Corporate Law* 148.

30 *Corporations Act 2001* (Cth), s 180(2).

31 See <https://www.petercostello.com.au/press/2007/3137-reviews-of-sanctions-in-corporate-law-and-infringement-notice-provisions>.

32 *Hodgson v Amcor* [2012] VSC 94.

33 *Grimaldi v Chameleon Mining NL (No 2)* (2012) 200 FCR 296; G Morgan, "De Facto Directors and Duties – Chameleon Mining" (2012) 64(3) *Keeping Good Companies* 222.

Are there Basic Legal Duties of Officers and Directors?

[2.120] In April 2010, the Australian Government's reform body for corporate law, the CAMAC[34] published a more detailed guide for directors.[35] This 2010 report outlined in detail the challenges facing directors and the various guidance to be drawn from legislation, the case law, the regulators and the ASX Corporate Governance Council. It provided an international comparison with the United Kingdom and North America.

There is a natural overlap between the legislation imposed by Parliament and the case law developed over the last couple of centuries. Companies have existed since the 1600s[36] but the modern, incorporated (after 1991 referred to in Australia as "registered") company can be traced back to 1844.[37]

Australia has, for the most part, followed the corporate laws of the United Kingdom but has only moved to registered corporations as part of the changes, in 1991, to a national system, under what is now the *Corporations Act 2001* (Cth).[38]

In Australia, the laws relating to officers and directors can be divided into three parts:

- statutory duties;
- common law duties (such as the duties of care, skill and diligence); and
- equitable fiduciary duties (conflicts of interests and secret profits).

The fundamental duties that are imposed on all officers of all registered companies, and can be illustrated by a simple Venn diagram (see Figure 2.2). The overlapping areas represent how the *Corporations Act* reflects aspects of both the common law and equitable principles.

Some duties are specifically laid out in statute, such as the prohibition on insider trading, under s 1043A. Other legal duties, such as when directors have interests in company contracts, are both statutory (s 191) and fiduciary duties (s 182).

34 CAMAC was disbanded as a budget saving measure, and corporate law reform is part of the Commonwealth Treasury Department or the Australian Law Reform Commission.

35 Corporations and Markets Advisory Committee, Parliament of Australia, *Guidance for Directors Report* (2010).

36 The Honourable East India Company, 1600 England.

37 *Joint Stock Companies Act 1844* (UK).

38 Previously, each State and Territory had its own *Companies Act*, which was similar in most provisions.

Figure 2.2: Updated Adams' overview of officers' duties[39] (1992)

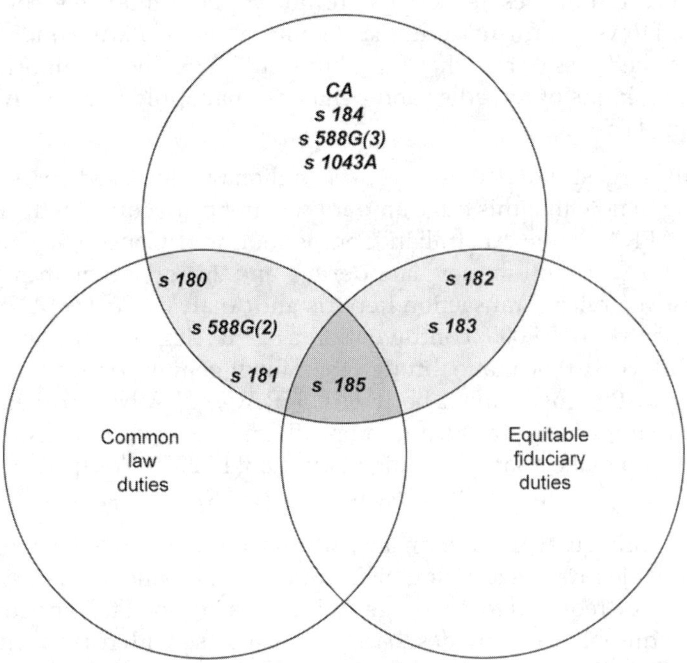

Other positive duties include the fact that directors must not allow the company to trade while insolvent, by virtue of s 588G. The directors are held personally liable if this occurs. There is a similar common law duty to consider creditors in times of financial trouble, as expressed in the High Court case of *Spies v The Queen*.[40]

The three circles intersect at s 185, which provides that the duties imposed by legislation are additional to, and not exclusive from, the duties imposed at common law and in equity. Thus, a director could be sued for all three bases of action, rather than just the *Corporations Act* or the common law/equity principles. An example of a director being held liable for all three types of actions occurred in *State of South Australia v Clark*.[41]

39 A Hargovan, M Adams and C Brown, *Australian Corporate Law* (LexisNexis Butterworths, 7th ed, 2021) 452.

40 *Spies v The Queen* (2000) 201 CLR 603.

41 *State of South Australia v Clark* (1996) 66 SASR 199.

The consequences of breaching ss 180–183 result in a civil penalty order, under s 1317E, but these sanctions are not applied under the common law or equity. However, further criminal liability may also arise under s 184, in relation to the types of breaches found in ss 181–183. This is important due to the different kinds of remedies and penalties, that apply to civil, civil penalty and criminal cases.

In 2018, the largest civil penalty of A$700 million was imposed on the CBA. It is interesting to note that this huge amount was not prosecuted by the regulators ASIC or APRA or the Australian Competition and Consumer Commission (ACCC), but the anti-money laundering and terrorism financing agency, known as Australian Transaction Reports and Analysis Centre (AUSTRAC).[42] CBA admitted to 54,000 contraventions of the legislation through cash-deposits above $10,000 made through their intelligent ATM machines, without disclosing to the government body (AUSTRAC). CBA has worked with the regulator to improve its fraud, anti-money laundering and terrorism financing protections, to make a safer banking institution. In 2020, Westpac was ordered to pay A$1.2 billion for similar breaches of AUSTRAC laws.[43]

It is worth noting that at common law, officers are expected to be honest and to take reasonable care in exercising their duties. At the same time, s 181 provides that officers are required to discharge their duties in good faith and for a proper purpose, while s 180(1) provides that they must do so with reasonable care and diligence. This is comparable to the tort of negligence, which was recognised in the corporate directors' context in *ASIC v Adler*.[44] The equitable principles of avoiding conflicts of interest and not taking advantage of confidential information are reflected in ss 182 and 183 respectively.

The HCA does not often examine corporate law cases, but one of the many One.Tel proceedings did get considered was *Rich v ASIC*.[45] This matter examined the importance of procedures in the area of civil penalties. The HIH Insurance cases around *ASIC v Adler*[46] also scrutinised in depth the civil penalty standards of directors' duties.

---

42 *AUSTRAC v CBA* [2018] FCA 930.

43 AUSTRAC, "AUSTRAC Applies for Civil Penalty Orders against Westpac" (Media Release, 20 November 2019) <https://www.austrac.gov.au/about-us/media-release/civil-penalty-orders-against-westpac>.

44 *ASIC v Adler* (2002) 168 FLR 253.

45 *Rich v ASIC* (2004) 220 CLR 129. For a detailed discussion on this case, see M Adams, "Whether to Protect or Punish: Legal Consequences of Contravening the Corporations Act" (2004) 56(9) *Keeping Good Companies* 592.

46 *ASIC v Adler* (2002) 168 FLR 253.

In particular, whether Mr Rodney Adler acted dishonestly (a breach of s 181) and the failure to take reasonable care and diligence (a breach of s 180) by Mr Ray Williams and Mr Adler. Unusually, a separate criminal prosecution was launched against Mr Williams[47] and Mr Adler,[48] resulting in a conviction and jail sentence. This was followed by the high-profile case of Steve Vizard, which involved the misuse of confidential information, from the boardroom of Telstra, for personal gain.[49] This case could have been brought under the insider trading laws, but was in fact brought under the directors' duties provision for misusing confidential information.

Close to the HIH Insurance group of cases were the GIO cases (the hostile takeover by AMP of GIO) which resulted in *ASIC v Vines*.[50] In this case the three CFOs of the various GIO group of companies were held liable for a breach of their duties as officers of the target company.

Thus, after a number of successful enforcements against directors in the civil and criminal courts, the regulator was challenged on a number of cases. The successful 2009 *James Hardie litigation*[51] resulted in an appellate court over-ruling Gzell J in a number of ways and exonerating most of the directors held liable. The case of *Morley v ASIC*[52] and *James Hardie Industries NV v ASIC*[53] was a challenging decision for the regulator.

The outcome of the final appeal was that the company (JHL) was found to have made misleading statements to the ASX in June 2002 and failed to comply with continuous disclosure obligations. The CFO at the time, Mr Morley, was in breach of his duty in advising the board and thereby limited the nature of the predicted analysis of compensation. Similarly, the company secretary and general counsel, Mr Shafron, had part of his appeal upheld, but was still found to be in breach of his duty to advise the board. The other non-executive directors, including the chair, Ms Hellicar, were successful in their appeals such that the finding of breaches of the officers' duty in s 180 were removed (in respect of the approved minutes of the board meeting, which became the ASX announcement on asbestos compensation). ASIC was criticised for not calling

47 *R v Williams* (2005) 216 ALR 113.

48 *R v Adler* [2005] NSWSC 274.

49 *ASIC v Vizard* (2005) 145 FCR 57.

50 *ASIC v Vines* [2005] NSWSC 738. For a detailed discussion of this case, see M Adams, "Officers' Duties under the Microscope" (2005) 57(8) *Keeping Good Companies* 516.

51 *ASIC v MacDonald (No 11)* (2009) 230 FLR 1 and penalties imposed at *ASIC v MacDonald (No 12)* (2009) 259 ALR 116.

52 *Morley v ASIC* (2010) 247 FLR 140.

53 *James Hardie Industries NV v ASIC* (2010) 274 ALR 85.

a particular witness (an external lawyer) who was present at the relevant board meeting of JHL.[54]

Then in 2012, the HCA finally ruled on the *James Hardie litigation* with a clear statement, holding the non-executive directors liable in *ASIC v Hellicar*.[55] The matter was also remitted to the NSW Court of Appeal for the determination of the appropriate penalty for the non-executive. But the executive director that appealed, the company secretary and general counsel, was dismissed and the person was held to have failed to advice the CEO and board of information from the professional advisors and the famous media release of 16th February 2001, in *Shafron v ASIC*.[56]

Are Laws Derived from Older Principles?

[2.130] Many of the principles of law discussed above can be derived from the basic legal duties which were borrowed, by way of an analogy to the duties owed by the trustees to the beneficiaries, from *Re German Mining Co; Ex parte Chippendale*.[57] Although the *Corporations Act* in many ways codifies the common law and equitable duties, there is still an overlap even though they have different outcomes in terms of remedies or sanctions.

Around the world, consumers and citizens are increasingly concerned about environmental problems. Consequently, they are becoming more and more conscious of the impact their purchasing decisions may have on the environment.[58] This has led the "green" market to expand drastically over the last few years.

---

54 For more detailed discussions, see A Hargovan, "Directors' and Officers' Duty of Care Following James Hardie" (2009) 61(7) *Keeping Good Companies* 586; R Head, "Directors and Officers Still in the Firing Line – A Guide to Managing Risk" (2010) 62(1) *Keeping Good Companies* 57.

55 *ASIC v Hellicar* (2012) 86 ALJR 522; see M Adams, "Lessons for Non-Executives from James Hardie Litigation" (2012) 64(2) *Keeping Good Companies* 263.

56 *Shafron v ASIC* (2012) 86 ALJR 584; see A Hargovan, "Raising the Bar for General Counsel and Company Secretaries – High Court Decision in James Hardie" (2012) 64(2) *Keeping Good Companies* 260.

57 *Re German Mining Co; Ex parte Chippendale* (1853) 43 ER 415.

58 National Geographic, "Greendex 2010: Consumer Choice and the Environment – A Worldwide Tracking Survey" (June 2010) <https://www.nationalgeographic.com/greendex/assets/GS_NGS_Full_Report_May09.pdf> and updated reports at <https://globescan.com/tag/greendex/>; for example <https://greengrowthindex.gggi.org/wp-content/uploads/2021/01/2020-Green-Growth-Index.pdf>; A Bodger and M Monks, "Getting in the Red over Green: The Risks with 'Green' Marketing" (2010) 3(3) *Journal of Sponsorship* 284.

For instance, the Australian market for sustainable products and services has surged from $12 billion in 2007 to $21.5 billion in 2010. It is predicted that the market will be valued at over $30 billion.[59] Consequently, green marketing has become popular as such marketing may attract environmental conscious consumers to buy green products. Green marketing may be defined as the "marketers attempt to develop strategies targeting the 'environmental consumer'".[60]

This is important as green marketing may be accompanied with the concept of "greenwash"[61] where the manufacturer or retailer promotes the green credentials of a product but overstates the benefits and potentially misleads the end consumer.

The 2011 introduction of the *Australian Consumer Law*[62] brings the laws all under one umbrella. Today, s 18 of the *Australian Consumer Law* has replaced s 52 of the *Trade Practices Act 1974*. However, overlapping provisions in the *Corporations Act 2001* (Cth)[63] and the *Australian Securities and Investments Commission Act 2001* (Cth) (*ASIC Act*)[64] regarding misleading and deceptive conduct in the financial service area continue to exist. The CSR notions, such as green marketing have become popular.[65] This approach to marketing is paralleled with the prevailing view that corporations should behave in a socially responsible manner.[66]

A number of definitions for CSR have developed over the years. These definitions have related to different stakeholders and have centred on some or all of the following five dimensions:[67]

---

59 Mobium Group, "Green Market – State of Play – Research Project Summary – Australia" (May 2011) 4 <https://www.mobium.com.au>.

60 S McDaniel and D Rylander, "Strategic Green Marketing" (1993) 10(3) *Journal of Consumer Marketing* 4.

61 M Nehme and M Adams, "Section 18 of the Australian Consumer Law and Environmental Issues" (2012) 24(1) *Bond Law Review* 30.

62 Schedule 2 of the *Competition and Consumer Act 2010* (Cth), which came into force on 1 January 2011.

63 *Corporations Act 2001* (Cth), s 1041H.

64 *Australian Securities and Investments Commission Act 2001* (Cth), s 12DA.

65 MacDaniel and Rylander.

66 P Bronn and A Vrioni, "Corporate Social Responsibility and Cause-Related Marketing: An Overview" (2001) 20 *International Journal of Advertising* 207; I Maignan, O Ferrell and L Ferrell, "A Stakeholder Model for Implementing Social Responsibility in Marketing" (2005) 9 *European Journal of Marketing* 956.

67 A Dahsrud, "How Corporate Social Responsibility Is Defined: An Analysis of 37 Definitions" (2008) 15(1) *Corporate Social Responsibility and Environmental Management* 1.

- the environmental dimension;
- the social dimension;
- the economic dimension;
- the stakeholder dimension; and
- the voluntariness for actions and reporting dimension.

Additionally, the related concepts such as corporate citizens[68] and corporate social performance[69] have been debated since the 1950s.[70] However, there is no consensus on a definition for CSR[71] and this highlights the complexity of the concept itself.

CSR may be viewed as involving only purely voluntary acts. The Manne and Wallich defined this term as "a condition in which the corporation is at least in some measure a free agent. To the extent that any of the foregoing social objectives are imposed on the corporation by law, the corporation exercises no responsibility when it implements them".[72] Alternatively, CSR may also be referred to as a business approach by which an organisation considers the manner in which its activities may impact different stakeholders.[73]

---

68 D Matten and A Crane, "Corporate Citizenship: Toward an Extended Theoretical Conceptualization" (2005) 30(1) *The Academy of Management Review* 166; D Matten, A Crane and W Chapple, "Behind the Mask: Revealing the True Face of Corporate Citizenship" (2003) 45 *Journal of Business Ethics* 109.

69 D Wood, "Corporate Social Performance Revisited" (1991) 16(4) *Academy of Management Review* 691; M Clarkson, "A Stakeholder Framework for Analyzing and Evaluating Corporate Social Performance" (1995) 20 *Academy of Management Review* 92.

70 H Bowen, *Social Responsibilities of the Businessman* (New York University Press, New York, 1953) xi; A Carroll, "Corporate Social Responsibility: Evolution of a Definition Construct" (1999) 38(3) *Business and Society* 268; R Briggs, "Corporate Social Responsibility and Sustainability" in T Gillis (ed), *The IABC Handbook of Organizational Communication: A Guide to Internal Communication, Public Relations, Marketing and Leadership* (John Wiley and Sons, San Francisco, 2nd ed, 2011) 79. However, it is important to note that as early as the 1930s, the concept of CSR has been referred to. However, the publication of Bowen's book in 1953 led to the start of a modern era of CSR. A Carroll, "A Three-Dimensional Conceptual Model of Corporate Performance" (1979) 4(4) *The Academy of Management Review* 497.

71 Corporations and Markets Advisory Committee, *The Social Responsibility of Corporations Report* (2006) 13.

72 H Manne and H Wallich, *The Modern Corporation and Social Responsibility* (Washington American Enterprise Institute for Public Policy Research, Washington, 1973) 106.

73 Corporations and Markets Advisory Committee, *The Social Responsibility of Corporations Report* (2006) 13.

Influence of ASX Corporate Governance Principles

[2.140] The eight principles prescribed in the fourth edition of ASX Principles of Good Corporate Governance. While the word leadership has been repeatedly mentioned in Principle 1, it focuses on the foundations for management and oversight.[74] It is in Principle 3, that leadership is mentioned in the context of acting ethically and responsibly. The tenant of the recommendations was that: "A listed entity's reputation is one of its most valuable assets and, if damaged, can be one of the most difficult to restore." Therefore, ethical behaviour is reduced to preserve the reputation of organisations and not because acting ethical is the "right thing" to do.

The ASX suggested contents for a code of conduct states among other things that, clearly states the organisation's expectation that all directors, senior executives and employees will:

- act in the best interests of the entity;
- act honestly and with high standards of personal integrity;
- comply with the laws and regulations that apply to the entity and its operations;
- not knowingly participate in any illegal or unethical activity;
- not enter into any arrangement or participate in any activity that would conflict with the entity's best interests or that would be likely to negatively affect the entity's reputation;
- not take advantage of the property or information of the entity or its customers for personal gain or to cause detriment to the entity or its customers; and
- not take advantage of their position or the opportunities arising therefrom for personal gain.

On closer inspection of the above list it places the entity's best interests as the first on the list and "not knowingly engages in illegal or unethical conduct" as the ethical standards by-line. Further, it offers no measurements of what constitutes "act honestly and with high standards of personal integrity".

The 2016 South African King Report IV on corporate governance offers more direction and help in how ethical leadership is part and parcel of good corporate governance. The key author of the report, Professor Mervyn King emphasises

74 ASX Corporate Governance Council, "Corporate Governance Principles and Recommendations" (3rd ed, 2014) <http://www.asx.com.au/documents/asx-compliance/cgc-principles-and-recommendations-3rd-edn.pdf>.

that, "the overarching objective of King Report IV is to make corporate governance more accessible and relevant to a wider range of organisations, and to be the catalyst for a shift from a compliance-based mindset to one that sees corporate governance as a lever for value creation".[75] One of the objectives of the King Report IV are to promote corporate governance as integral to running an organisation and delivering governance outcomes such as ethical culture, good performance, effective control and legitimacy.

This report also defined corporate governance in the following terms: ethical culture, good performance, effective controls and legitimacy. Further in Principle 2 of the report it states that, "The governing body should govern the ethics of the organization in a way that supports the establishment of an ethical culture." While it did offer a list of recommendations to establish an ethical culture, the solutions include institute a code of conduct and assignment of managerial responsibilities. Such a structural approach to ethics only goes so far instituting policies, procedures and practices. At the heart of culture is "people", and shaping behaviour requires good leadership to lead the way.

In 2007, Adams and Young argued that, "Leadership is not governance. Instead leadership should be viewed as a facet of governance. Leadership in an organisational context can be defined as the ability to influence others or direct the activities of a group of people towards a common shared goal or outcomes."[76] The role of leadership is thus a yardstick for ethical conduct aided by corporate governance principles as framework to establish good practice and legal rules as default rules and penalty for misconduct.

The United Kingdom has taken a different approach with the enactment of s 172 of the *Companies Act 2006* (UK). There has been a plethora of debate surrounding the approach to directorial decision-making in the scheme of corporate governance. A divergence has emerged between numerous schools of thought as to whose interests the directors are to consider in conducting the company's management. The English law approach was to codified under s 172 which professes an "enlightened shareholder value" approach to corporate governance. This has given rise to scrutiny and challenge from numerous critics but most notably from proponents of the "stakeholder management" stance.[77]

---

75 See <https://www2.deloitte.com/za/en/pages/africa-centre-for-corporate-governance/articles/kingiv-report-on-corporate-governance.html>.

76 M Adams and A Young, "Regulating Corporate Governors: Rethinking Board Responsibilities and Liabilities" (2007) 59(1) *Keeping Good Companies* 11.

77 A Keay, "The Duty to Promote the Success of the Company: Is It Fit for Purpose?" (2011) 32 *The Company Lawyer* 1.

Section 172 inaugurated an "enlightened shareholder value" approach so that directors, in fulfilling their duty towards *the company* are required to "act in the way [they] consider, in good faith, would be most likely to promote the success of the company for the benefit of its members as a whole, and in doing so have regard" to other factors insofar as they promote the company's interests; thus, the legislation equates the interests of the shareholders with the company's success.

Although other factors such as, *inter alia*, the company's employees, suppliers and customers, the long-term consequences etc are to feature in decision-making, these factors will be subordinate to the interests of the shareholders. Thus, the intention of the provision is not to engender a surreptitious adoption of "stakeholder management", as the assertion suggests, since the interests of other stakeholders are only instrumental to ensuring that the company is profitable which is causatively linked to the members' interests.[78]

The imposition of a subjective standard by requiring "good faith" appears *prima facie* to be counterproductive to consistency as it does not appear to set any threshold standard for directors. Nonetheless, the legislative guidance illustrates that compliance with s 172 is supplemented by the "duty of care" embodied in statute, with an objectivity given that directors are required to act with a degree of "reasonable care, skill and diligence".

In *Regentcrest v Cohen*,[79] Parker J articulated that a subjective standard necessitates a consideration of what the director "genuinely" and "honestly" believed was conducive to promoting the company's success. This, in conjunction with good commercial reasons for acting entitled the UK court to conclude that a policy to excuse the debts of the directors was advancing the success of the company.

The courts seem reluctant to interfere with directorial decisions on the premise that corporate entities should be largely administered by internal management save to the extent that legal input is unavoidable. Directors are in a better position to meet the demands of the individual company in *R v HM Treasury*[80] and the courts thus adopt a non-interventionist stance.

The view that a company is "organised and carried on primarily for the profit of the [shareholders]" has been articulated in the US decision of *Dodge v Ford*

---

78 R Williams, "Enlightened Shareholder Value in UK Company Law" (2012) 35(1) UNSW Law Journal 360.

79 *Regentcrest v Cohen* [2001] BCC 494.

80 *R v HM Treasury* [2009] EWHC 3020.

Motor Co (1919)[81] but the UK position is now different to Australia and the United States. Thus, s 172 can arguably be viewed as an effective development in ensuring that the company's success is *always* at the forefront of decision-making. A key question is whether Australia should adopt a similar provision to the UK's enlightened shareholder in s 172.

So what does ESG Mean?

[2.150] There is a growing trend in the 21st century which may be a shift away from CSR as the driver for CSR or perhaps a redefinition of its place in the corporate governance framework. The trend has been two-pronged; one is the rise and rise of the influence of institutional investors globally and in each national jurisdiction and their use of socially responsible investment principles using the lenses of environmental, social and governance issues, collectively known as ESG.

ESG is now an accepted "concept" applied by institutional investors such as banks, pension systems, superannuation funds and fund managers across the globe, departments in these organisations are staffed by teams of professionals managing the wealth of beneficial members – retirees, pensioners and superannuants valued in the trillions of dollars.[82]

The second prong is the shift of CSR from the voluntary governance codes of the 1990s to corporate governance compliance becoming mandatory and set in legislation, and stock exchange listing rules also backed by law.[83] Together with this shift has been the acceptance of risk management practices as integral to corporate governance and also enshrined in legislation such as the requirement of all Australian financial institutions to maintain risk management systems.[84]

Finally, there is the concept of "sustainability" in that the strategy and or activity of the company must be focused beyond the short or medium term. Together these two prongs are supported by the growing trend in the rise of the application of ESG by institutional investors globally that has incorporated CSR into the ESG concept, as applied by institutional investors in their assessment of

---

81 *Dodge v Ford Motor Co*, 170 NW 668 (Mich, 1919).

82 R G Eccles, M D Kastrapeli and S J Potter, "How to Integrate ESG into Investment Decision-Making: Results of a Global Survey of Institutional Investors" (2017) 29(4) *Journal of Applied Corporate Finance* 125.

83 S J Griffith, "Corporate Governance in an Era of Compliance" (2016) 57(6) *William & Mary Law Review* 2075.

84 *Corporations Act 2001* (Cth), s 912A.

their portfolio of investments in all jurisdictions and in many ways converging a local approach to corporate governance to a global approach.

Institutional investors have a fiduciary responsibility to act in the best interests of the beneficial or ultimate owners of the funds under their management. The shift of these funds from investing in companies that are not only profitable but continue to have a growing trend to profits to being more concerned with how these profits are achieved and the internal governance of the company and the company's relationship with other stakeholders. The exponential growth of shareholdings and subsequent influence on companies of institutional investors demands the attention of corporate citizens far more intently than does the social pressure of being responsible, as directors also have duties and responsibilities to be totally responsive to their shareholders.[85]

The Growth and Importance of Information Governance

[2.160] Information governance, data protection and security, privacy, cybersecurity and artificial intelligence (AI) have all become critical topics for boards and government bodies to consider. Historically, the issues tended to be dealt with under either "information technology (IT)" issues or records and information compliance issues. In recent years, the importance of cybersecurity, AI and data analytics together with changing privacy regulations have brought new governance challenges to the forefront of the minds of directors.

There are common themes in the surveys of top issues confronting boards of directors, which have been carried out in recent years. These include the opportunities and challenges arising from technology innovation and disruption, the overriding concern of cybersecurity and data breach, which is highlighting the importance of information security, and regulatory compliance including changing privacy regulations.

The Akin Gump Lawyers group in the US report an annual "Top 10 Topics for Directors" each year, which is published in the *Harvard Law School Forum on Corporate Governance and Financial Regulation* website.[86] The 2020 report, that came out in January 2020, placed cybersecurity at number 7 (the 2019 report had it as the number 8 issue). Similarly the EY Centre for Board Matters ranked

85 P Iliev et al, *Shareholder Voting and Corporate Governance around the World* (Oxford University Press on behalf of The Society for Financial Studies, 2015).

86 Akin Gump, *Top 10 Topics for Directors in 2020* (9 January 2020) <https://www.akingump.com/en/experience/practices/corporate/ag-deal-diary/top-10-topics-for-directors-in-2020-executive-summary.html>.

"prioritizing cybersecurity and data privacy" as their number 4 key issue for boards.[87]

To add further evidence to the importance of this topic, Diligent, in its 2020 *Foresight: Year Ahead in Corporate Governance* report sets out that, "[t]echnology, processes and insights are the foundation of modern governance, enabling boards to effectively navigate this changing landscape".

The top law firm, King & Wood Mallesons, in its 2016 *Directions* report had listed digital disruption at number 3. By the release of its 2019 *Directions: Navigating a New Order*[88] report, the issue of managing IT and cybersecurity had moved to the number 2 spot as a priority for boards.

In 2019, the Governance Institute of Australia released its own paper, entitled "The Future of the Governance Professional"[89] and had three major themes – technological disruption was the third highest priority for governance changes into the future (2025). Over 75% of the respondents agreed that the issue was vital or very important due to "the use of new technology and its effects on the workforce, and also because the rate of change and implementation of these technologies is accelerating".[90] The other themes of complexity and regulatory change are top of mind for many directors and governance professionals.

However, it is the impact of technological disruption that is having far-reaching consequences. This is seen by the growing use of AI and its earlier incarnation, machine learning, in business to change the role of the governance and compliance professional. There is a role for humans and that is perceived to oversee machines and to make qualitative judgments.

There is acceptance that machines will be better than humans at some tasks, including taking minutes, gathering vast amounts of information and highlighting what is relevant for directors. But there will still be a need for emotional intelligence and creativity, which humans bring to the table (with bias and other unconscious attitudes). As well as AI, the developments in

---

87 EY Center for Board Matters, *Eight Priorities for Boards in 2020* (Harvard Law School Forum on Corporate Governance, 14 January 2020) <https://corpgov.law.harvard.edu/2020/01/14/eight-priorities-for-boards-in-2020/>.

88 King & Wood Mallesons, *Directions 2019: Navigating a New Order* <https://www.kwm.com/en/au/knowledge/hubs/directions-non-executive-directors>.

89 GIA, *The Future of the Governance Professional* (August 2019) <https://www.governanceinstitute.com.au/media/884166/govinst_the-future-of-the-governance-professional_august-2019.pdf>.

90 Corporations and Markets Advisory Committee, *Report on Personal Liability for Corporate Fault* (26 September 2006) 9.

real-time information flows, big data analysis, increased automation and improved "regtech" with blockchain and voice recognition to all affect the governance role. The 2019 report notes that 39% of respondents thought it would make the governance professional role more interesting and high level, as well as 25% thought it would improve the quality of information that the board receives in its papers.

Corporate Governance in the Digital Economy

[2.170] Previously, the author examined the link between corporate governance and the digital economy in *Governance Directions*.[91] The definition of information governance has generally been accepted as:

> the activities and technologies that organisations employ to maximise the value of information while minimising associated risks and costs.

This definition has been affirmed by 90% of the Information Governance ANZ (InfoGovANZ) survey report, published in 2019.[92] The 2021 survey report accepted the definition by 81% of the respondents.[93] This survey built on the 2017 edition[94] and reinforced that information governance is an umbrella concept that describes all information management activities.

Traditional governance processes are just not fit for their purpose now and what stakeholders, including governments, regulators, owners and employees actually expect. There is a distinction between governance practices in the digital age and a framework for contemporary governance.

Information Governance Core to Good Business Management

[2.180] The 2021 InfoGovANZ survey report had 338 (2019 survey had 340) industry participants and highlights the importance of an information governance framework. Implementing such a framework was seen by 46% of industry professionals as the most important issue (see Figure 2.3). The survey

91 M Adams and S Bennett, "Corporate Governance in the Digital Economy: The Critical Importance of Information Governance" (2018) 70(10) *Governance Directions* 631.

92 Information Governance ANZ, *IG Industry Survey* (July 2019) <https://www.infogovanz.com/wp-content/uploads/2020/01/IGANZ2019ReportFinal.pdf>.

93 Information Governance ANZ, *IG Industry Report* (May 2021) <https://www.infogovanz.com/wp-content/uploads/2021/05/InfoGov_IndustrySurvey_MAY2021.pdf>.

94 Information Governance ANZ, *IG Industry Survey* (August 2017) <https://www.infogovanz.com/wp-content/uploads/2020/01/IGANZ_Industry_Survey_AUGUST_2017.pdf>.

Figure 2.3: Changes in reasons for implementing an information governance framework

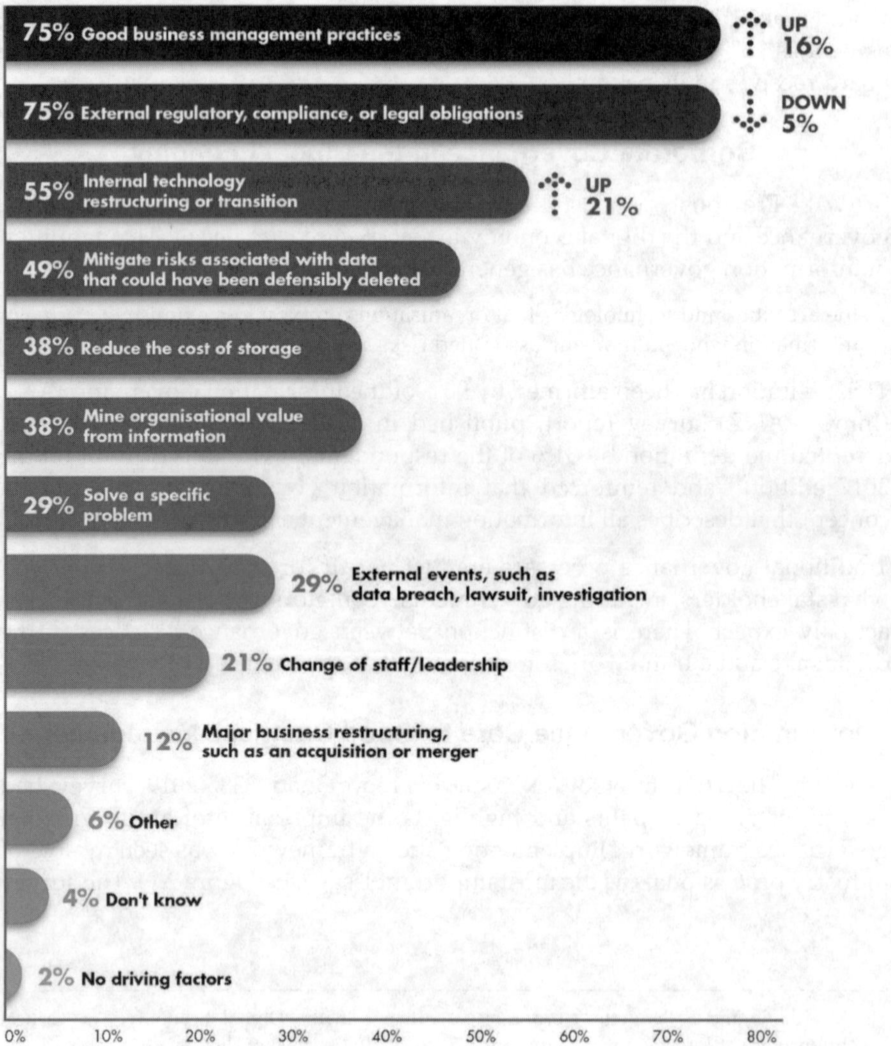

derived that the three main drivers for information governance projects were as follows:

- **Good business management practices** – 75% respondents in 2019, which reflected a 16% increase from the 2017 survey;
- **External regulatory, compliance or legal obligations** – 75% respondents in 2019, which was 5% lower than the 2017 survey; and
- **Internal technology restructuring or transition** – 55% respondents in 2019, which was a massive 21% increase from the 2017 survey.

Over half of all respondents said that their organisations, both private and government, had information governance framework with policies and procedures in place. About 75% of participants had identified specific information governance projects to be underway or planned for 2020.

Information governance programs in organisations are now maturing, 54% of respondents indicated their programs were intermediate of advanced.

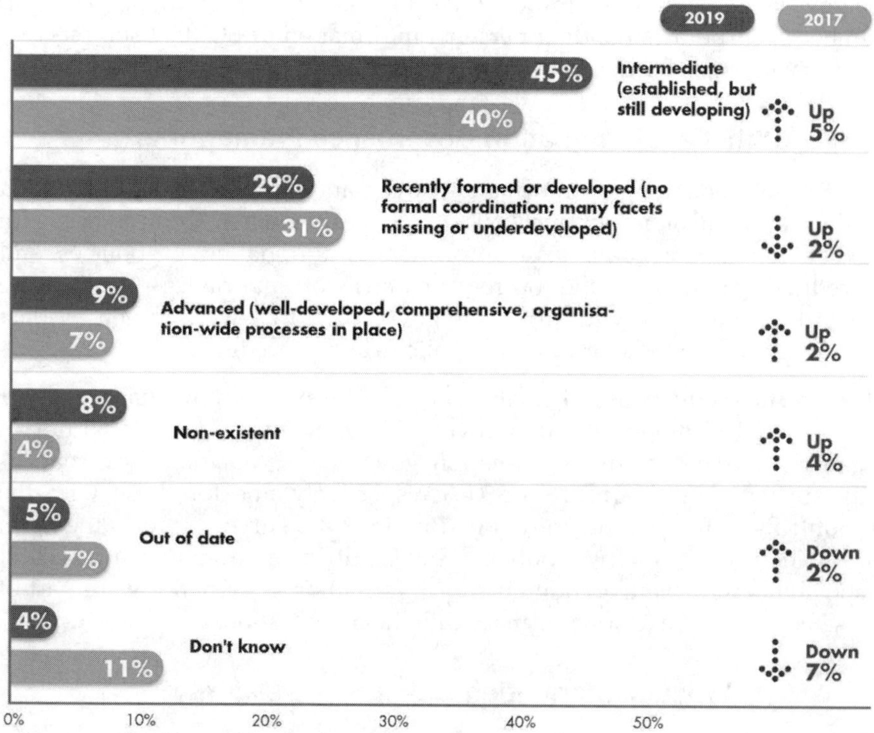

Impact of Privacy Regulations

[2.190] It was noted that 40% of the respondents stated that recent changes to privacy regulations had been a driver for their current projects in information governance. This could be identified by two significant changes that occurred in 2018. The first was the European Union's General Data Protection Regulation (GDPR), which came into force on 25 May 2018, imposing a significant change to privacy laws in Europe. Organisation that fail to comply with GDPR requirements (including non-EU country organisations) can face fines of up to 20 million Euros or 4% of global turnover. The other factor in Australia was the implementation of the Notifiable Data Breaches Scheme (NDB Scheme) that came into force on 22 February 2018. The NDB Scheme requires organisations to notify the Australian Information Commissioner and individuals whose personal information is involved in a data breach that is likely to result in serious harm.

An interesting aspect is that those industry professionals that worked in the private sector (55%) were more driven by these changes to privacy laws than the government employed professionals (36%). This may be due to a greater number of corporates handing personal information of EU data subjects and dealing with cross-border transfers of personal data as a result of the GDPR.

What are Information Governance Frameworks?

[2.200] Implementing an information governance framework was identified as the key area of importance by 46% of respondents. Compliance with privacy regulations, data loss prevention and updating of policies and procedures rounded out the top four key areas of importance – 16.2% were driven by compliance with privacy regulations, 10.4% were driven by data loss prevention and 9% for updating policies and procedures.

Most participants believed that a chief information governance officer was essential to the information governance frameworks success within an organisation. The words "information governance" or "data governance" only appeared in about 12% or 11% respectively title for those with the accountability for the organisation. But in 2017 survey report, the term information governance was only in 5% of job titles. More significantly, 41% of respondents who were accountable for information governance were part of the senior executive (c-suite) team within the organisation.

What is Information Governance Maturity?

[2.210] Information governance programs in organisations appear to be maturing with 54% indicating their programs were intermediate or advanced.

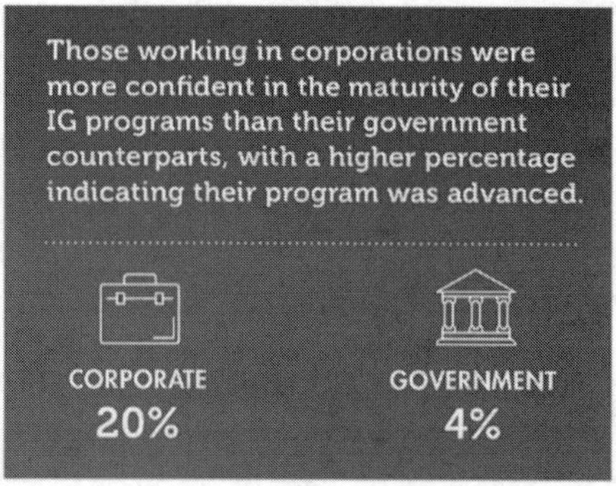

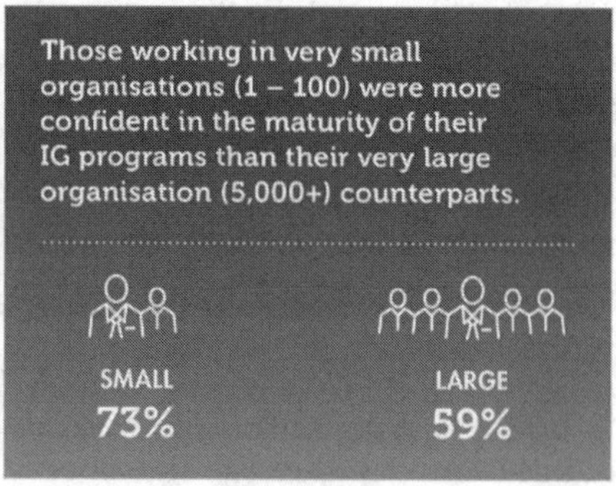

Responses indicated a fairly even split between proactive and reactive approaches to information governance. This was most in line with the previous survey results, however, participants appeared to have better clarity of their programs, with only 7% indicating they did not know compared to 16% in the previous survey.

This data can be compared to the United States, where ARMA International has published survey results in the *Information Governance Maturity Index Report 2020*.[95] This survey had over 1,200 responses, which were subject to a gateway question (of qualifications and skills) and checks for duplications and incomplete answers to establish 912 full responses. The scale applied for all the domains were from level 1 (a non-existent framework) to level 5 (transformational). The middle level 3 was stated to be essential (which equates to a basic requirement in information governance to do the job).

Across all domains measured, including infrastructures, supports, processes, capabilities and a steering committee, 66.2% stated that their organisations were essential (level 3) or higher. Within particular domains or attributes, ARMA found that having a Steering Committee, with information governance leadership, and links to information management and business unit applications, scored a maturity index of 62.7%. In the area of authorities, meaning authoritative frameworks, privacy requirements and best practices, 72.1% scored essential level 3 or higher.

Finally, for the attribute supports, including change management and project management, the maturity score was 67.7% for level 3 and above. The ARMA report highlights that a clear majority of respondents reported that their organisations have the essentials in place or better with respect to each

95 ARMA International, *Information Governance Maturity Index Report 2020* <https://www.arma.org/page/ig-report>.

of the domains and for their overall information governance programs. All this data indicates the growing maturity of information governance within organisations and allows information governance professionals to assess how their organisation is tracking against the survey results of the InfoGovANZ and ARMA reports.

So Alignment is the Key to Information Governance?

[2.220] The key to good information governance is to align data and information governance with overall strategic objectives. This requires organisations to identify and coordinate different IG areas and activities. The *Elements of Information Governance* diagram (see Figure 2.4) illustrates the various areas, which can be adjusted as necessary, to provide a clearer understanding of how the overarching information governance framework enables alignment of policies, procedures, people and technologies.[96]

Figure 2.4: Information governance framework (InfoGovANZ)

The elements link to the icons and the IG centre in a continuous chain. All of the elements must combine and connect to provide an effective information governance system. The elements on the top and middle rows to the left

96 Information Governance ANZ, *Information Governance: Optimising the Lifeblood of Organisations* (November 2019) <https://www.infogovanz.com/information-governance/information-governance-optimising-the-lifeblood-of-organisations/>.

reflect people-focused activities, while those to the right are data-focused activities. The elements on the bottom row are information-focused and reflect foundation services.

The icons surrounding the IG centre represent information governance and the elements to be aligned:

- innovation and technology initiatives (lightbulb);
- optimising the value of data and minimising costs by reducing risk (dollar sign);
- technologies, systems and people across organisational silos (cog/gear);
- data and information security (lock);
- people skills and collaborative culture with supporting structures (the information governance committee or equivalent) across organisational silos to meet information governance and organisational objectives, and an external focus on customers and citizens and the handling of their personal information and transparency (people); and
- policies and procedures (house).

The house icon services as a reminder that robust information governance requires a top-down strategic approach building on a strong foundation of clear policies and procedures. The information governance framework enables directors and senior executives to achieve organisational objectives and to optimise the value of data and information while minimising risks and costs by:

- identifying all the areas and technologies – that is, the information governance elements in your organisation;
- putting strategic objectives and priorities in place for managing, controlling and securing the data and information your organisation collects, uses and stores;
- optimising the opportunities of new technologies and innovations to harness value and insights from data;
- implementing appropriate risk management to minimise costs, such as those associated with a data breach and eDiscovery in litigation and legal proceedings;
- implementing measures to protect the organisation's intellectual property; and
- complying with regulatory and legal obligations including, record keeping obligations and, in particular, changing privacy regulations.

What is the Impact of Cybersecurity and DAO Developments?

[2.230] GRC2020 published "2021 Trends: Governance, Risk Management & Compliance (GRC): An Integrated Focus on Business Integrity and Resiliency" in January 2021. This document explains the lessons learnt from 2020 with GRC functions. Governance needs reliably achieve objectives and risk management to address uncertainties. Compliance must act with integrity and there is a need for interconnected risk analysis. Disruption has become the norm and only dynamic and agile businesses can survive. The 2021 will without doubt rely upon integrity, resilience and integration.

Information security from cybersecurity issues will be the number one issue for the next few years. The 2020 pandemic has required greater focus on health and safety, as well as the broader environment. Similarly, the greater use of GRC technology to address these changing trends. There will be greater engagement with stakeholders, in particular, with consumers and employees, but also with the regulatory authorities globally.

It has been reported that cyber ransom threats have been made to 1,500 key bodies in Australia in 2021.[97] The organisations have been governments, schools, healthcare providers, law firms and other entities. Data has been stolen by cyber criminals or held to ransom. More than 75,000 organisations worldwide have failed to update their Microsoft Exchange email servers following the discovery of a major vulnerability in January 2021. It is believed that Chinese state-sponsored hacking group, called "Hafnium" was behind the majority of the cyber attacks. Although Microsoft released multiple security updates, had 92% update the vulnerability by March 2021, that still left a major hole to be exploited.

This same issue hit the Prime Minister's office in Malaysia, the US Chemical Safety/Hazard Board and the Michigan Supreme Court, to name a few organisations. No Australian federal or state government domain is identified as being at risk. However, 32 Australian healthcare providers have not updated their servers and are at risk, as well as 18 law firms and 24 private schools.

In September 2021, a government report was released that showed the Australian Cyber Security Centre received 67,500 reports, last financial year, of attacks – up 13% on the previous year. It appears that China is responsible for more than two-thirds of state-sponsored cyber attacks around the world.[98]

---

97 L Mendes, "Cyber Ransom Threat to 1500 Key Bodies", *The Australian* (16 September 2021).

98 A Galloway, "China behind Majority of Cyber Attacks", *Sydney Morning Herald* (16 September 2021).

Additionally, in September 2021 a former UNSW student has been sentenced to seven years imprisonment for pleading guilty to stealing A$123 million (US$90 million) from investors in a cryptocurrency fraud. Mr Stefan Qin was born in Canberra and was convicted in a New York Court for deliberately falsifying account statements from over 100 investors for personal gain. The then 20-year-old ran a crypto fund called Virgil Sigma Fund from Sydney in 2017 through a company (Virgil Capital). He was reported to have made 500% over 12 months for his clients by the *Wall Street Journal*.[99]

The latest challenge to the legal status of investments and the meaning of corporations and/or securities (shares) is the development of decentralised autonomous organisations (DAO). DAO are a type of cryptocurrency, that are based on blockchain technology and create units or tokens, which can give rights, such as voting or dividends. There is some confusion in the public mind, as one of the first DAO in April 2016 was launched with the entity's name "The DAO" from a crowdfunding campaign. It was based on a particular blockchain, known as Ethereum (ETH) and raised over US$150 million. In June 2016, hackers attacked the DAO vulnerabilities and they gained access to 3.6 million ETH, worth about US$50 million at the time. After massive and contentious arguments among DAO investors, a compromise was found and funds were repaid to investors. In July 2017, the US Securities and Exchange Commission (SEC), which has federal control of securities, found the sale of DAO tokens on the ETH blockchain was violating parts of the US securities law.

However, apart from the entity known as The DAO, the concept of DAO has started to grown again in 2021 due to the US State of Wyoming basing legislation that allows such tokens to be created and issued to investors. The Maker Foundation, an icon in the crypto industry as the original champion of DAO, announced it was officially turning operations over to MakerDAO (the creator of the DAI stablecoin) and would then dissolve.

One of the most challenging aspects of DAO is agreeing on a definition. The one adopted by Harvard academics Hassan and de Filippi is:

> A DAO is a blockchain-based system that enables people to coordinate and govern themselves mediated by a set of self-executing rules deployed on a public blockchain, and whose governance is decentralised (independent from central control).[100]

---

99 J Sier, "UNSW Dropout Jailed for $123m Crypto Scam", *Australian Financial Review* (17 September 2021).

100 S Hassan and P de Filippi, "Decentralized Autonomous Organization" (2021) 10(2) *Internet Policy Review*.

There are this moment in time approximately seven DAO operating from dVest Labs DAO to Index Coop DAO, Dash, Augur, Steem, BanklessDAO and The DAO. It is worth noting that depending upon English dialect, there are a variety of spelling of DAO, which includes distributed autonomous organisation and decentralised autonomous company.[101]

Organisational theory has an abundance of literature on decentralised organisations of several kinds.[102] Yet, the first reference to actual DAO only emerged in the 1990s to describe multi-agent systems in the Internet of Things environment.[103] However, the modern application of DAO or DAC (distributed autonomous corporations) meaning can be traced to the appearance of Bitcoin.[104] DACs were described as a new corporate governance form, using tokens tradable like shares and providing dividends to stakeholders. In theory, shareholders could via the token enjoy a share of the profits and participate in its growth and have a say in how the business is run. The ideal was that blockchains do not need regulation, as the owners do not want to regulate them. This is quoted by Vitalik Buterin, who would later be the co-founder of the ETH platform of blockchain, which traded The DAO and other cryptocurrencies and tokens.

While it could be argued that Bitcoin was effectively the first DAO in 2014, the term today is understood to be the network or organisation rather than the product or outcome token. The current academic literature on DAOs is fairly limited, but there is much more in the technical blockchain discipline. This may rapidly change with the US State of Wyoming passing legislation blockchain laws in 2019 and then a *Decentralized Autonomous Organizations Act 2020* (Wyoming) (*DAO Act*),[105] which came into force on 1st July 2021. Wyoming has been a world leader with DAO and builds on its amendments to the business form, known as a limited liability company (LLC). Although the US has a *Uniform Commercial Code*, Wyoming made a number of amendments to make virtual currencies and digital securities and tokens to be issued to investors.[106]

---

101 As an Australian book, the "decentralised autonomous organisation" is applied for DAO.

102 M Shubik, "Incentives, Decentralized Control, the Assignment of Joint Costs and Internal Pricing" (1962) 8(3) *Management Science* 325; J R Freeland and N R Baker, "Goal Partitioning in a Hierarchical Organization" (1975) 3(6) *Omega* 673.

103 W Dilger, "Decentralized Autonomous Organization of the Intelligent Home According to the Principle of the Immune System" (1997) *1997 IEEE International Conference on Systems, Man, and Cybernetics* 351.

104 S Nakamoto, *Bitcoin: A Peer-to-Peer Electronic Cash System* (2008).

105 *Decentralized Autonomous Organizations Act 2020* (Wyoming).

106 Wyoming Statutes, Title 17, "Chapter 29 – Wyoming Limited Liability Company Act" (Arts 1–11).

In terms of governance, there are diverse scholars have started to investigate the opportunities of blockchain technology and smart contracts to experiment with open and distributed governance structures;[107] along with the challenges and limitations of such forms. Although the use of the term "DAO" is now fairly established in the blockchain space, yet there are still many misconceptions and unresolved legal issues under discussion around the term of art.

It is particularly challenging whether the tokens that are issues are the same or equivalent of "securities". If they are, as has been argued, then the Federal jurisdiction rather than State laws should be applied and the SEC has indicated that it is their opinion, but this is sure to be challenged in the US Supreme Court at some point in the future.

Conclusion – The Future of Corporate Governance

[2.240] As this chapter has examined, the competing concepts of corporate governance, including CSR and ESG, as well as due diligence and compliance, are challenging. The principles are applied to all companies, but a greater focus on public companies (in particular, those listed on a stock exchange).

Some of the commentary that indicates confusion is led by the public listed companies that have to deal with a constantly changing environment. Specifically, there is a power play between the board and its stakeholders, as it impacts on employees, suppliers, local communities and the broader physical environment. Additionally, may ordinary people, either directly as an investment or via their superannuation fund, have mandates to invest in an ethical way. Thus, the importance of institutional investors and trillion-dollar super funds with clear mandates around fossil fuels or gambling or sustainability are changing the future directions and strategies of corporations.

The key to good corporate governance is a strong information governance framework aligned to achieve organisational objectives with top-down leadership. Effective information governance is when policies, technologies and people all align and work together to enable data and information to be optimised and regulatory compliance of privacy, record keeping and other information regulations to increase the overall performance of the organisation. The key issues for directors confronting both opportunities from technology innovations, AI and data analytics and challenges arising from cybersecurity,

107 K Jones, "Blockchain in or as Governance? Evolutions in Experimentation, Social Impacts, and Prefigurative Practice in the Blockchain and DAO Space" (2019) 24(4) *Information Policy* 469.

data breach, privacy and other regulatory drivers can be met with strong information governance.

Professor Bill Black, while at the University of Texas, wrote a guide to help corporate governance across a range of issues, dealt with in this chapter. The 2005 book, *The Best Way to Rob a Bank Is to Own One*, reflected on the US savings and loans financial debacle, but could be applied to the contemporary investigations into misconduct in the Australian financial services industry.[108]

He coins the term "control fraud" to mean when the CEO is actually the primary person controlling the corporate governance and fraud preventions, but uses their power for their own benefit.

Black's top 15 lessons from an earlier financial disaster are:

- fraud matters and control systems pose unique risks;
- critical to understand fraud mechanisms, and few regulators have fraud training (not taught in business schools);
- control frauds occur in waves and not random, as fit what criminologists know increase crime (opportunistic environments, which you can control);
- waves of control fraud cause immense damage;
- control fraud converts conventional restraints on abuse into aids for fraud;
- conflicts of interest really matter;
- deposit insurance was not essential to the frauds, but helped;
- systemic capacity' problems became endemic (and followed in the global financial crisis' and contemporary banking scandals);
- regulatory policy and highest political leadership is vital;
- ethics and social forces are critical restraints on fraud;
- deregulation and assets matter in the equation of fraud;
- why do regulatory agencies (SEC[109] and in Australia, ASIC) not have a chief criminologist, to understand white-collar crime?
- control frauds defeat traditional corporate governance protections;
- stock (shares) options increase the actual looting by control frauds (the link between short- and long-term remuneration, paid as bonuses); and
- there is a need to reinvent in the government policies that actually work and positively act to prevent control fraud and other opportunities to exploit corporations.

---

108 W Black, *The Best Way to Rob a Bank Is to Own One* (University of Texas Press, 2005).

109 Securities and Exchange Commission, Federal body, United States.

As is often said, will directors and investors look back and learn the lessons of history especially when we consider the overwhelming debacle that was the South Sea Bubble Company, arguably the progenitor of the modern-day corporate governance scandal, such scandals continue to call for a renewed focus from age to age of better governance and responsibility of the corporate citizen:

> During all this time the public excitement was extreme. We learn, from Coxe's Walpole, that the very name of a South-Sea director was thought synonymous with every species of fraud and villainy … there were cries of justice due to an injured nation.[110]

Andres Sormon-Nisson, the Futurist and founder of Thinque,[111] poses five questions for organisations for the 2020s, as follows:

- How can I get two times the result with half the effort (through technology and human creativity)?
- Which old analogue processes do not offer me any actionable data insights and need upgrading immediately?
- What is the compound effect of my competition adopting the right exponential technology, while we do not by 2025?
- What is the "analogue baby" in my business that must not be thrown away with the digital bathwater, and which can be further amplified and augmented through technology?
- What would our competition not want us to do next?[112]

110 C Mackay, *Memoirs of Extraordinary Popular Delusions* (Richard Bentley, 1841) reproduced by Wordsworth Press 2006.

111 See <https://www.anderssorman-nilsson.com/>.

112 Governance Institute of Australia, "Sustaining Innovation" (2021 Annual Conference (virtual), 2 September 2021).

Chapter 3

Conflicting Values and Competing Laws: Jurisdiction and the Internet

Monique Cormier*

Introduction

[3.10]

> It is very difficult to do business if you have to wake up every day and say "OK, whose laws do I follow?" We have many countries and many laws and just one internet.[1]

Jurisdiction is a complex, multifaceted concept and a key consideration in the regulation of cyberspace. In a nutshell, jurisdiction determines which state,[2] which laws and which courts are allowed to exercise their powers over which persons and which matters. The transnational nature of the internet and the sheer number and scope of online activities present significant challenges for traditional jurisdiction paradigms. Take a simple example to illustrate the seemingly endless jurisdictional possibilities: An Australian citizen, while visiting New Zealand, uploads a short post to her Facebook account. Which state has the right to regulate the content of this post and to exercise jurisdiction over any legal issue that might arise in relation to it? The state of the poster's nationality (Australia)? The state where the poster was physically located when she uploaded the post (New Zealand)? The state where Facebook is headquartered (US)? Any of the states in which her Facebook friends viewed

---

* School of Law, University of New England, Armidale, New South Wales. The author would like to thank Robert Brown for his invaluable research assistance on this chapter.

1 Heather Killen, former Yahoo Vice-President, quoted in J Tessler, "Online Auction of Nazi Items Sparks Debate Issue: National Laws on Global Web", *San Jose Mercury News* (25 July 2000).

2 Unless otherwise specified, the term "state" in this chapter is used to mean "nation state" or country.

the post? What if those friends then share the original poster's content with their friends who are based in other countries? Can those states assert jurisdiction? What about states in which Facebook servers are located? Or cloud servers? The spectre of global liability looms large over ordinary internet transactions which are potentially subject to a multitude of national laws and jurisdictions.

Since the early days of the internet, states and their courts have been grappling with how to balance competing jurisdictional claims in online regulation. The results have been uneven to say the least, highlighting the legal uncertainty that characterises jurisdiction over cyberspace. The ubiquity of smart phones, the portability of tablets and even the connectivity of household appliances are erasing the boundaries between the physical and online worlds. The aim of this chapter is to provide an overview of some of the key challenges and issues that arise when state-based jurisdiction confronts this online global interconnectivity. It is not intended to be a comprehensive examination of rules or case law, but rather a snapshot of some of the core themes that have emerged over the past few decades. Select cases and other examples are used to illustrate how and why states have taken divergent approaches to questions of jurisdiction in the internet age and the consequences of this for a global internet.

This chapter first looks at some of the reasons why internet regulation is necessary. The state-centric nature of global society and the fact that humans have local needs and cultures defeated the ideal of a completely free and unregulated global internet. This then introduces the central conflict arising from the assertion of jurisdiction over transborder online activities: the clash of cultural values.

This chapter then provides an overview of the different concepts and terminology associated with the law of jurisdiction. The traditional jurisdiction principles found in public and private international law are useful for understanding the legal basis on which courts make decisions in disputes involving online activities.

The third part of the chapter uses select cases to exemplify how the traditional jurisdiction principles have been used in the internet age, demonstrating that they are easily manipulated to allow for outcomes that prioritise a state's territorial sovereignty and cultural values. This part first examines a number of early, high profile court decisions involving criminal speech offences and online defamation before turning to more recent examples of how states are fighting to enforce local jurisdiction in the borderless online environment.

The final part offers some brief concluding remarks on current approaches to managing competing jurisdictional claims in the internet era.

The Jurisdiction Problem in Cyberspace

Why regulate the internet?

[3.20] Jurisdiction, as a concept, is difficult to define with any precision. In broad terms, it is understood to mean a state's legal competence to exercise authority over territory and persons by virtue of its sovereignty.[3] In more narrow terms, jurisdiction concerns the exercise of judicial powers by courts and associated entities of the domestic judicial system. Courts represent a mechanism through which a state exercises certain of its sovereign powers over persons and territory.[4] Courts are given particular judicial competences by a state's domestic legal framework. To say that a court has jurisdiction over someone or over a particular geographical area means that it has the legal right to exercise certain judicial powers over that person or over activities that occur in that territory. Jurisdiction, therefore, is traditionally the purview of nation states, rooted in sovereignty and tied to a particular geographical space. The notion of a global and borderless internet seems inherently incompatible with the very idea of jurisdiction.

In the early days of the World Wide Web,[5] its existence outside the realm of the state was considered to be a key feature of the internet. Developers and early internet users saw cyberspace as a potential global utopia; open to everyone and free from government interference. They fought to ensure that communications and other activities conducted in cyberspace were not beholden to any state.[6] It did not take long for optimism to give way to cynicism, as the libertarian dream of a totally free and unregulated internet was exposed as naivety. Cyberspace quickly became a platform for numerous abuses, including privacy violations, defamation, fraud, harassment, hacking

---

3 I Brownlie, *Principles of Public International Law* (Oxford University Press, 7th ed, 2008) 291; F A Mann, "The Doctrine of Jurisdiction in International Law" (1964) 111 *Recueil des Cours de l'Academie de Droit Internationale* 1, 9.

4 R Liivoja, "The Criminal Jurisdiction of States – A Theoretical Primer" (2010) 7 *No Foundations* 27, 35; M Hirst, *Jurisdiction and the Ambit of the Criminal Law* (Oxford University Press, 2003). See discussion at [3.50]–[3.90].

5 The World Wide Web was developed in 1991 by Tim Berners-Lee, allowing the internet to be much more navigable and accessible. See T Berners-Lee and M Fischetti, *Weaving the Web: The Original Design and Ultimate Destiny of the World Wide Web by Its Inventor* (Harper Collins, 1999).

6 See, for example, J P Barlow, *A Declaration of the Independence of Cyberspace* (1996) <https://www.eff.org/cyberspace-independence>; D J B Svantesson, *Solving the Internet Jurisdiction Puzzle* (Oxford University Press, 2017) 92; J Goldsmith and T Wu, *Who Controls the Internet? Illusions of a Borderless World* (Oxford University Press, 2006) 3.

and wide-ranging criminal activity.[7] There was concern about the pervasive influence of foreign cultures and values antithetical to one's own. Perhaps least surprising, is that the need for internet regulation also arose from the simple fact that the human race is not a homogenous global population.

Internet users began demanding diversity of languages, cultures and currencies online, and a recognition that they live and work in a particular geographical location. When someone residing in South Korea checks a weather website, they want to know, in Korean, if they will need an umbrella in Seoul. They do not want to see the forecast for New York, in English. A person in New Delhi wanting to order Domino's Pizza online, is not going to want the website of a Domino's franchise in Sydney. To accommodate such local requirements, advances in geo-location technologies from the early 2000s[8] made it easier to pinpoint where a particular internet user is located, and to tailor information that ostensibly takes into account their specific geographical, linguistic and cultural requirements. Such advances in technology represented early efforts of internet self-regulation[9] aimed at simplifying e-commerce activities to enable goods and services to be marketed and sold in local languages and currency. But it also coincided with a rise in online disputes and the first major attempts by states to assert jurisdiction and apply national laws to conflicts arising in cyberspace.

Protecting national values

[3.30] One of the earliest and most well-known cases to grapple with issues of jurisdiction over an online dispute was the *Yahoo* case, sometimes referred to as the Nazi memorabilia case.[10] In early 2000, Marc Knobel, a Jewish French citizen, was browsing an auction site hosted by yahoo.com when he discovered a vast cache of Nazi memorabilia for sale, including SS weapons, concentration camp photos and items emblazoned with the swastika. Yahoo is an American web services provider and was one of the largest internet companies of the time. The auction page was hosted on Yahoo's American servers[11] and the sale

---

7 T Schultz, "Carving Up the Internet: Jurisdiction, Legal Orders, and the Private/Public International Law Interface" (2008) 19(4) *European Journal of International Law* 799, 804.

8 Internet & Jurisdiction Policy Network, *Internet & Jurisdiction Global Status Report* (Report, 2019) 155–158 <https://www.internetjurisdiction.net/uploads/pdfs/GSR2019/Internet-Jurisdiction-Global-Status-Report-2019_web.pdf>.

9 Internet & Jurisdiction Policy Network, *Internet & Jurisdiction Global Status Report* (Report, 2019) 49.

10 *La Ligue Contre le Racisme et l'Antisémitisme (LICRA) et l'Union des Etudiants Juifs de France (UEJF) v Yahoo! Inc et Yahoo France*, Trib de 1re Instance, Paris, interlocutory orders of 22 May 2000, 22 August and 20 November 2000.

11 Later discovered to be located in Sweden: Goldsmith and Wu, n 6, 7.

of Nazi items is protected by the First Amendment of the US Constitution, making it perfectly legal in the United States. In France, however, displaying or selling Nazi memorabilia is a criminal offence,[12] and the items on the Yahoo auction site were available for sale in France. Knobel initiated proceedings in the Paris Court of First Instance on behalf of several anti-racism and anti-Semitism associations. Yahoo lawyers objected to the proceedings on the grounds that it would be impossible to identify the nationality of all its customers or to control who can access its site. The French judge held that Yahoo had violated French law by allowing Nazi items to be available for sale in France, and rejected Yahoo's "impossibility" defence, given the advent of geo-location technology. Yahoo was ordered to take reasonable steps to block French users from the site. While Yahoo initially refused to comply, it backed down once the French court threatened substantial fines, potentially enforceable through seizure and sale of sizeable Yahoo assets in France.[13] Yahoo removed all Nazi memorabilia from its websites by the court-imposed deadline.

This early case demonstrated that extending a national court's jurisdiction to cyber activities was possible but controversial.[14] In addition to raising concerns about the conflict of national laws, it shone a spotlight on the internet's ability to amplify the conflict of fundamental values at an international level.[15] The *Yahoo* case is just one of many national court decisions in which a clash of cultures was the subject of litigation. Some of these, like the *Yahoo* case, involved a conflict between constitutionally protected freedom of expression on one side and laws designed to protect against hate speech or other offensive conduct on the other. In the early 2000s, for example, a French citizen was convicted by a UK court for the offence of "publishing an obscene article".[16] The defendant was the director of an American company and operated a freely accessible pornographic website which was hosted on a US server. He argued unsuccessfully that the major steps to publish the website were taken in the United States, where the site was legally protected by the First Amendment of the Constitution. The Crown Court and the England and Wales Court of Appeal disagreed, and held that the availability of the website in the United

---

12 Article R645 of the *French Penal Code*.

13 J Pelline, "Yahoo to Charge Auction Fees, Ban Hate Materials", *CNet News* (29 March 2002).

14 L Guernsey, "Welcome to the Web. Passport, Please?", *New York Times* (15 March 2001).

15 H M Watt, "Yahoo Cyber-Collision of Cultures: Who Regulates Special Feature – Cyberage Conflicts Law" (2002) 24(3) *Michigan Journal of International Law* 673. The *Yahoo* case will be discussed further in [3.170].

16 *R v Perrin* [2002] EWCA Crim 747; *Obscene Publications Act 1959* (UK).

Kingdom meant that it was subject to the local obscenity laws which were in place "for the legitimate purpose of protecting morals".[17]

Another instance of conflicting "morality" laws was a 2006 German case, in which the Federal Court of Justice held that a Dutch website selling drugs was subject to German advertising laws. It was legal to sell the drugs in The Netherlands, and illegal to sell them in Germany. The German Court held that the Dutch site had to display a disclaimer that made it unequivocally clear that the drugs would not be delivered to states where they were prohibited. If the seller dishonoured this requirement, it would be liable for prosecution under German law.[18] The court viewed the potential sale of drugs to Germans as a matter of national health and safety.[19]

Further examples of where states assert jurisdiction at least partly on the basis of morality is in relation to online gambling. The Australian *Interactive Gambling Act 2001* (Cth) bans the provision of online games of chance to customers "physically present in Australia".[20] The purpose of the legislation is to "limit the harmful effects of gambling on the Australian community",[21] although as Uta Kohl observes, the national regulation of online gambling services is also about "controlling a lucrative industry".[22] Disallowing foreign gambling providers is, on the one hand, a protective measure against its negative social effects and, on the other hand, a way of ensuring that any revenue from gambling services stays in the country.

Conclusion

[3.40] As the above examples demonstrate, despite the intrinsically borderless nature of the internet, geographical territory and sovereign jurisdiction remain relevant in cyberspace. There is always a delicate balance to be struck whenever a national court or legislature asserts jurisdiction over a transnational matter, and resistance to a jurisdictional claim is to be expected when differing cultural values are involved.

17 *R v Perrin* [2002] EWCA Crim 747, [46].

18 *Arzneimittelwerbung im Internet* (BGH, 30 March 2006) I ZR 24/03.

19 U Kohl, "Jurisdiction in Cyberspace" in N Tsagourias and R Buchan (eds), *Research Handbook on International Law and Cyberspace* (Edward Elgar Publishing, 2015) 30, 39.

20 *Interactive Gambling Act 2001* (Cth), s 8.

21 Department of Infrastructure, Transport, Regional Development and Communications, *Interactive Gambling* <https://www.communications.gov.au/what-we-do/internet/internet-governance/online-gambling>.

22 Kohl, n 19, 40.

While international law has traditionally provided guidance as to how contested jurisdictional claims might be managed, as Dan Jerker B Svantessen writes, "there is a clash between the modern Cyber-landscape and the jurisdictional dinosaur rules sought to be applied to it".[23] The difficulties with applying the long-established principles of jurisdiction to modern cyber disputes is the focus of the remainder of this chapter. First, however, it is necessary to provide a brief overview of the international laws of jurisdiction to contextualise the ensuing analysis.

Traditional Jurisdiction Rules (a Primer)

[3.50] Broadly speaking, the difference between public international law and private international law is that the former regulates relations between states themselves, and private international law regulates relations between individuals or companies located in different states. Both public and private international law have rules of jurisdiction that govern cross-border disputes, some of which may be applicable to cyber issues. Public international law provides the overarching legal framework for when a state can assert jurisdiction; directly applicable in matters of criminal jurisdiction. Private international law provides jurisdictional guidance on private law matters (torts, contracts, commerce, etc).[24] There is a veritable labyrinth of terminology and sub-concepts that have to be navigated in order to reach an understanding of how jurisdiction is traditionally determined. This section provides a nutshell treatment of these concepts in order to understand and critique how they have been applied in cyber disputes. It begins with a breakdown of the principles and rules of jurisdiction under public international law, before turning to the tenets of jurisdiction in private international law.

Jurisdiction in public international law

To prescribe, adjudicate and enforce

[3.60] The traditional starting point for jurisdiction in public international law is the division of a state's power to prescribe, adjudicate and enforce laws.[25] To say that a state has jurisdiction to prescribe means that it has authority to make

23 Svantesson, n 6, 92.

24 There is disagreement among scholars and jurists as to whether public international law only regulates jurisdiction over criminal matters, or if it extends to civil disputes. See Kohl, n 19, 31–32.

25 *Restatement of the Law Fourth, Foreign Relations Law of the United States* (American Law Institute, 2017) §401.

laws "applicable to the activities, relations, or status of persons, or the interests of persons".[26] Jurisdiction to adjudicate is the power of a state "to subject persons or things to the process of its courts or administrative tribunals".[27] Jurisdiction to enforce refers to a state's power "to induce or compel compliance or to punish noncompliance with its laws or regulations".[28] In criminal matters, for example, jurisdiction to prescribe encompasses a state's right to enact laws proscribing particular conduct as criminal. Jurisdiction to adjudicate gives states the right to apply those laws to certain persons and territory. Jurisdiction to enforce comprises a state's power to investigate and collect evidence, to issue subpoenas, to arrest and retain custody over a defendant, to convene a trial, to incarcerate, etc.[29] The question of which persons and territory a state may exercise such powers over is then a matter of whether any of the five permissive principles of jurisdiction are applicable.

Principles of jurisdiction

[3.70] Alongside the division of a state's power into the categories of prescription, adjudication and enforcement, there are five principles in international law which govern when a state may exercise its jurisdictional powers: territoriality, nationality, passive personality, protection and universality. The following brief discussion looks first at the principle of territoriality, before providing an overview of the extraterritorial principles as a separate grouping.

The principle of territoriality

[3.80] The territoriality principle, at its core, is the idea that a state may exercise prescriptive, adjudicative and enforcement jurisdiction over conduct that takes place within its physical territory. Where conduct takes place

---

26 *Restatement of the Law Fourth, Foreign Relations Law of the United States* (American Law Institute, 2017) §401.

27 *Restatement of the Law Fourth, Foreign Relations Law of the United States* (American Law Institute, 2017) §401.

28 *Restatement of the Law Fourth, Foreign Relations Law of the United States* (American Law Institute, 2017) §401.

29 Not all writers agree on the tripartite division of powers, but the totality of the jurisdictional powers remains the same no matter how they are categorised. See generally, R Higgins, "The Legal Bases of Jurisdiction" in C J Olmstead (ed), *Extra-Territorial Application of Laws and Responses Thereto* (International Law Association in association with ESC, 1984) 3, 4; J Crawford and I Brownlie, *Brownlie's Principles of Public International Law* (Oxford University Press, 8th ed, 2012) 456; Liivoja, n 4; R O'Keefe, "Universal Jurisdiction: Clarifying the Basic Concept" (2004) 2(3) *Journal of International Criminal Justice* 735, 737.

entirely within the geographical border of a state, such conduct clearly falls within the jurisdiction of the territorial state. This principle of territorial jurisdiction is usually not contentious because territory is synonymous with a state's sovereignty. A state has the sovereign right to exercise jurisdiction over its territory. The assertion of territorial jurisdiction becomes more complicated when conduct is not limited to just one state's territory.

Acknowledging that activity does not always take place entirely within a state's borders, public international law recognises the notion of "subjective territoriality" which allows a state to assert jurisdiction over an action that was commenced within the territory of the state claiming jurisdiction, but completed in another state. The classic example is where someone in State A shoots a gun across the border, which injures or kills a person in State B. State A would be able to assert jurisdiction over the shooter on the basis of the subjective territoriality principle. This concept is sometimes also referred to as the "origin approach" to jurisdiction, because it is the state where the action originated that has jurisdiction.

There is also the "objective territoriality" principle which originally meant that the state in which an act was completed (despite being commenced elsewhere) could assert jurisdiction over it. State B would be able to assert jurisdiction over the cross-border shooting incident because the victim was shot on the territory of State B.[30] In criminal matters, objective territoriality has been broadened to allow a state to exercise jurisdiction when a "constituent element" of a crime has taken place on the territory of the prosecuting state.[31] What is meant by a "constituent element" of a crime has been left up to individual states to determine under their domestic law.[32]

Finally under the banner of the territoriality principle of jurisdiction is the "effects doctrine" in which a state may assert jurisdiction if economic effects or other negative consequences of activity conducted abroad are experienced in the territory of the state claiming jurisdiction. For decades, the effects doctrine was used extensively by the United States in antitrust litigation, and it remains a particularly controversial aspect of territorial jurisdiction because of the often tenuous nexus between the act and the state asserting jurisdiction.[33] Notably,

---

30 State B would not, however, be able to exercise personal jurisdiction over the shooter situated in the territory of State A, without State A's cooperation (see [3.90] for an overview of the personal jurisdiction principles).

31 *"SS Lotus" (France v Turkey) (Judgment)* [1927] PCIJ (ser A) No 10, 23.

32 M Vagias, *The Territorial Jurisdiction of the International Criminal Court* (Cambridge University Press, 2014) 17–18.

33 Vagias, n 32, 17–18.

the territorial effects doctrine has been repurposed for use in jurisdictional claims over cyber disputes.[34] Both the objective territoriality principle and the effects doctrine have sometimes been repackaged as the "destination approach" to jurisdiction which gives priority to the state of destination in a cross-border matter.

Extraterritorial principles

[3.90] The other four jurisdiction principles are collectively known as the extraterritorial jurisdiction principles, because they determine when and how a state may exercise its powers beyond its own borders. States traditionally place high value on their sovereignty and are resistant to any form of intervention by other states in matters within their territorial realm. This means that enforcement jurisdiction is strictly territorial because a state may not enforce its laws or judgments on the territory of another state.[35] There are, however, certain circumstances in which a state may exercise its jurisdiction to prescribe or adjudicate over matters that take place outside its territory.

For example, in accordance with the "nationality" principle, a state may exercise jurisdiction over its own nationals, even for conduct that occurs entirely abroad.[36] This is one of two types of "personal jurisdiction" under public international law, which denote circumstances in which a state can assert jurisdiction over particular individuals. The other category of personal jurisdiction falls under the principle of "passive personality" which allows a state to assert jurisdiction over crimes that take place outside its territory when one or more of its nationals is a victim of those acts.

Under the "protective" principle of jurisdiction, a state may assert jurisdiction over extraterritorial acts of non-nationals if they threaten the national security or key interests of that state. The protective principle has been used for offences such as drug smuggling[37] and illegal immigration,[38] for example. The

---

34 See discussion in [3.160].

35 Although see [3.190] for a discussion of whether states are asserting *de facto* extraterritorial jurisdiction in cyber matters.

36 Under Div 272 of the Australia's *Criminal Code Act 1995* (Cth), for example, it is a criminal offence for Australian citizens to participate in child sex tourism overseas.

37 *United States v Newball*, 524 F Supp 715 (EDNY, 1981): "Drug smuggling threatens the security and sovereignty of the United States by affecting its armed forces, contributes to widespread crime, and circumvents federal customs and laws" (at 720).

38 *Naim Molvan, Owner of Motor Vessel "Asya" v A-G (Palestine)* [1948] AC 351 [United Kingdom]; *Giles v Tumminello* [1963] SASR 96 [Australia].

final principle of jurisdiction under public international law is universality, which gives rise to universal jurisdiction. This allows for a state to extend its laws to any person, of any nationality, for conduct that takes place anywhere in the world. "Universal" jurisdiction is only exercisable in very limited circumstances where particularly serious international crimes such as genocide and crimes against humanity have been committed.[39]

How public international law jurisdiction principles have been applied by national courts to cross-border cyber activity will be discussed in [3.160]–[3.230] of this chapter. As will be seen, states have continued to rely heavily on the territorial principle when asserting jurisdiction over matters involving the internet, but increasingly such decisions have extraterritorial implications. The next section provides a brief overview of the jurisdiction regime of private international law.

Jurisdiction in private international law

[3.100] The body of international, national and local laws and conventions that govern transborder private relationships is known as private international law. When it comes to the issue of jurisdiction over foreign persons or matters, there are conceptual overlaps between public and private international law, although the latter is more concerned with exercise of jurisdiction at the level of local courts rather than by the sovereign state itself.[40] In this section, Australian laws and cases are used as examples.

Personal jurisdiction

[3.110] In civil proceedings involving cross-border litigation, a court with subject matter jurisdiction[41] must first establish personal jurisdiction over the foreign defendant which is typically secured by serving an originating process in accordance with the rules of the issuing court (or "forum"). Usually, service can only be effected if the defendant is physically present on

39 See M C Bassiouni, "The History of Universal Jurisdiction and Its Place in International Law" in S Macedo (ed), *Universal Jurisdiction: National Courts and the Prosecution of Serious Crimes under International Law* (Pennsylvania University Press, 2004) 39; O'Keefe, n 29.

40 Many of these private international rules of jurisdiction also apply to cross-border litigation that arises internally in federations. See, for example, J Allsop and D Ward, "Incoherence in Australian Private International Laws" [2013] *Federal Judicial Scholarship* 8.

41 This is simply a question of the type of matter a court is allowed to hear (ie, criminal, family, commercial, etc). In Australia, this is governed by the Constitution and by statute. See B Fitzgerald et al, *Internet and E-Commerce Law, Business and Policy* (Thomson Reuters, 2011) 84–89.

the territory that is within the issuing court's jurisdiction. There are, however, circumstances in which a court may serve an originating process on a foreign defendant outside of national borders, via "long-arm" jurisdiction rules. In Australia, these rules (which vary among courts) set out grounds on which the plaintiff must establish a nexus between the subject matter of the action and the desired Australian jurisdiction. In a contractual dispute, for instance, process may be served outside Australia if the contract in issue was made or broken within the relevant Australian jurisdiction or is governed by the law of the forum.[42] In matters relating to a tort, service of process may be effected outside Australia in situations where the act that gave rise to the cause of action occurred on the jurisdictional territory of the serving court.[43] The practicalities of implementing these rules and serving documents in a foreign nation is achieved through diplomatic channels or under multilateral international service conventions. For example, Australia is a party to the 1965 *Hague Convention on the Service Abroad of Judicial and Extrajudicial Documents in Civil or Commercial Matters* (*Hague Service Convention*) which provides a blueprint for consistent and efficient cross-border service among the 78 states parties.[44]

Choice of law

[3.120] If a court with subject matter jurisdiction has also established personal jurisdiction over a transborder civil dispute, it must then determine what law to apply. Usually the choice of law is between the law of the forum and the law of another jurisdiction, although it can sometimes be between the laws of two external jurisdictions.[45] In Australia, there are existing choice of law rules for disputes of a particular nature. In matters of tort, for example, the High Court has held that choice of law turns on where the tort occurred – the *lex locus delicti*.[46] In contractual disputes, the contract usually contains a choice

---

42 Fitzgerald et al, n 41, 63.

43 Fitzgerald et al, n 41, 65–66. See also *Dow Jones & Co Inc v Gutnick* (2002) 210 CLR 575.

44 *Convention on the Service Abroad of Judicial and Extrajudicial Documents in Civil or Commercial Matters*, opened for signature 11 November 1965, 658 UNTS 163 (entered into force 10 February 1969). For more on the *Hague Service Convention*, see R Garnett, *Substance and Procedure in Private International Law* (Oxford University Press, 1st ed, 2012) 75–80.

45 Fitzgerald et al, n 41, 90.

46 *John Pfeiffer Pty Ltd v Rogerson* (2003) 203 CLR 503; *Regie National des Usines Renault SA v Zhang* (2002) 210 CLR 491. There are also statutes that govern choice of law rules in particular matters. For example, the uniform defamation laws in Australian states.

of law clause that will be upheld and applied by Australian courts unless there are "countervailing reasons" for not doing so.[47]

Choice of forum

[3.130] Even where the court determines that the laws of the forum are applicable, the doctrine of *forum non conveniens* may mean that the court nevertheless declines to exercise jurisdiction on the basis that it is not the appropriate forum for the matter. In Australia, the High Court has held that the standard to be applied is the "clearly inappropriate forum" test which involves consideration of factors including whether there are significant connections between the chosen forum and the subject matter of the proceedings, if the chosen forum provides a legitimate advantage to the plaintiff, and whether alternate forums are available.[48]

Recognition and enforcement of foreign judgments

[3.140] As mentioned in [3.90], under public international law, a state's power to enforce is only exercisable within its territorial jurisdiction. This also applies to cross-border private litigation, meaning that any extraterritorial enforcement of judgments can therefore only be managed via transnational cooperation and mutual consent. In Australia, one of the ways that this can be done is through the *Foreign Judgments Act 1991* (Cth) which allows for reciprocal recognition and enforcement of certain types of foreign judgments from certain foreign courts.[49] Foreign judgments generally will not be enforceable on grounds of fraud, denial of natural justice or public policy.[50]

Conclusion

[3.150] It should be noted that a strict separation between public and private international law is not always evident (or necessary) when it comes to jurisdiction, particularly in matters involving the internet.[51] However, as

---

47 *Oceanic Sun Line Special Shipping Co Inc v Fay* (1988) 165 CLR 197. Such reasons may include where the performance of the contract would be unlawful in the country where the contract is to be performed, or where the choice of law is not bona fide.

48 *Voth v Manildra Flour Mills Pty Ltd* (1990) 171 CLR 538.

49 Fitzgerald et al, n 41, 138–141. See also *Convention on the Recognition and Enforcement of Foreign Judgments in Civil and Commercial Matters*, opened for signature 2 July 2019 (not yet in force).

50 See, for example, s 7 of the *Foreign Judgments Act 1991* (Cth); Art 7 of the *Convention on the Recognition and Enforcement of Foreign Judgments in Civil and Commercial Matters*.

51 Svantesson, n 6, 7.

will be seen in the next part, courts still tend to frame jurisdictional claims in the language of either public or private international law, depending on the subject matter of the dispute. It is therefore helpful to have an understanding of the main concepts and common terminology used to describe and justify jurisdiction. How the traditional principles of jurisdiction have been applied in the cyber age is the focus of the next part of this chapter.

Using (and Abusing) Jurisdiction Principles in the Cyber Age

[3.160] The principles and conventions of jurisdiction in public and private international law are complex and contested at the best of times. The internet has presented unprecedented challenges to, and magnified the shortcomings of, the traditional notions of territoriality-rooted jurisdiction.[52] The first section in this part uses a handful of well-known older cases to illustrate the diverse, sometimes conflicting, approaches to jurisdiction among courts in different countries. This is followed by a discussion of some of the more recent attempts by courts and legislatures to expand their extraterritorial reach online and the problems that such jurisdictional extension is causing.

Asserting jurisdiction in cyber disputes

Selling Nazi memorabilia in France and denying the Holocaust in Germany

[3.170] Returning first to the *Yahoo* case discussed in [3.30],[53] the decision of the French court to exercise adjudicative jurisdiction by applying French laws to Yahoo's auction website was essentially an application of the effects principle of territoriality. While the website was owned, established and maintained by a US company and US nationals, the French court held that "harm was suffered on the territory of France" by the availability of Nazi items for sale in France.[54] As a result of the website's accessibility on French territory, the court held that French laws applied. This rationale is also an example of the destination approach to jurisdiction, due to the fact that a state of destination for the online activity has asserted the right to apply its laws to that activity.

52 Y A Timofeeva, "Worldwide Prescriptive Jurisdiction in Internet Content Controversies: A Comparative Analysis" (2004) 20(2) *Connecticut Journal of International Law* 199, 201.

53 *La Ligue Contre le Racisme et l'Antisémitisme (LICRA) et l'Union des Etudiants Juifs de France (UEJF) v Yahoo! Inc et Yahoo France*, Trib de 1re Instance, Paris, interlocutory orders of 22 May 2000, 22 August and 20 November 2000.

54 Kohl, n 19, 38.

Yahoo unsuccessfully argued for an exclusively origin approach to jurisdiction which would allow only the laws of the state of the online activity's origin to apply. The benefits of an exclusive origin rule of jurisdiction are evident for an online corporation. Ensuring that only the laws of the corporation's home state apply would significantly limit the "regulatory burden" on such businesses and provides greater predictability and certainty with respect to potential liability.[55] States have not, however, been amenable to such a curtailment of jurisdiction, preferring to assert jurisdiction on the basis of the origin approach and reserving the concurrent right to apply the destination approach to jurisdiction should the need arise. This is broadly consistent with the jurisdiction rules under public international law which recognise the coexisting rights of the state of subjective territory (origin) and the state of objective territory (destination).[56]

Another case from 2000 involved an Australian citizen named Frederick Toben, who wrote a number of anti-Semitic articles which he posted to a website hosted on an Australian server. While Toben was on holiday in Germany, he was prosecuted and convicted of Holocaust denial by the German Federal Court of Justice.[57] Because Toben's material was accessible in Germany, and Holocaust denial communications contravenes the *German Penal Code*, this was sufficient for the Court to exercise jurisdiction. *Toben* represents another early example of a Court asserting jurisdiction on the basis of the doctrine of territorial effects, as the Federal Court of Justice explicitly found that Toben's writing could have harmful effects in Germany.[58] As with the French court in the *Yahoo* case, the German Court took the destination approach to jurisdiction on the grounds that the offending material was accessible in Germany and could have possible harmful effects in German territory. But unlike the French court, there was some suggestion in the *Toben* decision of a narrower, "targeted" destination approach. The Federal Court of Justice found that the offending material was directed at Germans, despite the fact that it was in English, which bolstered its jurisdictional claim.[59]

Unsurprisingly, the *Yahoo* and *Toben* decisions came under fire from commentators in the United States who decried the rulings as attempts to

55 Kohl, n 19, 49.

56 Kohl, n 19, 50.

57 BGH 46, 212, Urteil vom 12.12.2000 [Decision of the Federal Court of Justice, 12 December 2000].

58 Timofeeva, n 52, 207.

59 Timofeeva, n 52.

impose limits on free speech beyond French and German borders.[60] Conversely, the Europeans denounced the US Constitution's First Amendment as "the new best friend of ... neo-Nazi groups", pointing to the fact that "the majority of those [neo-Nazi] sites – 90 percent – are nourished by American companies".[61] These examples illustrated early on how transnational jurisdiction disputes in the internet era would be dominated by cases involving a clash of fundamental values.[62]

Transborder litigation over online defamation: Australia and the United States

[3.180] Another early case in which the origin vs destination approach to jurisdiction played out is the Australian High Court case of *Dow Jones & Co Inc v Gutnick*.[63] *Gutnick* remains the most influential Australian case on the topic of jurisdiction and cyberspace.[64] In 2000, the online version of an American magazine published an article that made allegations of improper business dealings conducted by Australian resident Joseph Gutnick. Gutnick sued Dow Jones & Co Inc, the US publishing company of the magazine *Barron's Online*, for defamation. The action was brought in the Victorian Supreme Court which found in Gutnick's favour, and was then appealed to the High Court. The key issues in this case related to the Supreme Court's personal jurisdiction over Dow Jones, the choice of law, and choice of forum. The originating process was served on Dow Jones through the Victorian Supreme Court's long-arm jurisdiction rules which stipulated that service may be effected extraterritorially where "the proceeding is founded on a tort committed within Victoria" or where "the proceeding is brought in respect of damage suffered wholly or partly in Victoria".[65] The High Court held that damage to Gutnick's reputation was done when the online article was downloaded (published) in Victoria, and that Victoria was therefore the place where the tort of defamation was

---

60 P Finn, "Neo-Nazis Sheltering Websites in the US", *Washington Post* (21 December 2000) <https://www.washingtonpost.com/archive/politics/2000/12/21/neo-nazis-sheltering-web-sites-in-the-us/ad40e8ff-09ad-44b2-84ab-61a2e4764141/>.

61 Finn, n 60.

62 Timofeeva, n 52.

63 *Dow Jones & Co Inc v Gutnick* (2002) 210 CLR 575.

64 Recent cases that have applied *Gutnick* include *Google Inc v Duffy* (2017) 129 SASR 304 and *Stoltenberg v Bolton* [2020] NSWCA 45.

65 Rule 7.01 of the *Supreme Court (General Civil Procedure) Rules 1996* (Vic). These rules have been superseded by the *Supreme Court (General Civil Procedure) Rules 2015* (Vic) but r 7.01 remains the same in the latter.

committed.[66] Under the established choice of law rules, the law of Victoria was applicable as the place where the tort occurred.[67] As for the choice of forum, the High Court held that Dow Jones had not demonstrated that Victoria was a clearly inappropriate forum. The appeal was dismissed.[68]

The High Court approached the jurisdiction question in *Gutnick* through the lens of traditional private international law rules, with little regard to distinctive features of the internet. Dow Jones argued that online publishers should only have to comply with the laws of the place where the publication originated, that is, the place where the publisher maintained its servers.[69] To do otherwise would mean that online publishers would be potentially subject to the laws of any and every country or local jurisdiction where the material is downloaded. Given that this case was dealing specifically with a matter of defamation, the High Court rejected that argument on the grounds that a publisher would only need to heed the defamation law that is directly applicable to the person allegedly being defamed.[70] Like the *Yahoo* court, the High Court rejected an origin approach to jurisdiction in favour of a destination approach, which has its basis in the territorial effects doctrine. Parallels can also be drawn to the objective territoriality principle in that the uploading of the article in question was done in one state, and the downloading of it in another state completed the publication process.

The *Gutnick* decision drew criticism for its potential "chilling effect" on international free speech and concern that it "could reduce the level of speech protection to the lowest common denominator; the law of the country with the lowest level of speech protection would become the *de facto* law of the Internet".[71] Conversely, Callinan J viewed the High Court's approach as protecting Australians from "an American legal hegemony" over online

66 *Dow Jones & Co Inc v Gutnick* (2002) 210 CLR 575, [42]–[48] (Gleeson CJ, McHugh, Gummow and Hayne JJ).

67 *Dow Jones & Co Inc v Gutnick* (2002) 210 CLR 575. See discussion at [34]–[42] (Gleeson CJ, McHugh, Gummow and Hayne JJ).

68 The case was ultimately settled and there was no need for Gutnick to seek enforcement of the High Court decision in the United States.

69 *Dow Jones & Co Inc v Gutnick* (2002) 210 CLR 575, [20] (Gleeson CJ, McHugh, Gummow and Hayne JJ).

70 *Dow Jones & Co Inc v Gutnick* (2002) 210 CLR 575, [54].

71 N W Garnett, "Dow Jones & Co v Gutnick: Will Australia's Long Jurisdictional Reach Chill Internet Speech World-Wide Comments" (2004) 13(1) *Pacific Rim Law & Policy Journal* 61, 68. See also "Sue You – Internet Publishers Face a Dangerous Precedent", *The Times* (11 December 2002); "A Blow to Online Freedom", *New York Times* (11 December 2002).

publications.[72] Callinan J further sparked controversy with his rejection of the argument that "the ubiquity of the internet" distinguished it "from practically every other form of human endeavour".[73] As Kohl points out, what makes the internet unique is that anyone and everyone can potentially be a publisher, and the *Gutnick* decision places a high burden on independent or individual online publishers to consider all the possible laws their publications could be subject to.[74]

The significant value placed on freedom of speech in the United States has meant that US courts have preferred a narrower approach to the jurisdiction question in online disputes. In *Young v New Haven Advocate*,[75] the Fourth Circuit Court of Appeals came to a different conclusion to that of the Australian High Court despite the cases being factually similar and decided at about the same time. Two newspapers based in the state of Connecticut published allegedly defamatory online articles about Stanley Young, an individual living in the state of Virginia. In determining whether a Virginian court could assert long-arm personal jurisdiction over Young, the Court of Appeal had to consider the Fifth Amendment of the US Constitution, which requires "sufficient minimum contacts with the forum state". The Court of Appeal then applied the jurisdiction test it formulated in a previous case[76] by asking whether the newspapers "manifested an intent to direct their website content ... to Virginia" and decided that accessibility alone was not sufficient to give rise to jurisdiction in this case.[77] This targeted destination approach to jurisdiction

72 *Dow Jones & Co Inc v Gutnick* (2002) 210 CLR 575, [200].

73 *Dow Jones & Co Inc v Gutnick* (2002) 210 CLR 575, [186].

74 U Kohl, "Defamation on the Internet – Nice Decision, Shame about the Reasoning: Dow Jones & Co Inc v Gutnick" (2003) 52(4) *International & Comparative Law Quarterly* 1049, 1056. See also Svantesson, n 6, 97–98. For further discussion about the legacy of *Gutnick*, see B Fitzgerald, "Dow Jones & Co Inc v Gutnick: Negotiating 'American Legal Hegemony' in the Transnational World of Cyberspace" [2003] *Melbourne University Law Review* 21; D Rolph, "Publication, Innocent Dissemination and the Internet after Dow Jones & Co Inc v Gutnick Forum: Cyberlaw" (2010) 33(2) *University of New South Wales Law Journal* 562.

75 *Young v New Haven Advocate*, 315 F 3d 256 (4th Cir, 2003). Although *Young* was not an international matter, the rules of private international law govern cross-border intranational civil disputes in federal countries.

76 *ALS Scan Inc v Digital Service Consultants Inc*, 293 F 3d 707 (4th Cir, 2002). For some of the earliest US case law on internet jurisdiction, see *Calder v Jones*, 468 US 783 (1984) and *Zippo Manufacturing Co v Zippo.com Inc*, 952 F Supp 119 (1997).

77 *Young v New Haven Advocate*, 315 F 3d 256, 263 (Michael J) (4th Cir, 2003). For further details on the legal analysis in *Young* and the US approach to jurisdiction for online disputes, see Fitzgerald, n 74; Fitzgerald et al, n 41, 157–162.

requires the defendant to have deliberately targeted an audience in a particular state, in order for that state to exercise jurisdiction over the matter.

As the above cases demonstrate, national courts continue to ground their jurisdictional claims in territory, despite the global, non-territorial nature of the internet. States have exploited the wide range of territorial principles that have allowed them to exercise jurisdiction over foreign persons and largely external activities. The flexibility of territorial effects and creativity of accessibility-as-destination has therefore allowed states to prioritise and protect their national values, even if it comes at the expense of a cohesive standard for internet jurisdiction.

De facto extraterritorial enforcement jurisdiction

[3.190] As discussed in [3.90], enforcement jurisdiction is traditionally limited to a state's sovereign territory. In the internet age, one of the ways in which states have been able exert influence beyond its borders is by subjecting global internet intermediaries[78] to national jurisdiction. States that can compel "online enforcement" of their laws via these intermediaries can have jurisdictional reach well beyond territorial borders. This section explores some recent examples of states attempting to exercise such *de facto* extraterritorial enforcement jurisdiction.

Canada versus Google

[3.200] Nearly two decades after a Paris Court found that Yahoo was subject to French law, the Canadian Supreme Court held that another US-based multinational technology company – Google – was bound by the terms of a lower Canadian Court injunction. The 2017 case of *Google v Equustek*[79] saw Google caught up in an intellectual property dispute between two Canadian companies: Equustek and Datalink. Equustek accused Datalink of stealing trade secrets and of manufacturing and selling a competing product online. Despite orders in Equustek's favour from the Supreme Court of British Columbia, Datalink continued to manufacture and sell its knock-off product and moved its operations outside Canada. Equustek asked Google to remove Datalink's websites, but Google only delinked individual webpages accessible via google.ca. Equustek sought an injunction requiring Google to delink all of Datalink's websites from all global versions of the Google search engine. The

78 Intermediaries are service providers that facilitate internet interactions, and include search engines, social media platforms, Internet service providers, etc. See Internet & Jurisdiction Policy Network, *Internet & Jurisdiction Global Status Report* (Report, 2019) 65–68.

79 *Google Inc v Equustek Solutions Inc*, 2017 SCC 34.

Supreme Court of British Columbia granted the injunction[80] which was upheld by the Court of Appeal[81] and then upheld again by the Supreme Court of Canada, in a 7-2 decision in Equustek's favour. The crux of the majority of the Supreme Court's reasoning was that "[t]he Internet has no borders – its natural habitat is global. The only way to ensure that the interlocutory injunction attained its objective was to have it apply where Google operates – globally".[82]

Google argued that a global injunction could violate the laws of other countries and have freedom of speech implications, and sought its own injunction from a US District Court to prevent enforcement of the Canadian injunction. The US District Court for Northern California[83] found that the Canadian injunction could not be enforced under the US *Communications Decency Act* which specifies that "no provider or user of an interactive computer service shall be treated as the publisher or speaker of any information provided by another information content provider".[84] The US Court decided that the "balance of equities favor Google because the [Canadian] injunction would deprive it of the benefits of US federal law".[85] Google returned to the Supreme Court of British Columbia seeking to lift or modify the original injunction based on the US Court's decision. The Canadian Court refused on the grounds that the global de-indexing order against Google did not require it to violate US law, it was simply "being restricted in its ability to exercise certain rights".[86]

The entire *Equustek* affair raised important public policy questions surrounding the legal responsibility of US-based multinational intermediaries to respect the laws of countries in which they operate. It also reignited the debate about whether there should be limitations on national courts asserting jurisdiction with extraterritorial effects. In some corners, the Supreme Court decision was derided as "a cautionary tale" of excess domestic jurisdiction that would encourage other global take-down orders and give rise to lengthy cross-border litigation.[87] Michael Geist, for example, writes that "by opening the door to

80 *Equustek Solutions Inc v Jack*, 2014 BCSC 1063.

81 *Equustek Solutions Inc v Google Inc*, 2014 BCCA 448.

82 *Google Inc v Equustek Solutions Inc*, 2017 SCC 34, [41].

83 *Google LLC v Equustek Solutions Inc*, Case No 5:17-cv-04207-EJD, 2017 WL 5000834 (ND Cal, 2 November 2017).

84 *Communications Decency Act of 1996*, 57 USC §230.

85 *Google LLC v Equustek Solutions Inc*, Case No 5:17-cv-04207-EJD, 2017 WL 5000834 (ND Cal, 2 November 2017).

86 *Equustek Solutions Inc v Jack*, 2018 BCSC 610.

87 M Geist, "The Unintended Equustek Effect", *Centre for International Governance Innovation* (28 February 2019) <https://www.cigionline.org/articles/unintended-equustek-effect>.

global takedowns, the ruling leaves two possible problematic outcomes: local courts deciding what others can access online, or companies such as Google selectively determining which rules they will follow".[88]

Barry Sookman, conversely, excoriated the US District Court decision, writing that the California court "[failed] to subject the Equustek order to traditional principles that govern the enforcement of foreign judgments demanded by the principles of private international law".[89] In his opinion, the court "thumbed its nose at [Canada's] highest court and created what should be viewed as an international incident".[90] Sookman argued that the Canadian injunction should have been enforceable in the United States in accordance with its own principles of private international law.[91]

Despite pursuing protracted cross-border litigation to reverse the Canadian injunction, Google did begrudgingly comply with the take-down order, in essence giving extraterritorial effect to the Canadian ruling.

Ignoring New Zealand and Australian suppression orders

[3.210] While Canada may have "won" the jurisdiction battle over *Equustek*, Geist's prediction that companies like Google will selectively choose which rules and rulings that they obey has proven perceptive. In 2018, a man on trial in Auckland for a high profile murder was the subject of a name suppression order. New Zealand media and Google NZ were served with orders which prohibited publication of identifying information about the accused and required any content to be removed that would breach fair trial or privacy rights.[92] Within days of the order, thousands of subscribers received a Google "what's trending in New Zealand" email which named the accused in the item headline, and led to accusations that Google was "flipping the bird" at New Zealand courts.[93] Google NZ initially claimed that the matter was

---

88 Geist, n 87.

89 B Sookman, "US Court Thumbs Its Nose at Supreme Court of Canada: Google v Equustek" (2018) 30(3) *Intellectual Property Journal; Toronto* 375, 376.

90 Sookman, n 89, 377.

91 In that the ruling was neither "repugnant to public policy" nor "repugnant to fundamental notions of what is decent and just". See discussion in Sookman, n 89, 388.

92 S Hurley, "Google 'Thumbs Its Nose' at New Zealand Courts – Lawyer", *NZ Herald* (23 May 2018) <https://www.nzherald.co.nz/business/google-thumbs-its-nose-at-new-zealand-courts-lawyer/HM6IDHX46JK3BQI2I6PWRIAPO4/>.

93 C Anderson, "Google Accused of 'Flipping the Bird' at New Zealand Laws after Grace Millane Murder", *The Guardian* (3 July 2019) <https://www.theguardian.com/world/2019/jul/03/google-accused-of-flipping-the-bird-at-new-zealand-laws-after-grace-millane>.

out of its hands and proffered the well-worn argument that the only laws Google is bound by are those of California, where the global headquarters are situated.[94] New Zealand's Justice Minister, Andrew Little, alluded to national sovereignty and territoriality in his public admonitions of Google: "if they choose to publish in New Zealand, whether it's a server overseas or not ... they've got to respect our laws".[95] Perhaps as a result of local backlash, Google eventually apologised to Little for the "miscommunication" and committed to reviewing and suspending those systems that enabled the violation of the suppression order.[96] The apology, however, came more than six months after the suppression order and Google's publication of the accused's name, which made it seem that Google was doing little more than paying lip service to respecting New Zealand laws. It was an example of the internet giant choosing to comply with a foreign domestic court order in its own time, for reputational reasons, rather than obeying out of any sense of legal obligation.

While global tech companies often argue that compliance with the many and varied laws of the states in which they do business is "impossible", another recent example involving local suppression orders demonstrates the potential futility of states trying to enforce local rules in the internet era. In 2018, the Melbourne County Court issued an injunction to prevent the publication of any information about the criminal proceedings and guilty verdict against Cardinal George Pell for historical child sex abuse offences. The rationale for the order was to mitigate the "real and substantial risk of prejudice to the proper administration of justice" given that Pell was facing a second criminal trial on different charges.[97] While Australian media complied with the gag-order, it is estimated that more than 140 news reports were published

---

94 Hurley, n 92.

95 "NZ Suppression Orders May Become Enforceable Overseas", *Otago Daily Times* (10 August 2019) <https://www.odt.co.nz/news/national/nz-suppression-orders-may-become-enforcable-overseas>. The issue of whether internet platforms such as Google or Facebook are publishers remains hotly contested. See, for example, R Giles, "High Court Ruling in Voller Defamation Case Puts Media Companies Firmly in Firing Line", *The Guardian* (8 September 2021) <https://www.theguardian.com/commentisfree/2021/sep/08/high-court-ruling-in-voller-defamation-case-puts-media-companies-firmly-in-firing-line>.

96 C Overington, "One Man's War on Google's Contemptible Arrogance", *The Australian* (6 July 2019) <https://www.theaustralian.com.au/inquirer/one-mans-war-on-googles-contemptible-arrogance/news-story/bb7cfd11dbab07e4ad6a683078a7d2a7>.

97 A Meade, "Up to 100 Journalists Accused of Breaking Pell Suppression Order Face Possible Jail Terms", *The Guardian* (26 February 2019) <https://www.theguardian.com/media/2019/feb/26/dozens-of-journalists-accused-of-breaking-pell-trial-suppression-order-face-possible-jail-terms>.

in international outlets within 24 hours of Pell's conviction.[98] These stories were disseminated through social media and easily available to Australian readers. Only those international media companies with a physical presence in Australia felt compelled to comply with the suppression order. The rest, outside the reach of Australia's enforcement jurisdiction, justified their reporting of Pell's conviction as a matter of global public interest and derided the suppression order as antithetical to freedom of the press and "futile against the Internet".[99] Journalists in Australia resented the inequity of the order, with Richard Ackland opining that it was "evident that the internet does not stop at the sovereign borders of the nation", and that "[t]o make orders significantly beyond the power of judicial enforcement in this country smacks of futility".[100]

The difficulties of enforcing local suppression orders when information can be so easily disseminated and accessed online acutely demonstrates how the notion of territorial jurisdiction can be undermined. Without the cooperation of global internet intermediaries, attempts to apply national laws and court decisions to the internet at large is destined to fail.

Protecting Europe's online data

[3.220] In May 2018, the European Union's (EU) sweeping data protection law came into force.[101] The *General Data Protection Regulation* (*GDPR*) requires any company or organisation that collects, uses or stores personal data to ensure they conform to certain principles of privacy, security, fairness and accuracy. Data is only to be collected and used for specific purposes, and every piece of data must be justified under the regulation. In addition, individuals have

98 M Shields and T Akerman, "Suppression Order Failed to Block Overseas Reports", *The Australian* (27 February 2019) <https://www.theaustralian.com.au/business/media/suppression-order-failed-to-block-overseas-reports/news-story/ca6814794c8fc3376efb36baa5c7971c>.

99 P Farhi, "An Australian Court's Gag Order Is No Match for the Internet, as Word Gets Out about Prominent Cardinal's Conviction", *The Washington Post* (13 December 2018) <https://www.washingtonpost.com/lifestyle/style/an-australian-courts-gag-order-is-no-match-for-the-internet-as-word-gets-out-about-prominent-cardinals-conviction/2018/12/13/5137005c-fef5-11e8-83c0-b06139e540e5_story.html?noredirect=on&utm_term=.18770937f510>.

100 R Ackland, "Pell's Trial Shows Courts Can't Keep Secrets in the Internet Age", *The Guardian* (27 February 2019) <https://www.theguardian.com/australia-news/commentisfree/2019/feb/27/pells-trial-shows-courts-cant-keep-secrets-in-the-internet-age>.

101 *Regulation (EU) 2016/679 of the European Parliament and of the Council of 27 April 2016 on the Protection of Natural Persons with regard to the Processing of Personal Data and on the Free Movement of Such Data, and Repealing Directive 95/46/EC (General Data Protection Regulation)* [2016] OJ L 119/1.

significant rights to access and control their personal digital data. The *GDPR* is particularly notable as an example of the EU's assertion of extraterritorial prescriptive jurisdiction, and it has been described as "the world's most powerful and far-reaching privacy law".[102]

The *GDPR* applies to all companies or organisations that collect or process online data where they have an establishment in the EU.[103] This includes foreign companies with a European presence that satisfies the "establishment" criteria, and is a fairly typical manifestation of the origin approach, or subjective territorial principle of jurisdiction. Foreign companies without a European territorial presence will also be subject to the requirements of the *GDPR* in certain circumstances. For example, if any company or organisation in the world offers goods or services to "data subjects in the Union", then it must comply with the *GDPR*.[104] The European Data Protection Board has specified that a targeted destination approach is to be taken when determining whether the activity in question falls within the *GDPR*'s jurisdiction.[105] In other words, the goods or services offered by the foreign company must be intentionally targeted to the EU market. The term "data subjects in the Union" is broad, and includes any persons within the territory of the EU, whether or not they are EU citizens.[106] It also has extraterritorial application on the basis of the nationality principle, meaning that as long as a foreign company is offering goods or services targeting the EU, then it must also comply with the *GDPR* in respect of any data collected from EU citizens who are located outside the territory of the Union.[107]

The introduction of the *GDPR* left foreign and global companies with few options. They could withdraw from the lucrative European market entirely; they could attempt to comply with the *GDPR* only in relation to those "data

102 M Parker, "What Does GDPR Mean for Me? An Explainer", *The Conversation* (16 May 2018) <https://theconversation.com/what-does-gdpr-mean-for-me-an-explainer-96630>.

103 Article 3(1). See also European Data Protection Board, *Guidelines 3/2018 on the Territorial Scope of the GDPR (Article 3)* (version 2.1, 12 November 2019).

104 Article 3(2)(a). Such companies must also comply with the *GDPR* if they monitor the behaviour of data subjects "as far as their behaviour takes place in the Union": Art 3(2)(b).

105 European Data Protection Board, *Guidelines 3/2018 on the Territorial Scope of the GDPR (Article 3)* (version 2.1, 12 November 2019) 13; see also M Klar, "Binding Effects of the European General Data Protection Regulation (GDPR) on US Companies" (2020) 11 *Hastings Science and Technology Law Journal* 55.

106 European Data Protection Board, *Guidelines 3/2018 on the Territorial Scope of the GDPR (Article 3)* (version 2.1, 12 November 2019) 14.

107 Klar, n 105, 110.

subjects in the Union"; or they could implement the strict EU data protection laws for all users worldwide. Perhaps unsurprisingly, the majority of transnational companies have taken the third option, on the basis that "it is far more efficient to implement the rigid European regulations on a global scale, instead of trying to align digital markets with national borders".[108] The effect of the *GDPR* is perhaps the most pervasive example to date of *de facto* extraterritorial enforcement jurisdiction. The EU does not, and cannot, legally extend its laws beyond its territory or its citizens, and yet the nature of the internet has meant that it would be too onerous for companies to do anything other than adopt the *GDPR* for all their data collection and processing.

The EU has essentially set the global standard for data protection and, surprisingly, there was little pushback from intermediaries about the new regulations.[109] The same global tech companies that criticised decisions like *Yahoo* and *Gutnick* as facilitating a "lowest common denominator" approach to online freedom of speech protection, were content to allow the *GDPR* to become the *de facto* data protection law of the internet. One explanation is that the *GDPR* aligns with the culture of these intermediaries. According to a report in *The New York Times*, "[o]fficials from Facebook, Google and other companies said in interviews that they had been working to give people more control over what data they share anyway".[110] Another explanation is that the big tech companies foresaw that they would have a business advantage over their smaller competitors.[111] Whatever the reason for such acquiescence, the *GDPR* is a clear example of *de facto* European extraterritorial enforcement jurisdiction.

Conclusion

[3.230] The above is just a snapshot of a vast and growing tangle of jurisprudence and legislation relating to jurisdiction and the internet. Despite the inherently global and interconnected nature of the internet, states continue to prioritise their national interests by asserting jurisdiction largely on the basis of territory. Any exercise of territorial jurisdiction over internet matters

108 A Bendiek and M Römer, "Externalizing Europe: The Global Effects of European Data Protection" (2019) 21(1) *Digital Policy, Regulation and Governance* 32, 35.

109 S Frenkel, "Tech Giants Brace for Europe's New Data Privacy Rules", *New York Times* (28 January 2018) <https://www.nytimes.com/2018/01/28/technology/europe-data-privacy-rules.html>.

110 Frenkel, n 109.

111 N Kostov and S Schechner, "GDPR Has Been a Boon for Google and Facebook", *Wall Street Journal* (17 June 2019) <https://www.wsj.com/articles/gdpr-has-been-a-boon-for-google-and-facebook-11560789219?mod=rsswn>.

will inevitably have extraterritorial effects and lead to conflicting values and competing laws.

The Future of Jurisdiction and the Internet

[3.240] Traditionally state-centric international law principles are facilitating an unsustainable unilateral approach to jurisdiction and the internet. As Kohl writes, "the blunt application of national law to the transnational internet cannot but lead to the territorial fragmentation of the internet into national cyberspaces with attendant costs for freedom of expression as well as for economic, political, social and cultural exchange".[112] The growing recognition of the consequences of jurisdictional fragmentation has led to calls for increased international cooperation to protect the internet's "cross-border and permission-less nature".[113]

Early proposals for a universal multilateral treaty to harmonise internet jurisdiction laws have fallen out of favour.[114] The notion of a "global internet jurisdiction" agreed to by all states is a pipe dream in a world in which sovereignty and territory retain primacy. Heterogeneity of laws and cultures means that jurisdictional fragmentation is inescapable, and the way forward will need to be through transnational coordination and interoperability. This is the approach urged by such global non-profit groups as the Internet and Jurisdiction Policy Network and the Internet Society. The importance of transnational collaboration and the identification and pursuit of common goals will be essential to mitigate jurisdictional challenges. It is not only states that need to work together, but businesses, civil society, intermediaries and other internet stakeholders.[115] How such a "multistakeholder" approach will work in practice, and how this might be reflected in the decisions of national courts remains to be seen. In the meantime, internet users should be vigilant of the fact that their online activity can fall within multiple jurisdictions and be subject to foreign laws.

---

112 Kohl, n 19, 54.

113 Internet & Jurisdiction Policy Network, *Internet & Jurisdiction Global Status Report* (Report, 2019) 36.

114 Svantesson, n 6, 115.

115 Internet & Jurisdiction Policy Network, *Internet & Jurisdiction Global Status Report* (Report, 2019) 41–42; Internet Society, *The Internet and Extra-Territorial Effects of Laws* (Report, 2018).

Chapter 4

The Evolution of Domain Name Law

Alpana Roy*

Introduction

[4.10] The exponential rise of e-commerce due to the ongoing shift of the marketplace to the internet in technologically advanced economies has resulted in a mounting demand to register and use domain names in order to trade online. Not surprisingly, this in turn has led to an increase in the number of disputes involving the contested rights and claims made by parties in relation to certain domain names. The increasing number of disputes over the last two decades has resulted in the evolution of legal and quasi-legal rules and institutional arrangements relating to policy-making, rule-making and management of internet domain names.

The Uniform Domain Name Dispute Resolution Policy (UDRP) stipulates the international legal framework for resolving domain name disputes, and applies to domain name extensions known as generic top-level domains (gTLDs). Familiar gTLDs include: .com, .net, .org, .biz, .info, .aero, .asia, .cat, .coop, .jobs, .mobi, .museum, .name, .pro, .tel and .travel.[1] The UDRP has been in operation since 24 October 1999,[2] and also applies to all new gTLDs.[3]

---

* Dean, Te Piringa Faculty of Law, University of Waikato, BA (Soc Sci) (UTS), LLB (Hons) (Syd), MA (Journalism) (UTS), DipLegPrac (College of Law), PhD (Syd), GCHETL (UTS), Solicitor and Barrister of the Supreme Court of NSW and the High Court of Australia, Accredited Mediator.

1 For a detailed scholarly analysis of gTLDs and the application of the UDRP, see D Lindsay, *International Domain Name Law: ICANN and the UDRP* (Hart Publishing, 2007) 1–128.

2 The UDRP is available online at <https://www.icann.org/resources/pages/policy-2012-02-25-en>.

3 For full details of the Internet Corporation for Assigned Names and Numbers (ICANN) New gTLD program, see ICANN, *New Generic Top-Level Domains* <http://newgtlds.icann.org>.

National authorities are responsible for domain name dispute resolution involving country code top-level domains (ccTLDs) – such as .au. In Australia, the relevant national authority for the administration of ccTLDs is .au Domain Administration Ltd (auDA), and the relevant national policy governing .au disputes is the .au Dispute Resolution Policy (auDRP).

The auDRP came into effect on 1 August 2002.[4] The auDRP closely follows the wording and underlying objectives of the international UDRP. The overall aim of both the UDRP and the auDRP is to provide an alternative to litigation for the quicker and cheaper resolution of disputes between the registrant of a domain name and a party with competing rights in the domain name. Both policies have been an effective method for resolving disputes using online arbitration processes, and since their inception some 60,000 or so decisions have been decided under the UDRP,[5] while 450 or so have been decided under the auDRP.[6]

Along with examining the international legal and regulatory framework for internet domain name disputes (ie, the UDRP), this chapter will also examine the national legal and regulatory framework as the auDRP has not been studied widely given the relatively smaller number of decisions. Apart from Roy's scholarship on Australian domain name law,[7]

---

4 The auDRP, including auDRP Rules, is available online at: auDA, *.au Dispute Resolution Policy (auDRP) (2016-01)* (Policy No: 2016-01, 15 April 2016) <https://www.auda.org.au/assets/pdf/auda-2016-01.pdf>.

5 This figure has been based on a WIPO publication which states that the total number of UDRP decisions filed (as at 8 August 2011) is 36,443. See WIPO, *The Uniform Domain Name Dispute Resolution Policy and WIPO* (August 2011) 3 <http://www.wipo.int/export/sites/www/amc/en/docs/wipointaudrp.pdf>.

6 See auDA, *auDRP Proceedings Database* <https://www.auda.org.au/au-domain-names/au-dispute-resolution-policy/audrp-proceedings-database>.

7 See A Roy, *Australian Domain Name Law* (Thomson Reuters, 2016); A Roy and A Marsoof, "A Critical and Comparative Review of auDRP and UDRP Domain Name Decisions" (2016) 19 (5–6) *Journal of World Intellectual Property* 203; A Roy and A Marsoof, "'Bad Faith' and 'Rights or Legitimate Interests' under Domain Name Law – Emerging Themes from the UDRP and auDRP" (2015) 20 *Media and Arts Law Review* 282; A Roy, "Navigating the Landscape of the .au Dispute Resolution Policy as It Enters Its Second Decade" (2014) 19 *Media and Arts Law Review* 1; A Roy, "Internet Domain Name Dispute Resolution in Australia" (2014) 36(8) *European Intellectual Property Review* 492; A Roy, "Reflections on the Uniform Domain Name Dispute Resolution Policy as It Enters Its Second Decade" (2012) 1(1) *International Journal of Technology Policy and Law* 15.

there have been few other articles,[8] chapters[9] or academic commentary[10] on auDRP decisions and policy. Indeed, the analysis of the auDRP has been limited to a few short paragraphs within an intellectual property law textbook chapter on trade marks,[11] or an alternative dispute resolution textbook chapter on online dispute resolution,[12] and is often only mentioned briefly in footnotes.[13]

8 Mark Bender provides a general overview of the auDRP in "Domain Name Disputes Involving Trademarks in Australia" in *Trademarks and Internet/Cyberspace* (Amicus Books, 2010), "Domain Name Disputes Involving Trademarks in Australia" (2007) 3(2) *Monash Business Review* 1, 1–10 and "What's in a Name: Domain Name Disputes Involving Trademarks in Australia" (2007) 3(3) *Monash Business Review* 38. Liz Williams traces the development of internet governance in Australia in "Internet Governance in Australia: Modelling Self-Regulatory Structures in the Domain Name System" (2003) 10(2) *Murdoch University Electronic Journal of Law* <http://www.murdoch.edu.au/elaw/issues/v10n2/williams102.html>.

9 A chapter on Australian domain name law is provided by A Payne and R Mohindra, "Australia" in T Bettinger (ed), *Domain Name Law and Practice: An International Handbook* (Oxford University Press, 2005) 57–75. See also P Catania, L Cohn and L Turner, *Domain Names and Trademarks* (Law Book Company, 2001) 107–116.

10 See J Selby, *Submission to "Review of the Structure and Operation of the .au Internet Domain Name"* (Department of Communications, Information Technology and the Arts, Canberra, 2006).

11 See, for example, T Berger, M Davison and A Freeman, *Shanahan's Australian Law of Trade Marks and Passing Off* (Thomson Reuters, 6th ed, 2016) [115.1760]–[115.2765]; R Burrell and M Handler, *Australian Trade Mark Law* (Oxford University Press, 2nd ed, 2016) 554–558; R Reynolds, N Stoianoff and A Roy, *Intellectual Property: Text and Essential Cases* (Federation Press, 5th ed, 2015) 626–628; A Stewart et al, *Intellectual Property in Australia* (LexisNexis Butterworths, 5th ed, 2014) 616–625; E Clark et al, *Cyber Law in Australia* (Kluwer Law International, 2010) 146–152; B Fitzgerald et al, *Internet and E-Commerce Law: Business and Policy* (Thomson Reuters, 2011) 603–737. The auDRP is not frequently referred to in international academic journals either, but see W Chik, "Lord of Your Domain, but Master of None: The Need to Harmonize and Recalibrate the Domain Name Regime of Ownership and Control" (2008) 16(1) *International Journal of Law & Information Technology* 8, 29, where a short description of the auDRP is provided.

12 See, for example, D Spencer and S Hardy, *Dispute Resolution in Australia: Cases, Commentary and Materials* (Thomson Reuters, 3rd ed, 2014) 649; T Sourdin, *Alternative Dispute Resolution* (Thomson Reuters, 5th ed, 2016) 412.

13 See, for example, K Bowrey et al, *Australian Intellectual Property: Commentary, Law and Practice* (Oxford University Press, 2nd ed, 2015) 617.

In contrast, the UDRP system has attracted significant academic commentary by numerous scholars, including Froomkin,[14] Mueller,[15] Geist,[16] Armon[17] and Efroni.[18] Criticisms of the UDRP have included:

- questions about its legitimacy "as an internationally binding, compulsory legal instrument drafted by a private US not-for-profit organization";[19]
- the apparent systematic bias towards complainants in the online UDRP system;[20]
- the limited opportunity provided by the UDRP for complainants to have their defeated claims reviewed by the courts;[21] and
- the inconsistencies in the application of the UDRP by panellists.[22]

There have been numerous suggestions on how the UDRP process could be vastly improved, including:

- greater procedural fairness and transparency in UDRP decision-making;[23]
- the establishment of an internal appellate process, and the random selection of panellists;[24] and

---

14 See, for example, A M Froomkin, "ICANN's 'Uniform Dispute Resolution Policy' – Causes and (Partial) Cures" (2002) 67(3) *Brooklyn Law Review* 605; A M Froomkin, "Wrong Turn in Cyberspace: Using ICANN to Route around the APA and the Constitution" (2000) 50 *Duke Law Journal* 17.

15 See, for example, M L Mueller, "Rough Justice: A Statistical Assessment of ICANN's Uniform Dispute Resolution Policy" (2001) 17(3) *The Information Society* 153.

16 See, for example, M Geist, "Fair.com?: An Examination of the Allegations of Systemic Unfairness in the ICANN UDRP" (2002) 27(3) *Brooklyn Journal of International Law* 903.

17 See, for example, O Armon, "Is This as Good as It Gets? An Appraisal of ICANN's Uniform Domain Name Dispute Resolution Policy (UDRP) Three Years after Implementation" (2003) 22(1) *The Review of Litigation* 99.

18 See, for example, Z Efroni, "Names as Domains, Names as Marks: Issues Concerning the Interface between Internet Domain Names and Trademark Rights" in P K Yu (ed), *Intellectual Property and Information Wealth: Issues and Practices in the Digital Age* (Praeger Publishers, 2007) <http://ssrn.com/abstract=957750>.

19 Efroni, n 18, 388.

20 See Geist, n 16; Mueller, n 15.

21 Froomkin, "ICANN's 'Uniform Dispute Resolution Policy'", n 14, 678–688. See also Efroni, n 18.

22 See Armon, n 17, 122–129. See also Efroni, n 18, 390; Froomkin, "ICANN's 'Uniform Dispute Resolution Policy'", n 14.

23 Froomkin, "ICANN's 'Uniform Dispute Resolution Policy'", n 14, 713–716.

24 Mueller, n 15.

- the introduction of quality control mechanisms to review the performance of panellists, and the creation of mandatory three-member panels (as opposed to single member panels).[25]

There have also been several in-depth studies of the UDRP system, including:

- Komaitis' analysis within a property law context of domain names as a *sui generis* form of an "e-property" right;[26]
- Lipton's exploration of the competing interests of domain names, trade marks, privacy and personality rights;[27] and
- Lindsay's study of the history and development of the UDRP and its growing body of decisions.[28]

Others have studied the UDRP model as a potential template to develop for resolving different types of online intellectual property disputes.[29] This chapter will cover the UDRP and auDRP so that the concerns of the users of the auDRP system are properly addressed, and not simply absorbed into the international (and particularly United States) critical literature on the UDRP.

This chapter will trace the evolution of international and Australian domain name law. To this end, this chapter will first provide an overview of domain names. It will then examine the international and national regulatory frameworks for internet domain name disputes – the UDRP and the .auDRP. This chapter will conclude with reflections on trends and policy implications for both international and Australian domain name law.

Domain Names

[4.20] Over the past two decades, a new terminology has evolved to describe the unique types of disputes that have emerged in the online space with the

25 Geist, n 16.

26 K Komaitis, *The Current State of Domain Name Regulation: Domain Names as Second-Class Citizens in a Mark-Dominated World* (Routledge, 2010).

27 J Lipton, *Internet Domain Names, Trademarks and Free Speech* (Edward Elgar Publishing, 2010).

28 See Lindsay, n 1.

29 See A Christie, "The ICANN Domain-Name Dispute Resolution System as a Model for Resolving Other Intellectual Property Disputes on the Internet" (2002) 1 *The Journal of World Intellectual Property* 105, 105–117.

rapid increase in the use of the internet. In order to understand the broader context in which the UDRP and auDRP operate, the key terms governing domain name disputes will be briefly outlined below.[30]

Stewart et al usefully describe domain names as:

> A domain name or URL (uniform resource locator) is an internet address, providing a shorthand way of locating and connecting to a website. The structure and allocation of such names is governed by a set of international protocols, effectively created under the auspices of the United States Government but sustained by the agreement of the various entities involved in the operation of the internet. The protocols do not have a legislative basis, but are no less effective for that. At an international level, the key regulatory role is played by ICANN, the Internet Corporation for Assigned Names and Numbers, a California based not-for-profit company.[31]

As the internet is a sequence of interconnected computer networks and systems, each computer has its own unique designation to enable data transmission and exchange. Organisations authorised to issue domain names provide alphanumerical aliases for the domain names because the numerical addresses are generally too difficult to remember. These alphanumerical aliases provide the technical internet address, and also fulfil the dual function of identifying the content of the internet address.[32]

Along with the relevant internet protocol, each URL consists of a secondary top-level domain (sTLD) and a gTLD. For example, for the URL http://www.microsoft.com/ "www" is the relevant internet protocol, "microsoft" is the sTLD and "com" is the gTLD. The gTLDs indicate the type of entity (or target audience) for which the website relates to. For example, ".com" relates to commercial operations, ".gov" relates to government bodies and departments, and ".edu" relates to educational institutions and establishments. Application for a domain name is made to the list of domain name registrars authorised by the Internet Corporation for Assigned Names and Numbers (ICANN) to issue domain names.[33] A URL may also contain an individual ccTLD, which

30 For a clear summary of other types on online disputes – such as metatags, linking and framing – which do not involve using the UDRP or the auDRP, see Berger, Davison and Freeman, n 11.

31 Stewart et al, n 11, 583.

32 See Berger, Davison and Freeman, n 11, [115.505].

33 For details of accredited registrars, see ICANN, "Information for Registrars" <http://www.icann.org/en/resources/registrars>.

identifies where the website is located. As noted in the Introduction at [4.10], the ccTLD for Australia is ".au".

The domain name system of registration is based on a first-come first-served basis, and it is problematic to prevent another entity from registering a domain name if they were the first in time to seek registration. Unlike trade mark law, there is no assessment of the nature of the registrant's interest in the particular domain name. Further, unlike trade mark law, where the same name can be registered for different classes of goods and/or services by different entities and bodies, each domain name is required to be unique and inimitable with only one entity able to obtain a particular domain name within an URL. As conveniently explained on ICANN's website:

> The Domain Name System (DNS) helps users to find their way around the Internet. Every computer on the Internet has a unique address – just like a telephone number – which is a rather complicated string of numbers. It is called its "IP address" (IP stands for "Internet Protocol"). IP Addresses are hard to remember. The DNS makes using the Internet easier by allowing a familiar string of letters (the "domain name") to be used instead of the arcane IP address. So instead of typing 207.151.159.3, you can type www.internic.net. It is a "mnemonic" device that makes addresses easier to remember.[34]

While "[a]n entire taxonomy" has emerged in the discourse on domain names, Berger et al accessibly identify three main types of disputes:[35]

- First, "squatters", where a party registers a domain name knowing that other parties with a legitimate interest may wish to register that same domain name.[36] Typically in these cases the registrant has registered a series of domain names illicitly, with the objective of transferring and selling the domain name to parties with a legitimate interest. These registrants are often also referred to as "cybersquatters".[37]
- Second, "parasites", where a party without a legitimate interest registers a domain name with the intent of drawing internet users to that website – often by registering a very similar domain name to another domain name

34 ICANN, "FAQs – What Is the Domain Name System?" <https://www.icann.org/resources/pages/faqs-2014-01-21-en#dns>.

35 Berger, Davison and Freeman, n 11, [115.555]. See also I S Nathenson, "Showdown at the Domain Name Corral: Property Rights and Personal Jurisdiction over Squatters, Poachers and Other Parasites" (1997) 58(4) *University of Pittsburgh Law Review* 911.

36 Berger, Davison and Freeman, n 11, [115.565].

37 See generally Lindsay, n 1, 95–99.

belonging to a party that has a legitimate interest in the name.[38] This is also referred to as "typosquatting".[39]

- Third, "twins", where two parties – both with legitimate interests – wish to register a specific domain name.[40] While the party first to register the domain name is likely to prevail, the party second in time may also attempt to assert a claim in the domain name given its legitimate interest in the name.[41]

The International and National Regulatory Frameworks for Internet Domain Name Disputes – the UDRP and the .auDRP

The international framework under the UDRP

[4.30] On the application of the US Government, and with approval of the Member States of the World Intellectual Property Organization (WIPO), in June 1998 WIPO undertook an international consultation to develop recommendations regarding the legal issues associated with domain names, including domain name dispute resolution. WIPO's recommendations were published in its Final Report – *The Management of Internet Names and Addresses: Intellectual Property Issues* (1999).[42] The recommendations contained in this Report were adopted by ICANN, and the UDRP was subsequently established as the international dispute resolution process for resolving domain name disputes.[43]

During this same period, the US Government reviewed the issue of the privatisation of the domain name system, and the transfer of its management from the US Government to a non-governmental newly established not-for-profit entity. On 5 June 1998, the US Department of Commerce published its Statement of Policy on the *Management of Internet Names and Addresses,*

38 Berger, Davison and Freeman, n 11, [115.570].

39 See generally Lindsay, n 1, 259–261.

40 Berger, Davison and Freeman, n 11, [115.560].

41 Berger, Davison and Freeman, n 11.

42 This Report is available online at <http://www.wipo.int/export/sites/www/amc/en/docs/report-final1.pdf>.

43 The UDRP is available on ICANN's website at <http://www.icann.org/en/udrp/udrp.htm>. The UDRP is available online at <https://www.icann.org/resources/pages/policy-2012-02-25-en>.

63 *Federal Register* 31741 (commonly referred to as the "White Paper").[44] The White Paper addressed the issue of the transition of management and privatisation of the domain name system, and also considered WIPO's role for developing recommendations for resolving disputes between trade mark holders and domain names:

> The US Government will seek international support to call upon the World Intellectual Property Organization (WIPO) to initiate a balanced and transparent process, which includes the participation of trademark holders and members of the Internet community who are not trademark holders, to (1) develop recommendations for a uniform approach to resolving trademark/domain name disputes involving cyberpiracy (as opposed to conflicts between trademark holders with legitimate competing rights), (2) recommend a process for protecting famous trademarks in the generic top level domains, and (3) evaluate the effects, based on studies conducted by independent organizations, such as the National Research Council of the National Academy of Sciences, of adding new gTLDs and related dispute resolution procedures on trademark and intellectual property holders. These findings and recommendations could be submitted to the board of the new corporation for its consideration in conjunction with its development of registry and registrar policy and the creation and introduction of new gTLDs.

In 1998, ICANN was established as the new not-for-profit entity to manage and administer the international domain name system.[45]

ICANN was established under Californian law with the overall mission to coordinate "the global Internet's systems of unique identifiers, and in particular to ensure the stable and secure operation of the Internet's unique identifier systems".[46] More specifically, ICANN's mission is to coordinate the allocation and assignment of the three sets of unique identifiers:

1. domain names;
2. internet protocol addresses and autonomous system numbers; and
3. protocol port and parameter numbers.

ICANN's mission also includes coordinating the development and operation of the domain name root name server system, and coordinating policies in

---

44 This Statement of Policy is available online at <https://www.icann.org/resources/unthemed-pages/white-paper-2012-02-25-en>.

45 The major agreements establishing ICANN are available online at <https://www.icann.org/resources/pages/agreements-en>.

46 ICANN's "Mission and Core Values" are stated in Art I of its *Bylaws*, available online at <http://www.icann.org/en/general/bylaws.htm#I>.

relation to these technical functions. This extends to implementing and developing policies to facilitate the security, stability, interoperability and resilience of the domain name system, and coordinating policy related to these technical functions.[47] On 24 October 1999, the ICANN Board approved the documents which established the new international domain name dispute resolution system: the UDRP and the *Rules for Uniform Domain Name Dispute Resolution Policy* ("UDRP Rules").[48] These documents established the international regulatory framework for dealing with domain name disputes.

The Australian framework under the auDRP

[4.40] The auDRP was drafted as part of a report by auDA into Australian ccTLDs (ie, .au domain names). auDA is the Australian policy and industry regulatory body which regulates .au domain names. Among its functions, auDA develops and implements policy for .au domain names, accredits and licenses registrars to make domain name registrations, and represents the .au domain name space at ICANN and other international bodies.[49]

Similarly to ICANN, auDA was established as a non-profit corporation. It was registered on 23 June 1997 with the purpose of administering the .au ccTLD for the benefit of the Australian community.[50] The object of auDA is set out in cl 3.1 of its Constitution, which provides:

---

47 ICANN's "Mission and Core Values" are stated in Art I of its *Bylaws*, available online at <http://www.icann.org/en/general/bylaws.htm#I>.

48 The *Rules for Uniform Domain Name Dispute Resolution Policy* (the "UDRP Rules") is available on ICANN's website at <http://www.icann.org/en/dndr/udrp/uniform-rules.htm>.

49 See auDA, *About auDA* <http://www.auda.org.au/about-auda/>. There is detailed information about auDA on its website. For all of auDA's published policies (both current and historical), see auDA, *Index of Published Policies* <http://www.auda.org.au/policies/index-of-published-policies/>. For information about the auDA Board, see auDA, *auDA Board* <http://www.auda.org.au/about-auda/our-org/board/>. For auDA's annual reports, see auDA, *Annual Reports* <http://www.auda.org.au/about-auda/our-org/annual-reports/>. For auDA's current and previous strategic plans, see auDA, *Strategic Plan* <http://www.auda.org.au/about-auda/our-org/strategic-plan/>. For information on auDA's international activities, see auDA, *International Activities* <http://www.auda.org.au/about-auda/our-org/international-activities/>. There is even detailed information about auDA's budget (see auDA, *Budget*); auDA's Board meetings (see auDA, *auDA Board Meetings* <http://www.auda.org.au/about-auda/our-org/board-meetings/>); and auDA's Annual General Meetings (see auDA, *Annual General Meetings* <http://www.auda.org.au/about-auda/our-org/agm/>).

50 *Constitution of .au Domain Administration Limited ACN 079 009 340* <https://assets.auda.org.au/a/2021-11/auDA%20Constitution-%20Approved%2016%20November%202021.pdf?VersionId=lf3VDyJL7yw4n9.00pyaJ_erde4Ac5AD>.

The principal purposes of auDA are:

a. to be the administrator of, and the Australian self regulatory policy body for the .au ccTLD and its associated Second Level Domains;
b. to maintain and promote the operational stability and utility of the .au ccTLD and more generally, the Internet's unique identifier system, and to enhance the benefits of the Internet to the wider community; (*Amended by Special Resolution, 14 August 2006*)
c. to ensure a cost effective administration of the .au ccTLD and its sub-domains;
d. to develop and establish a policy framework for the development and administration of the .au ccTLD including:
   i. rules governing the operations of second level domain registries;
   ii. the creation of second level domains;
   iii. rules governing the accreditation of registrars and registry operators; (*Amended by Special Resolution, 23 September 2002*)
   iv. rules governing the registration of names within second level domains and access to second level domain registries;
   v. ensuring that registrars have equal access to second level registry services.
e. to manage the operation of critical technical functions including:
   i. the primary and secondary .au name servers;
   ii. zone files for second level domains; and
   iii. a searchable data base containing information on registrations within the .au ccTLD.
f. to liaise with national and international bodies on issues relating to the development and administration of domain name systems.
g. to establish appropriate complaints handling and dispute resolution processes to provide for conciliation or redress of grievances on matters associated with the administration of the .au ccTLD.

As detailed in auDA's Constitution, auDA is a non-profit, membership based Australian company limited by guarantee. Accordingly, auDA is governed by both the *Corporations Act 2001* (Cth) and its own Constitution. auDA's structure – including composition of auDA's Board (see cl 18.2), and different classes of members (see cl 9), are set out in the Constitution. auDA is accountable to the Australian Federal Government.[51] As detailed on auDA's website, the organisation has conducted several reviews of its internal operations, governance structures and processes.[52] There have been two

51 See *auDA Transparency and Accountability Framework* (May 2019) <https://assets.auda.org.au/a/2020-11/auDA-Transparency-and-Accountability-Framework.pdf?VersionId=79BrRcoxJwxDITJ0QmqFZtLn7K4gadLP>.

52 See auDA, *Reviews of auDA* <http://www.auda.org.au/about-auda/our-org/reviews-of-auda/>.

internal reviews of the auDRP by auDA to date – the first one in 2007,[53] and the second one in late 2012.[54] auDA's complaint handling framework deals with complaints about breaches of auDA policies by domain name registrants, and also complaints about accredited registrars and resellers.[55] The complaints process is supported by an appeals process: the Registrant Review Panel (for reviews of decisions by auDA to cancel domain names due to breach of auDA policies), and the Registrar Review Panel (for reviews of decisions by auDA to suspend or terminate registrar accreditation).[56]

Leading from the accumulation of events from 1995, the auDA organisation was eventually established to manage the .au domain system in 1999.[57] On 31 December 2000, the Commonwealth formally endorsed auDA as the appropriate body "to hold the delegation of authority by the Internet Corporation for Assigned Names and Numbers (ICANN) for administrative authority of the au country code top level domain (ccTLD)".[58] In exchange for this endorsement, auDA was required to be bound by ICANN's policies, co-operate with the Commonwealth and/or ICANN in the case of any reassignment of authority from auDA to another party, and recognise the Commonwealth government as "the ultimate authority" for the administration and management of the .au domain name space.[59] The Commonwealth continues to have reserve powers in relation to domain names under the *Telecommunications Act 1997* (Cth).[60]

---

53 auDA Issues Paper, *.au Dispute Resolution Policy (auDRP) Review* (2007) 2 <https://archive.auda.org.au/news/auda-reviews-au-dispute-resolution-policy-audrp-2/>.

54 auDA Issues Paper, *.au Dispute Resolution Policy (auDRP) Review* (2012) <https://archive.auda.org.au/policies/policy-reviews/au-dispute-resolution-policy-review/>.

55 See auDA, *Submit a Complaint* <https://www.auda.org.au/au-domain-names/lodge-complaint/submit-complaint>.

56 See auDA, *Complaints Policy (2015-01)* (Policy No: 2015-01, 14 May 2015) <http://www.auda.org.au/assets/Policies/2015-01.pdf>.

57 See auDA, *About auDA* <http://www.auda.org.au/about-auda/>.

58 See letter from Richard Alston, Minister for Communications, Information Technology and the Arts to Greg Watson, Chairman of auDA (31 December 2000) <https://www.iana.org/reports/2001/au-redelegation/alston-to-watson-31dec00.html>.

59 See letter from Richard Alston, Minister for Communications, Information Technology and the Arts to Greg Watson, Chairman of auDA (31 December 2000) <https://www.iana.org/reports/2001/au-redelegation/alston-to-watson-31dec00.html>.

60 See auDA, *About auDA* <http://www.auda.org.au/about-auda/>.

As a result of another endorsement by the Commonwealth government,[61] an Internet Assigned Numbers Authority (IANA) report[62] and the ICANN Board's approval,[63] auDA and ICANN entered into a ccTLD Sponsorship Agreement on 25 October 2001 under which auDA was recognised as the "manager" for the .au ccTLD.[64]

In June 2001, the auDA Dispute Resolution Working Group presented a report to the auDA Board which recommended a dispute resolution policy and procedural rules closely based on ICANN's UDRP "as a mechanism for handling disputes between registrants and parties with competing legal rights in a .au domain name".[65] The recommendations were adopted by the auDA Board, and the dispute resolution policy for Australian ccTLDs (ie, the auDRP) commenced on 1 August 2002.[66]

While the auDRP is an adaptation of the UDRP, there are some significant differences between the two domain name dispute resolution policies. A key difference is that .au domain names must have an additional requirement, namely some connection to Australia at the registration stage. To this end, auDA's eligibility and allocation policy specifies certain requirements for the different types of .au domain names – such as com.au,[67] net.au,[68] org.au,[69]

---

61 Letter from Richard Alston, Minister for Communications, Information Technology and the Arts to Stuart Lynn, President and CEO of ICANN (4 July 2001) <http://www.iana.org/reports/2001/au-redelegation/alston-to-lynn-04jul01.html>.

62 See IANA, *IANA Report on Request for Redelegation of the .au Top-Level Domain* (31 August 2001) <http://www.iana.org/reports/2001/au-report-31aug01.html>.

63 See ICANN Board of Director's approval of the ccTLD Sponsorship Agreement (10 September 2001) <http://www.icann.org/en/groups/board/documents/prelim-report-10sep01-en.htm>.

64 *ccTLD Sponsorship Agreement (.au)*, Section 3.1. The agreement and its appendices are available on the auDA website: <http://www.icann.org/en/about/agreements/cctlds/au/sponsorship-agmt-25oct01-en.htm>.

65 auDA Dispute Resolution Working Group, *Proposed .au Dispute Resolution Policy (auDRP) and Rules* (2001) 2 <https://www.auda.org.au/have-your-say/policy-panels-and-committees>.

66 The auDRP, including auDRP Rules, is available online at <http://www.auda.org.au/policies/auda-2010-05/>.

67 auDA, *Domain Name Eligibility and Allocation Policy Rules for the Open 2LDs (2012-04)* (Policy No: 2012-04, 1 July 2018) Sch C <https://www.auda.org.au/have-your-say/policy-panels-and-committees>.

68 auDA, n 67, Sch E.

69 auDA, n 67, Sch F.

asn.au[70] and id.au.[71] For example, a .com.au and net.au second level domain name is intended for commercial/business purposes, and registrants must be:

a) an Australian registered company; or
b) trading under a registered business name in any Australian State or Territory; or
c) an Australian partnership or sole trader; or
d) a foreign company licensed to trade in Australia; or
e) an owner of an Australian Registered Trade Mark; or
f) an applicant for an Australian Registered Trade Mark; or
g) an association incorporated in any Australian State or Territory; or
h) an Australian commercial statutory body.[72]

The following section will detail the key provisions in both the international and Australian domain name dispute resolution policies.

The UDRP and auDRP: Relevant provisions

[4.50] Decisions by panellists under both the UDRP and auDRP have been extensively considered elsewhere.[73] The purpose of this section is to merely outline the key provisions under both the international and Australian domain name dispute resolution policies.

Both the UDRP and auDRP domain name dispute resolution policies have been designed to provide an alternative dispute resolution process for relatively straightforward cases – and are explicitly not intended for cases that involve complex disputes where more than one party can demonstrate legitimate rights in the domain name. The underlying purpose of the auDRP, like the UDRP, "is to provide a cheaper, speedier alternative to litigation for the resolution of disputes between the registrant of a .au domain name and a party with competing rights in the domain name".[74] Paragraph 4(k) in both the UDRP and auDRP provide that the mandatory jurisdiction of the policies do not preclude the parties from submitting to a court of competent jurisdiction for independent resolution of the dispute before the UDRP or auDRP proceedings are commenced or after such proceedings are concluded.[75]

---

70 auDA, n 67, Sch B.

71 auDA, n 67, Sch D.

72 auDA, n 67, Schs C and E.

73 See, for example, Lindsay, n 1; Roy, *Australian Domain Name Law*, n 7; Roy and Marsoof, "A Critical and Comparative Review", n 7; Roy and Marsoof, "'Bad Faith' and 'Rights or Legitimate Interests'", n 7.

74 See auDRP, n 4, para 1.2.

75 auDRP, n 4, para 2.3. See auDRP, n 4, Sch A, para 4(k). See n 48 for UDRP, para 4(k).

The procedural rules for both policies (known as the UDRP Rules and the auDRP Rules) prescribe the way in which these proceedings (referred to in the policies as "mandatory administrative proceedings") are required to be administered, including relevant timelines for lodging complaints and filing responses, the relevant fees associated with the proceedings, and so on.

The originating process for initiating a complaint under both the UDRP and the auDRP policies is relatively straightforward. The process is driven by the complainant, and they are required to select an approved or authorised "provider" by submitting the complaint to that provider: see UDRP and auDRP, para 4(d).[76] A number of "providers" or organisations, such as WIPO, have been approved by ICANN and auDA to provide a dispute resolution service under the UDRP[77] and auDRP[78] respectively. Providers are required to apply the domain name dispute resolution policies to the dispute, as well as their own supplemental rules.[79] The two providers approved by auDA are the Resolution Institute (formerly LEADR & IAMA) and WIPO – with WIPO being the only provider approved by both ICANN and auDA. Complainants are required to submit to the jurisdiction of the respective domain name dispute resolution policies, and adjudicating panellists are required to adhere to the policies when deciding a dispute.

A key section of both the UDRP and auDRP is provided in para 4(a), which stipulates the three separate (but related) elements the complainant must establish in order to prove breach. Under the Australian auDRP, the complainant is required to establish that:

1. the domain name is identical or confusingly similar to a name (which refers to the complainant's personal name, company, business or other legal or trading name) trade mark or service mark in which the complainant has rights; *and*
2. the domain name registrant has "no rights or legitimate interests in respect of the domain name"; *and*
3. the "domain name has been registered or subsequently used in bad faith".

---

76 auDRP, n 4, para 3.

77 See ICANN, *List of Approved Dispute Resolution Service Providers* <http://www.icann.org/en/dndr/udrp/approved-providers.htm>.

78 See auDA, *auDRP Providers* <https://www.auda.org.au/policies/audrp/>.

79 The supplemental rules for each provider are available on the respective websites. See n 77 and n 78.

The corresponding para 4(a) of the UDRP is almost identical, except that para 4(a)(i) does not include a complainant's name, and only refers to the complainant's trade mark or service mark. Further, para 4(a)(iii) of the UDRP provides that the domain name holder is required to both register *and* use the domain name in bad faith (as opposed to the requirement under the auDRP which states that the "domain name has been registered *or* subsequently used in bad faith" (emphasis added)).

Paragraph 4(b) of both policies non-exhaustively outline some of the circumstances which would provide evidence of the registration and use of a domain name in bad faith for the purposes of para 4(a)(iii). Under the auDRP, these include the following (without limitation):

1. where the domain name has been registered or acquired primarily for the purpose of selling, renting, or otherwise transferring the registration to another person for valuable consideration in excess of out-of-pocket costs (instead of "another person", the corresponding provision in the UDRP provides "the complainant who is the owner of the trademark or service mark or to a competitor of that complainant"); or
2. the domain name has been registered to prevent the owner of a name, trade mark or service mark from reflecting that name or mark in a corresponding domain (the corresponding provision in the UDRP also requires the respondent to "have engaged in a pattern of such conduct", and for obvious reasons does not include "name"); or
3. the domain name has been registered "primarily for the purpose of disrupting the business or activities of another person" (again, instead of "another person", the corresponding provision in the UDRP refers to "a competitor"); or
4. the domain name has been registered to intentionally attract users to a website or other online location for commercial gain "by creating a likelihood of confusion with the complainant's name or mark as to the source, sponsorship, affiliation, or endorsement of that website or location or of a product or service on that website or location" (the corresponding UDRP provision uses the words "your web site" – the auDRP thus differentiates itself from the UDRP by providing that attracting users to any websites, and not just websites owned by the respondent, will amount to bad faith); or
5. if any representations or warranties with respect to eligibility or third party rights provided on application (or renewal) are (or subsequently become) false or misleading (there is no corresponding para 4(b)(v) in the UDRP).

Under para 3(b)(iv) in both the UDRP Rules and the auDRP Rules, the complainant is required to elect whether to have the dispute decided by a single-member or a three-member panel. There are additional costs if the panel is enlarged to a three-member panel: see UDRP and auDRP, para 4(g). In the event of multiple disputes, either party may petition to consolidate the disputes before a single panel – provided that the disputes being consolidated are governed by the respective policies: as provided in UDRP and auDRP, para 4(f). The Rules for both policies stipulate that the complainant is required to:

- specify the name, trade mark or service mark on which the complaint is based: auDRP Rules, para 3(b)(viii) (the corresponding paragraph in the UDRP Rules does not include "name");
- specify the grounds on which the complaint is made: UDRP and auDRP Rules, para 3(b)(ix);
- specify the remedies sought: UDRP and auDRP Rules, para 3(b)(x); and
- state whether any other legal proceedings have been commenced or terminated relating to the complaint: UDRP and auDRP Rules, para 3(b)(xi).

Within 20 days the respondent is required to respond to the complaint by explaining their rights and legal interest in the domain name, or face a likely default judgment and transfer of the domain name: see UDRP and auDRP Rules, para 5. The respondent must also state in their response whether any other legal proceedings have been commenced or terminated in connection with the complaint: UDRP and auDRP Rules, para 5(b)(vi). Under both policies, the complaints to date have nearly always been dealt with on written submissions, although para 13 of the UDRP Rules and the auDRP Rules provide for in-person hearings where the panel deems it necessary. In the event that legal proceedings are commenced prior to or during a hearing, it remains within the panel's discretionary power to suspend or terminate the hearing, or hand-down a decision: see UDRP Rules and auDRP Rules, para 18(a).

The remedies available under both policies are limited to cancelling the registration of the domain name or transferring the registration to the complainant: see UDRP and auDRP, para 4(i). The panel is required to forward its decision to the provider within 14 days of its appointment: UDRP and auDRP Rules, para 15(b), and the provider is then required to communicate the decision to each party – within three days under the UDRP Rules (see para 16(a)), or five days under the auDRP Rules (see para 16(a)), after receiving the decision from the panel. Importantly, the provider is also required to publish the full text of the decision on a publicly accessible website: UDRP and auDRP Rules, para 16(b). Panel decisions under both the UDRP and auDRP are binding, and there is regrettably no appeals process (this is discussed in further detail below).[80] Any claim for damages is required to be made through separate court proceedings. As noted above, the policies do not preclude the availability of court proceedings either during or after the mandatory administrative proceeding: see UDRP and auDRP, para 4(k). If the domain name is cancelled, it simply becomes available again for registration on a first to file basis. Importantly, domain names are not actually "owned" by registrants – but rather "held" as renewable licences. As the entitlement to hold a domain name is based in contract law (ie, as a licence), it is permissible to transfer the licence for a domain name to other entities.

While there is no formal doctrine of precedent applied in UDRP and auDRP proceedings, all written decisions of panellists are publicly available and frequently referred to – particularly where consensus has emerged about particular issues.[81]

auDA and WIPO have also now produced an overview of panel decisions: the *auDA auDRP Overview 1.0* published in July 2014,[82] and the *WIPO Overview of WIPO Panel Views on Selected UDRP Questions* ("*WIPO Jurisprudential Overview 3.0*") published in 2017, which is now in its third edition.[83] The *auDA auDRP Overview 1.0* is an informal overview of auDRP panel opinions on key procedural and substantive issues that have arisen since the inception of the policy. The *auDA auDRP Overview 1.0* is directly based on the *WIPO Jurisprudential Overview 3.0*. Lindsay states that the *WIPO Overview*:

> takes the form of a concise statement of the views of panellists on a number of significant issues that have arisen in the application of the UDRP, coupled with the citation of a small number of decisions that support the propositions in the overview. The statement of views identifies those issues in relation to which a consensus has emerged among UDRP panellists, as well as qualifications to the consensus views.

---

80 See auDRP, n 4, para 7.1.

81 For a summary of consensus views by auDRP and UDRP panels on key legal and procedural issues, see auDA, *auDA Overview of Panel Views on Selected auDRP Questions First Edition* ("auDA auDRP Overview 1.0") (2014) <https://assets.auda.org.au/a/2020-11/auDRP-Overview-2014b.pdf?VersionId=yjOrxJkeDYxTarz7Uc8EOpML_5KCE9z1>; and WIPO, *WIPO Overview of WIPO Panel Views on Selected UDRP Questions, Third Edition* ("WIPO Jurisprudential Overview 3.0") (2017) <https://www.wipo.int/amc/en/domains/search/overview3.0/>.

82 A Christie, *auDA Overview of Panel Views on Selected auDRP Questions First Edition* ("auDA auDRP Overview 1.0") (auDA, July 2014) <https://assets.auda.org.au/a/2020-11/auDRP-Overview-2014b.pdf?VersionId=yjOrxJkeDYxTarz7Uc8EOpML_5KCE9z1>.

83 See WIPO, *WIPO Overview of WIPO Panel Views on Selected UDRP Questions, Third Edition* ("WIPO Jurisprudential Overview 3.0") (2017) <https://www.wipo.int/amc/en/domains/search/overview3.0/>.

> The statement also identifies those issues where there is no consensus among UDRP panellists and, where appropriate, provides a statement of the views of the majority and minority of panellists on the relevant issue. Finally, the overview identifies issues where neither a consensus nor a majority view has yet to emerge, and which continue to divide UDRP panellists.[84]

The *auDA auDRP Overview 1.0* does precisely the same.

As there is no formal doctrine of precedent under the auDRP and UDRP, the *Overviews* are not binding. Nevertheless, as Lindsay suggests:

> the interests of fairness and consistency mean that, in practice, panellists will not generally depart from a Consensus View, even if they disagree with it. Where there is no Consensus View on an issue but it is possible to identify a majority view, it seems that the majority view will usually be applied, unless the UDRP panel finds an argument not to apply the majority view to be compelling.[85]

Conclusion: Trends and Policy Implications for International and Australian Domain Name Law

[4.60] While both the UDRP and auDRP have arguably been successful on certain fronts, both domain name dispute resolution policies have also widely been criticised.

One of the most significant criticisms of both the UDRP and auDRP relate to the quality of justice administered under both dispute resolution policies. With respect to the UDRP, Froomkin states that "[t]he decisions themselves do bear varying indicia of quality".[86] Roy argues that this is also the case under the auDRP – where there are significant differences in the application of the auDRP and the auDRP Rules in panel decisions.[87] Furthermore, "[w]hile a large number of decisions cited the auDRP and the Rules, and supported their decisions with authority, a considerable number of decisions did not refer to any authority at all".[88] In auDA's internal review of the auDRP in 2012, auDA outlined a number of reforms in its response that it was willing to consider further. One such reform related to quality checks of the dispute resolution providers, and auDA agreed that it would be beneficial to conduct "a formal periodic review of Providers. Not only might this have some practical use for

84 Lindsay, n 1, 128.

85 Lindsay, n 1.

86 See Froomkin, "ICANN's 'Uniform Dispute Resolution Policy' ", n 14, 708.

87 See Roy, "Navigating the Landscape", n 7, 25–28.

88 Roy, "Navigating the Landscape", n 7, 26.

auDA and Providers from a procedural perspective, it would also serve to enhance the integrity and credibility of the auDRP".[89] Roy suggests that while it is not clear in auDA's response whether a periodic review of providers would also include a review of the decisions of individual panellists, a procedural review of panellists to ensure greater consistency in the quality of auDRP decisions is strongly recommended.[90] Given the significant variations in the quality of UDRP and auDRP decisions, the introduction of an appeals process within the UDRP and auDRP system has been frequently recommended by scholars.[91] Some jurisdictions have an appeals process built within the ccTLD domain name dispute resolution policy – like New Zealand.[92] Under the auDRP, auDA has rejected suggestions for an appeals process in its response to its 2012 review on the following grounds:

> an appeals process would add cost, complexity and delay to what was designed to be a relatively inexpensive and expedited dispute resolution process. We note that parties to an auDRP proceeding have recourse to the courts if they do not agree with the Panel's decision. We also note that (in contrast to ICANN's administration of the UDRP) auDA reserves the right to intervene where there has been a clear and substantive procedural flaw in an auDRP proceeding, which provides a limited appeals process of sorts.[93]

Roy has criticised this reasoning by auDA and argues that *not* having an auDRP appeals process raises serious questions in relation to procedural fairness – given the significant variations in the quality of auDRP decisions.[94] Indeed, the preservation of procedural fairness is fundamentally important if the process is to be championed as a genuine alternative dispute resolution system that saves time and money.

Schultz et al suggest that "[t]he main concern about independence in online dispute resolution is the existence of lists".[95] This concerns issues such as who

---

89 See Roy, "Navigating the Landscape", n 7, 55, auDA Issues Paper (2012).

90 Roy, "Navigating the Landscape", n 7, 25.

91 Roy, "Navigating the Landscape", n 7, 28. See also Mueller, n 15.

92 See New Zealand's domain name *Dispute Resolution Service Policy*, which is issued by the Domain Name Commission Limited on behalf of InternetNZ, Internet New Zealand Incorporated: <https://www.dnc.org.nz/resource-library/policies/65>.

93 See auDA's response to the review (published in May 2013), n 89, 2.

94 Roy, "Navigating the Landscape", n 7, 28.

95 See T Schultz et al, *Online Dispute Resolution: The State of the Art and the Issues* (E-Com Research Project of the University of Geneva, Geneva, 2001) [11]–[18]; cited in Spencer and Hardy, n 12, 659.

constitutes the list and is it mandatory, who chooses the actual dispute resolver from the list for a given dispute, how many potential arbitrators are listed, and so on.[96] The issue of lists in UDRP and auDRP proceedings has also received significant comment. For example, with respect to panellists' caseloads under the UDRP, Froomkin states:

> There is no question that a small number of arbitrators have heard a disproportionate number of cases and that others have heard very few. The UDRP should require that arbitration service providers use neutral, documented, and transparent criteria to select the arbitrator for any given case. ... Finally, much greater thought needs to be given to how arbitrators are selected in the first place – and what it takes to get an arbitrator removed from a provider's list. No amount of random selection will suffice if a provider's entire list is drawn from a like-minded community of trademark lawyers with large institutional clients.[97]

Similarly, with respect to the auDRP lists, Roy argues:

> a small number of panelists decide a disproportionate number of proceedings. Indeed, the same names appear time and again in auDRP decisions. It was also noted that very few female panelists are used. There should certainly be greater transparency with respect to how individual panelists are chosen by providers, and what criteria is applied to select panelists for particular proceedings. Greater openness in the panelist selection process will perhaps answer these questions and shed some light on what appears to be a rather small (male) club of auDRP decision-makers.[98]

Despite the numerous criticisms of the UDRP and auDRP, both policies have proven to be quick and relatively inexpensive methods for resolving domain name disputes. With the exponential increase in the use of the internet across the globe there is little doubt that these policies will be used more frequently as the years progress, and successful processes such as the UDRP and auDRP should be willing to actively engage with relevant stakeholders and be open to criticism and reform as necessary. If this occurs effectively, not only will the UDRP and auDRP continue to provide an effective form of dispute resolution, but it is also likely that this specific dispute resolution model will be replicated in other areas of disputes (particularly online disputes) where litigation has failed to serve stakeholder needs.

96 Schultz et al, n 95.

97 See Froomkin, "ICANN's 'Uniform Dispute Resolution Policy'", n 14, 710–711.

98 Roy, "Navigating the Landscape", n 7, 26.

Chapter 5

Cyber-Dependent and Cyber-Enabled Crime: Legal Responses and Challenges

Monique Cormier and Simon McKenzie*

Introduction

[5.10] The term "cybercrime" is any crime committed using computers or online networks.[1] It is more constructive, however, to consider cybercrime in two categories: cyber-dependent crime and cyber-enabled offences. Cyber-dependent crimes (sometimes called "pure" cybercrime) are those offences that can only be committed using communication and information technologies. They are crimes that are directed against computers and networks and include such illicit activities as hacking, spreading malware or ransomware and causing distributed denial of service attacks.[2] Cyber-enabled offences are continuations or varieties of existing types of offences, committed using digital technologies, such as online fraud, cyberstalking or harassment. The risk of not recognising the difference between pure cybercrime and cyber-enabled crime is that there is the potential to miss how cyber-enabled crime fits into existing patterns of offending. We should avoid fetishising the technology and instead focus on the most prevalent forms of cybercrime, and the perpetrators responsible for it. It is important to recognise when the internet is a "new medium for

---

* Monique Cormier is a Senior Lecturer in the School of Law at the University of New England, Armidale, New South Wales; and Simon McKenzie is a Research Fellow in the School of Law at the University of Queensland, Brisbane, Queensland. The authors would like to thank Robert Brown and Isabelle Peart for their excellent research assistance during the preparation of this chapter.

1 Australian Cyber Security Centre, "ReportCyber" <https://www.cyber.gov.au/acsc/report>.

2 C Teunissen, I Voce and R Smith, "Estimating the Cost of Pure Cybercrime to Australian Individuals" (Statistical Bulletin No 34, Australian Institute of Criminology, 2021).

'old' practices; and where in other cases it facilitates actions that would not be perpetrated 'offline'".[3]

First, a note of caution: any categorisation and assessment of the legal responses to cybercrime should account for the reality of how cyberspace forms part of everyday life.[4] Most people in the developed world have ongoing internet access through their phones, their computers, as well as through their televisions, tablets, even sometimes fridges and vehicles. In addition to revolutionising work, business and commerce, people carry out their most intimate and important personal tasks through the internet. Relationships are formed, sustained and ended via digital means; if a person is sick, a common first step is to search the internet for explanations or book a doctor's appointment online; banking and shopping online is now routine. Our online and offline lives are thoroughly and – at least for some of us – irretrievably intertwined. We are not disembodied in digital spaces "because digital life is in fact lived through our bodies in the way we use and engage with technology".[5]

This means that while it is useful to differentiate between cyber-dependent and cyber-enabled crimes, it is also important to recognise that the boundaries between online and offline spaces is blurred. We should be attentive to the fact that thinking of cyberspace as a separate, alternative, disembodied space does not accurately reflect digital technologies which are "very real, very material, and very grounded geographies".[6]

With such caveats in mind, this chapter explores legal responses to cybercrime using two distinctly different types of cyber offending to demonstrate the diversity under the umbrella concept of cybercrime. It focuses on the cyber-dependent crime of deploying ransomware and the suite of cyber-enabled crimes that facilitate family violence and digital coercive control. Ransomware and family violence are in many ways opposite ends of the spectrum of cyber offending, but they provide diverse examples to demonstrate how digital technologies are facilitating, transforming and escalating the commission of criminal offences. They also provide examples of the various challenges that cybercrime presents for law and law enforcement, and demonstrate why a one-size-fits-all response to different types of cyber offending is problematic.

3 B A Harris and D Woodlock, "Digital Coercive Control: Insights from Two Landmark Domestic Violence Studies" (2019) 59(3) *British Journal of Criminology* 530, 532.

4 A Powell and N Henry, *Sexual Violence in a Digital Age* (Palgrave Macmillan UK, 2017) 52.

5 Powell and Henry, n 4, 60.

6 M Graham, "Geography/Internet: Ethereal Alternate Dimensions of Cyberspace or Grounded Augmented Realities?" (2013) 179(2) *Geographical Journal* 177, 181.

This chapter begins with an overview of how cyber-dependent crime is conceptualised, in broad terms, before turning to the specific example of ransomware attacks. Ransomware has wide-ranging scope and the potential for devastating real-world impact. It is categorised as a cyber-dependent crime because it is, at its core, an attack on a computer system or network, but it can have significant consequences for individuals, business and industry, public infrastructure and national security. In this first part, the chapter provides a snapshot of both the international and Australian legal frameworks that deal with cyber-dependent crime and examines how and why the problem of ransomware has proven to be almost immune to legal responses.

The chapter then turns to the example of cyber-enabled crime, exploring how the internet has provided a new means for committing old crimes of family violence. Focusing on the example of family violence, it demonstrates how perpetrators use digital technologies in a variety of ways – some crude, some creative – to perpetuate ongoing abuse and control against their family members. This second part reviews Australian legal responses to cyber-enabled family violence (including conduct such as image-based sexual abuse and online harassment) and emphasises the importance of recognising the real harm caused by such conduct.

This chapter concludes by identifying common shortcomings of the legal responses to both cyber-dependent and cyber-enabled crime. It also considers some of the current policy responses to cybercrime and suggests that a more holistic approach is needed.

Cyber-Dependent Crimes

[5.20] "Computer crimes", "pure cybercrimes" or "cyber-dependent crimes" are various labels for the type of cybercrime that targets computers or networks. It includes computer access crimes and computer disruption crimes.[7] Access crimes include those in which a perpetrator unlawfully accesses (hacks) a computer or network for the purposes of removing, acquiring or otherwise using information or data that they have no right to access. Disruption crimes are those which prevent the computer or network from functioning properly. Common disruption crimes include distributed denial of service attacks, circulation of computer viruses and deployment of ransomware. This section explores international and domestic legal responses to cyber-dependent crime, using ransomware as the primary example. It demonstrates how the ever-increasing volume of cyber-dependant crime and the transborder nature of

---

7 Teunissen, Voce and Smith, n 2, 2–3.

such activities provide particular challenges for criminal prosecution of this type of cybercrime.

What is ransomware?

[5.30] Ransomware is a type of malware that works by encrypting files on a user's machine as well as files on any connected devices. It displays an image on the screen with instructions for the user to pay a ransom to have their files decrypted. If the user does not pay by a certain time, their files are usually destroyed or their systems remain otherwise inaccessible.[8] Thanks to the proliferation of what is called "ransomware-as-a-service", someone wanting to perpetrate a ransomware attack does not have to possess any particular technical skills. Ransomware specialists offer their code and expertise to novice hackers for either a nominal fee or a cut of the ransom, meaning that ransomware-as-a-service is quite readily available and easily accessible.[9]

Ransomware is deployed by a range of actors: individuals, organised criminal groups, loosely affiliated criminal networks and states.[10] There is also a long and growing list of victims of ransomware attacks, including individuals, small businesses, large corporations, hospitals, banks, utilities, schools and government departments. Ransomware is now a multi-billion-dollar industry, with estimates that by 2020 it had cost the global economy more than US$1 trillion.[11] The use of ransomware has grown to become one of the top global cybercrime concerns, fuelled no doubt by its ease of use and its success rate.

There are reportedly well over a thousand different variants of ransomware, most are deployed indiscriminately and some can spread rapidly by self-replicating. Others are highly targeted; flooding the internal systems inside a particular organisation and effectively grinding all operations to a halt until a bulk ransom is paid to decrypt all the systems of that organisation. Other strains of ransomware are clearly deployed for non-financial purposes, and maliciously delete data or release it even after the ransom is paid.[12]

8 M Harkins and A M Freed, "The Ransomware Assault on the Healthcare Sector" (2018) 6(2) *Journal of Law & Cyber Warfare* 148, 151.

9 Harkins and Freed, n 8, 152.

10 This chapter mostly focuses on the legal issues relating to cybercrimes committed by individuals or criminal groups. For legal analysis of cyberattacks attributable to states, see, for example, N Tsagourias, "Cyber Attacks, Self-Defence and the Problem of Attribution" (2012) 17 *Journal of Conflict and Security Law* 229.

11 "New McAfee Report Estimates Global Cybercrime Losses to Exceed $1 Trillion", *McAfee* (7 December 2020) <http://www.mcafee.com/en-au/consumer-corporate/newsroom/press-releases/press-release.html?news_id=6859bd8c-9304-4147-bdab-32b35457e629>.

12 Australian Cyber Security Centre, *Ransomware in Australia* (Report, 2 October 2020) 6.

While relatively small-scale ransomware incidents continue to plague individuals and small businesses or organisations, cybersecurity experts are concerned that ransomware is increasingly being used to "hunt big game entities" which are those targets perceived as "high profile, high value, and/or those that provide critical services".[13] In May 2021, for example, there was a significant ransomware attack on critical infrastructure in the United States, when cybercriminals targeted Colonial Pipeline, operator of the US's largest fuel pipeline system. Colonial Pipeline was forced to shut down the fuel delivery system which caused petrol shortages to the east coast for several days. It led to panic buying and gasoline price surges and had flow on effects for the transport and aviation industries. The company reportedly paid US$4.4 million dollars in ransom to resume normal operations,[14] and it has since been labelled "the largest attack on the US energy system in history".[15]

The ability of ransomware to disrupt critical infrastructure and essential services makes it significantly more dangerous than "ordinary" crimes relating to blackmail or extortion. The added component of cyber enables criminals to increase the stakes of the threat, which in turn increases the odds that the ransom will be paid. The fact that so many public and private services rely on networked systems to function mean that they are vulnerable to hacking and malware, and a prime target for ransomware. The nature of cybercrime also allows for criminal activity to be coordinated across national borders and have increasingly wide-reaching and transnational effects.

One of the most infamous global ransomware incidents to date was the 2017 Wannacry ransomware attack. Wannacry was a self-replicating ransomware cryptoworm that spread rapidly and indiscriminately, eventually infecting at least 200,000 computers in over 150 countries.[16] Of particular concern was the fact that Wannacry infected parts of the National Health Service (NHS) network in the United Kingdom, locking patient databases and shutting down medical equipment. The NHS estimated nearly 20,000 patient appointments

---

13 Australian Cyber Security Centre, *ACSC Annual Cyber Threat Report 2020–21* (Report, 15 September 2021) 31 (*ACSC Annual Cyber Threat Report 2020–21*); K Keneally and T Watts, *Beyond the Blame Game* (Policy Paper, February 2021) <http://www.timwatts.net.au/media/187357/beyond-the-blame-game-ransomware-discussion-paper.pdf>.

14 *ACSC Annual Cyber Threat Report 2020–21*, n 13, 33.

15 J Bardoff, "The Colonial Pipeline Crisis Is a Taste of Things to Come", *Foreign Policy* (17 May 2021) <http://www.foreignpolicy.com/2021/05/17/colonial-pipeline-crisis-cyberattack-ransomware-cybersecurity-energy-electicity-power-grid-russia-hackers/>.

16 L J Trautman and P C Ormerod, "Wannacry, Ransomware, and the Emerging Threat to Corporations" (2019) 86(2) *Tennessee Law Review* 503, 505.

including surgeries were cancelled, ambulances had to be diverted and 1,200 pieces of diagnostic equipment were infected.[17] There were no reported cases of physical harm to patients caused by this disruption, but one can imagine how this could quite easily have contributed to patients' deaths or exacerbation of medical conditions. While the NHS might have been the most high profile victim of Wannacry, there were many, many others including companies in Japan, universities in Canada, ministries in Russia, police departments in India and individuals all over the world.[18] In 2021, it is still considered "the most notorious ransomware attack of all time".[19]

In Australia, ransomware is a growing cybersecurity concern, with the Australian Cyber Security Centre labelling ransomware as "one of the most significant threats" facing the Australian cybersecurity landscape.[20] Millions of dollars are reportedly being paid in ransom by Australian organisations,[21] and cybercriminals are now ramping up their hunt of big game in Australia. In March 2021, for example, Eastern Health, one of Melbourne's public health services which runs several hospitals, was the victim of a ransomware attack which caused the postponement of elective surgeries and prevented staff from accessing patient medical histories for weeks.[22] While ransomware incidents remain a relatively small proportion of cybercrime in Australia, ransomware is considered the most serious type of cybercrime "due to its high financial impact and disruptive impacts to victims and the wider community".[23]

The escalating threat presented by cyber-dependent crime more broadly, and ransomware specifically, has arguably reached a tipping point. Ciaran Martin,

---

17 O Hughes, "WannaCry Impact on NHS Considerably Larger than Previously Suggested", *Digital Health* (27 October 2017) <https://www.digitalhealth.net/2017/10/wannacry-impact-on-nhs-considerably-larger-than-previously-suggested/>.

18 Trautman and Ormerod, n 16.

19 P Haskell-Dowland and A Woodward, "Is Australia a Sitting Duck for Ransomware Attacks? Yes, and the Danger Has Been Growing for 30 Years", *The Conversation* (13 July 2021) <http://www.theconversation.com/is-australia-a-sitting-duck-for-ransomware-attacks-yes-and-the-danger-has-been-growing-for-30-years-161818>.

20 *ACSC Annual Cyber Threat Report 2020–21*, n 13, 9.

21 J Purtill, "Australian Organisations Are Quietly Paying Hackers Millions in a 'Tsunami of Cyber Crime'", *ABC News* (16 July 2021) <http://www.abc.net.au/news/science/2021-07-16/australian-organisations-paying-millions-ransomware-hackers/100291542>.

22 M Cunningham, "Staff Unable to Access Patient Files after Eastern Health Cyber Attack", *The Age* (29 March 2021) <http://www.theage.com.au/national/victoria/staff-unable-to-access-patient-files-after-eastern-health-cyber-attack-20210329-p57eyj.html>.

23 *ACSC Annual Cyber Threat Report 2020–21*, n 13, 16.

the former director of the UK's National Cyber Security Centre articulated the urgency of this matter:

> It's time to do something because we're getting cleaned out left, right and centre. Services are being disrupted and millions of pounds are being lost ... We need to do something to catapult ransomware up the priority ladder for cybersecurity agencies, governments and industry people who care about cybersecurity.[24]

With such high global stakes, there is a concerted push for both a coordinated international and targeted domestic response. The next section evaluates both the international and Australian legal responses to cyber-dependent crime.

Legal responses to cyber-dependent crime

[5.40] At present, the most pressing challenges created by ransomware are seen to be technological: how to protect against such attacks, how to minimise damage when they occur, how to identify who is behind them. But legal responses are also needed and given the unprecedented transborder effects of ransomware, it needs to involve both international and domestic actors. This section first provides an overview of the current international legal framework for addressing cybercrime, before demonstrating that Australia's criminal laws are *prima facie* sufficient to deal with cyber-dependent offences such as ransomware attacks.

The international legal response to cyber-dependent crime

[5.50] It goes without saying that the internet and digital technologies have created an unprecedented level of transnational connectivity. This shrinking of geographical distance and the borderless nature of cyberspace has fostered innovation in commerce, science and education. It has also become a playground for enterprising criminals, with the territorial reach of criminal activity only being limited by the extent of internet connectivity, necessitating an international approach to combat cybercrime. While there is no global cybercrime treaty at present, there are several regional cybercrime instruments, the most comprehensive of which is the Council of Europe Convention on Cybercrime, also known as the *Budapest Convention*.[25]

Although regional in origin, the *Budapest Convention* is open to all states and is the closest thing the world has to a comprehensive international

---

24 M Gooding, "Pay Ransom, Face Sanctions? US Treasury Warning Divides Industry", *Tech Monitor* (15 October 2020) <https://www.techmonitor.ai/cybersecurity/ransomware-sanctions-treasury>.

25 *Convention on Cybercrime*, opened for signature 23 November 2001, 2296 UNTS 167 (entered into force 1 July 2004).

cybercrime treaty. In recognising "the profound changes brought about by the digitalisation, convergence and continuing globalisation of computer networks", the aim of the *Convention* is to pursue "a common criminal policy aimed at the protection of society against cybercrime".[26] To that end it requires parties to criminalise certain cybercrime activities, and it sets out a relatively comprehensive framework on cyber investigations, international cooperation and jurisdiction – including an obligation on parties to extradite or punish alleged offenders found on their territory.

The *Budapest Convention* has several shortcomings, however, including the fact that, at the time of writing, it only has 66 states parties and only 21 of those are from outside Europe. Australia ratified the *Budapest Convention* in 2015, but is one of only four countries in the Asia-Pacific region to have done so.[27] The *Convention* does not provide a model law, and gives states significant leeway in how they implement the legal framework. The *Convention* also gives states the right to require that the proscribed conduct must result in serious harm and leaves it to states to determine what constitutes "serious harm".[28] The *Convention* recommends that states criminalise the following:

- illegal access to any part of a computer system;
- illegal interception of private transmission of computer data;
- interference with computer data or a computer system;
- misuse of devices;
- computer-related forgery and fraud;
- use of a computer system in relation to child pornography; and
- copyright infringement.[29]

None of these provisions explicitly mention ransomware or cyber extortion of any kind. It is conceivable that an offence of illegal access to a computer system and a prohibition on data interference (which includes the suppression of computer data) would be applicable. But it does not address the "ransom" aspect of ransomware attacks, nor does it acknowledge the potentially debilitating indirect effects that suppressing data can have. The fact that the *Convention*'s

26 *Convention on Cybercrime*, opened for signature 23 November 2001, 2296 UNTS 167 (entered into force 1 July 2004), Preamble.

27 The only other parties in the Asia-Pacific region are Japan, Tonga and the Philippines.

28 *Convention on Cybercrime*, opened for signature 23 November 2001, 2296 UNTS 167 (entered into force 1 July 2004), Art 4(2).

29 *Convention on Cybercrime*, opened for signature 23 November 2001, 2296 UNTS 167 (entered into force 1 July 2004), Arts 2–10.

substantive law is underinclusive and not sufficiently particularised, and the fact that it only has 66 states parties has led some commentators to argue for an entirely new cybercrime convention developed by international consensus.[30] But developing new multilateral treaties can take decades, which is time the world does not have when facing rapid, widespread and increasingly destructive cybercriminal activity. The *Budapest Convention* provides a good starting point for developing a more comprehensive transnational cybercrime framework. What it does need, however, is a model law, and there may already be a solution to this issue.

The International Telecommunication Union's (ITU) Toolkit for Cybercrime Legislation is essentially a ready blueprint for such a model law. Developed in consultation with technical experts, various industry and government representatives, and the American Bar Association, the toolkit was produced with the aim of helping "to advance a harmonized global legal framework, facilitate international cooperation, resolve jurisdictional and evidentiary issues and deter cyber-criminal behaviour".[31] It provides what it calls "sample language" for a raft of cyber offences including multiple provisions that would apply to ransomware. To give a few examples, there are provisions that make it an offence to use computers to extort money;[32] that make it a crime to interfere with or impair medical care,[33] another one that deals with unauthorised access to critical infrastructure.[34] Most specify the mental element of intention, but for some it is sufficient that the perpetrator has "knowledge that such conduct could cause" the particular harm, which is akin to the mental element of recklessness.[35] This would cover ransomware

30 See, for example, J Hakmeh, "Building a Stronger International Legal Framework on Cybercrime", *Chatham House* (6 July 2017) <https://www.chathamhouse.org/2017/06/building-stronger-international-legal-framework-cybercrime>. In December 2019, the UN General Assembly adopted a resolution in which it decided "to establish an open-ended ad hoc intergovernmental committee of experts, representative of all regions, to elaborate a comprehensive international convention on countering the use of information and communications technologies for criminal purposes". This represents a first step towards a possible global cybercrime treaty: *Countering the Use of Information and Communications Technologies for Criminal Purposes*, GA Res 74/247, UN GAOR, UN Doc A/RES/74/247 (20 January 2020, adopted 27 December 2019).

31 International Telecommunications Union, "Toolkit for Cybercrime Legislation" (Report, February 2010) 8 <https://www.combattingcybercrime.org/files/virtual-library/assessment-tool/itu-toolkit-for-cybercrime-legislation-%28draft%29.pdf>.

32 International Telecommunications Union, n 31, s 9.

33 International Telecommunications Union, n 31, s 6(f).

34 International Telecommunications Union, n 31, ss 2(c), 3(d).

35 For example, s 4(c), (d) and (e).

deployed indiscriminately; hackers could not claim that they did not intend for their ransomware to hit any particular target. It would also cover situations like the Colonial Pipeline attack in which the group responsible claimed that it did not mean to "[create] problems for society" its only goal was "to make money".[36] There are also provisions in the ITU Toolkit that make it an offence to "produce, sell or procure" a computer program intended primarily for committing various cyber offences,[37] which would apply to those providing ransomware-as-a-service. In addition, there is a comprehensive range of procedural provisions that deal with issues of jurisdiction, expedited mutual assistance and due process.

Without a model law, the *Budapest Convention's laissez-faire* approach to defining cybercriminal acts reflects the variable state of domestic laws. A 2013 survey of cybercrime legislation conducted by the UN Office on Drugs and Crime found that laws relating to illegal access to computer systems differed widely with respect to both the physical and fault elements of the offences. Some specify that illegal access must be for a particular objective – for example, to damage, delete, alter, suppress or transfer data. Some laws criminalise mere access to a computer system, others require criminal intent to cause a particular harm.[38]

As the next section demonstrates, however, a comprehensive domestic legal framework on cyber-dependent crime is never going to be sufficient in and of itself to ensure that such offending is prosecuted. The complexity of criminal investigation and difficulty of transnational enforcement require a multifaceted response to the challenge of cyber-dependent crime.

The Australian legal response to cyber-dependent crime

[5.60] Criminal law in Australia is largely a matter for the states and territories, but there is also a separate Australia-wide Commonwealth criminal jurisdiction. This means that there are nine different criminal law regimes in Australia, any of which may be applicable to cybercrime with or without some kind of jurisdictional connection to the offence.[39] This section provides a brief overview of the types of criminal offences codified in various Australian

---

36 M A Russon, "US Fuel Pipeline Hackers 'Didn't Mean to Create Problems'", *BBC News* (10 May 2021) <http://www.bbc.com/news/business-57050690>.

37 International Telecommunications Union, n 31, s 6(b).

38 United Nations Office on Drugs and Crime, "Comprehensive Study on Cybercrime" (Draft Report, February 2013) Ch 4.

39 The relevant legislation will usually specify jurisdiction. In the *Criminal Code Act 1983* (NT), for example, computer offences in Pt VII Div 10 require there to be a territorial nexus to the Northern Territory (s 276F). See Chapter 3 on "Jurisdiction".

jurisdictions that may be appropriate for prosecuting cyber-dependent crimes, including ransomware. It then turns to discuss the considerable challenges for enforcing such laws.

As Australia is a party to the *Budapest Convention*, its suite of dedicated Commonwealth cyber offences complies with the broad requirements of that treaty. Part 10.7 of the *Commonwealth Criminal Code* criminalises certain "computer offences" including:

- unauthorised access to, or modification of, data held in a computer;[40]
- unauthorised impairment of electronic communication;[41] and
- possession or control of data, or producing, supplying, or obtaining data, with intent to commit a computer offence.[42]

Under such offences the computer itself, and/or the data it contains, is the target of the criminal activity. These laws are designed for archetypal cyber-dependent activity such as hacking and data breaches and would be appropriate for prosecuting use of ransomware. Under s 477.1, for instance, it is an offence to cause unauthorised access to data held in a computer with intent to commit a serious Commonwealth, State or Territory offence. A serious offence is one punishable by imprisonment for five or more years.[43] This provision, used in conjunction with a state or territory offence of extortion or blackmail, would allow for the prosecution of someone using ransomware by Commonwealth prosecuting authorities. For example, s 249K of the *Crimes Act 1900* (NSW) criminalises blackmail, requiring an accused person to have made "any unwarranted demand with menaces"[44] and with the intention of "obtaining a gain or of causing a loss".[45] Section 415 of the *Criminal Code Act 1899* (Qld) provides that a person commits the crime of extortion if he or she makes a demand without reasonable cause, with the intent "to gain a benefit for any person" or "cause a detriment to any person" with a threat to cause a detriment.[46] The use of ransomware to extort payment in exchange for release

40 *Criminal Code Act 1995* (Cth), Sch 1 ss 477.1–477.2.

41 *Criminal Code Act 1995* (Cth), Sch 1 s 477.3.

42 *Criminal Code Act 1995* (Cth), Sch 1 ss 478.3–478.4.

43 *Criminal Code Act 1995* (Cth), Sch 1 s 477.1(9).

44 "Menaces" is defined as "an express or implied threat of any action detrimental or unpleasant to another person": *Crimes Act 1900* (NSW), s 249M.

45 Maximum penalty is 10 years: *Crimes Act 1900* (NSW), s 249K.

46 Maximum penalty is 14 years: *Criminal Code Act 1899* (Qld), s 415; the *Criminal Code Act 1899* (Qld) also provides that the maximum penalty may be increased to life imprisonment if the extortion threat is likely to cause serious personal injury to someone, or likely to cause

of data or to regain control of a computer system, would invariably satisfy the elements of such serious offences.

Each Australian state and territory also has its own suite of codified computer offences that largely mirror those in the *Commonwealth Criminal Code*. This means that there are also laws at the state and territory level which criminalise such cyber-dependent activities as unauthorised access to, modification of, or impairment to computer function or data.[47] In some jurisdictions, such activities are penalised if they are committed with the intent to commit a serious (non-cyber) offence.

There are also state or territory-specific computer offences without direct equivalents in the other Australian jurisdictions. For instance, the *Queensland Criminal Code* provides a variable penalty regime for "computer hacking and misuse" depending on the value of damage caused or benefit gained. A person who accesses a computer or network without consent, and who "causes or intends to cause detriment or damage, or gains or intends to gain a benefit" is liable to imprisonment for five years. The penalty increases to 10 years imprisonment if the unauthorised access or use of the computer system causes damage or provides a benefit to the accused to the value of more than $5,000.[48] Such a provision would be directly applicable to use of ransomware. The *Criminal Law Consolidation Act 1935* (SA) criminalises the possession, production, supply or obtaining of computer viruses where there is intent "of committing or facilitating the commission (either by that person or someone else) of, a serious computer offence".[49] This provision would apply to persons creating and selling ransomware-as-service as well as anyone purchasing or possessing the ransomware virus with the intent to use it.

The above snapshot of the Australian legal framework demonstrates that it contains a range of offences designed broadly for cyber-dependent crime, some of which may be used in conjunction with "serious offences" of the non-cyber-variety, such as blackmail or extortion. A person accused of committing a cyber-dependent crime would likely face multiple different charges under the relevant Australian legal regime given the complexity of cyber offending. Under the *Crimes Act 1900* (NSW), for instance, someone accused of deploying ransomware could conceivably face, *inter alia*, the following charges:

"substantial economic loss in an industrial or commercial activity". It is conceivable that such high sentences could be imposed in relation to a conviction for using ransomware.

47 See, for example, *Crimes Act 1900* (NSW), s 308C; *Criminal Code Act 1983* (NT), ss 276B–276C; *Criminal Law Consolidation Act 1935* (SA), s 86E; *Crimes Act 1958* (Vic), s 247B.

48 *Criminal Code Act 1899* (Qld), s 408E(2)–(3).

49 *Criminal Law Consolidation Act 1935* (SA), s 86I.

- unauthorised access, modification or impairment with intent to commit a serious indictable offence;[50]
- unauthorised modification of data with intent to cause impairment;[51]
- unauthorised impairment of electronic communication;[52]
- possession of data[53] with intent to commit a serious computer offence;[54]
- producing, supplying or obtaining data with intent to commit a serious computer offence;[55] and
- blackmail.[56]

The Australian legal framework applicable to cyber-dependent crimes therefore appears to be relatively comprehensive and fit-for-purpose. Why, then, is cyber-dependent crime so notoriously difficult to prosecute? The next section addresses some of the challenges to criminal prosecution of cyber-dependent crime in Australia and elsewhere.

Challenges to prosecuting cyber-dependent crime

[5.70] A recent assessment by the Australian Labor Party concluded that "[r]ansomware is largely a crime of impunity in Australia today".[57] Despite the existence of appropriate criminal offences to cover a range of cyber-dependent criminal activities, cybercriminals are able to target Australian individuals, businesses and other entities with few consequences.

One of the concerns in relation to cyber-dependent crime, and the rise of ransomware, is that it is now so widespread as to present an almost insurmountable challenge for traditional law enforcement. Individuals and entities targeted by ransomware are frequently now paying the ransom as the most expedient and cost-effective way to regain access to their data or systems.[58] This is not helped by the burgeoning cyber insurance market

---

50 *Crimes Act 1900* (NSW), s 308C.

51 *Crimes Act 1900* (NSW), s 308D.

52 *Crimes Act 1900* (NSW), s 308E.

53 "Data" is defined in s 308 as "information in any form" or "any program (or part of a program)" which would likely include a ransomware program: *Crimes Act 1900* (NSW), s 308.

54 *Crimes Act 1900* (NSW), s 308F.

55 *Crimes Act 1900* (NSW), s 308G.

56 *Crimes Act 1900* (NSW), s 249K.

57 Keneally and Watts, n 13, 8.

58 Purtill, n 21.

which encourages businesses targeted by ransomware to pay the ransom.[59] Cyber security experts and policy makers warn against paying any ransom to cybercriminals on the grounds that there are no guarantees that those behind the threat will not destroy data or permanently impair systems once paid.[60] Furthermore, payment of ransoms has only emboldened cybercriminals to increase the frequency of attacks, raise the amount of ransom and pursue big game targets.[61] The success of ransomware attacks has also contributed to the proliferation of ransomware as a "weapon of choice" for other cybercriminals.

In addition to the considerable volume of cybercrime, there is the added law enforcement challenge of being able to identify perpetrators who go to great lengths to hide their identities and cover their tracks online. It takes specialist technical skills and computer forensics resources to determine who is behind cybercriminal activity. Such resources are usually well beyond the budget and capabilities of local police and prosecuting authorities.[62] Furthermore, it can be hard to convince local law enforcement that it is an important enough issue to investigate and prosecute, and those tasked with carrying out investigations and prosecutions are often ill-equipped to handle the technical complexity.[63]

Even when a cybercriminal can be identified and located, the principal challenge to law enforcement of cyber-dependent crime is jurisdiction. Enforcement of criminal law, including prosecution and punishment, is the territorial prerogative of sovereign states.[64] Where the perpetrators of cybercrime are located overseas, it is almost impossible to investigate and prosecute such crimes without international coordination and cooperation. The prospects for law enforcement in relation to cyber-dependent crimes is

59 J Lemnitzer, "Ransomware Gangs Are Running Riot – Paying Them Off Doesn't Help", *The Conversation* (17 February 2021) <http://www.theconversation.com/ransomware-gangs-are- running-riot-paying-them-off-doesnt-help-155254>.

60 Australian Cyber Security Centre, n 12.

61 Keneally and Watts, n 13, 14–15.

62 A Peters and A Jordan, "Countering the Cyber Enforcement Gap: Strengthening Global Capacity on Cybercrime" (2019–2020) 10(3) *Journal of National Security Law and Policy* 487, 514.

63 Peters and Jordan, n 62; A Leppänen and T Kankaanranta, "Cybercrime Investigation in Finland" (2017) 18(2) *Journal of Scandinavian Studies in Criminology and Crime Prevention* 157, 170–172; Commonwealth of Australia, Comment to Intergovernmental Expert Group on Cybercrime, *Seventh Session of the Open-Ended Intergovernmental Expert Group to Conduct a Comprehensive Study of the Problem of Cybercrime* (22 March 2021) <https://www.unodc.org/documents/organized-crime/cybercrime/Cybercrime-April-2021/Comments/7th_IEG_Cyber_-_MS_comments.pdf>.

64 See Chapter 3 on "Jurisdiction".

therefore going to be contingent on increased international cooperation among domestic investigating and prosecuting agencies alongside the establishment of well-resourced multinational cybercrime task forces.[65]

An example of such a task force is the European Union's Joint Cybercrime Action Taskforce (J-CAT) which was established in 2014. J-CAT's purpose is "to drive intelligence-led, coordinated action against key cybercrime threats and targets by facilitating the joint identification, prioritisation, preparation, initiation and execution of cross-border investigations and operations by its partners".[66] One of J-CAT's recent successes against ransomware was a coordinated campaign to take down a virtual private network (VPN) service, thereby disrupting "a safe haven" used by ransomware groups to hide their identities and locations.[67]

Yet actual criminal prosecutions for cybercrime remain rare, even where there is well-resourced cross-border cooperation and no jurisdictional issues. Gathering admissible digital evidence that sufficiently links an identified perpetrator to the criminal act is a complex task and does not guarantee a successful prosecution.[68] Another contributing factor to impunity for cyber-dependent criminals is underreporting by individuals and businesses. Reasons for not reporting cybercrime can include embarrassment of becoming a victim; uncertainty about how and where to report cyber incidents, a belief that police cannot do anything; and businesses making the decision to simply deal with the fallout of a cyberattack internally to minimise loss of time and money.[69] At present, however, the main impediments to successful legal responses to cyber-dependent crime are jurisdictional hurdles and the sheer volume of incidents that make it impossible for police to mount time-consuming and resource-intensive cross-border investigations.

---

65 F Hanson, "Time to Admit We're Failing on Cybercrime", *ASPI Strategist* (16 February 2018) <https://www.aspistrategist.org.au/time-admit-failing-cybercrime>; see also Commonwealth of Australia, n 63.

66 Europol, "Joint Cybercrime Action Taskforce" <https://www.europol.europa.eu/activities-services/services-support/joint-cybercrime-action-taskforce>.

67 Europol, "Coordinated Action Cuts Off Access to VPN Service Used by Ransomware Groups" (Press Release, 30 June 2021) <https://www.europol.europa.eu/newsroom/news/coordinated- action-cuts-access-to-vpn-service-used-ransomware-groups>.

68 Peters and Jordan, n 62, 515.

69 Federal Bureau of Investigation, "Ransomware Victims Urged to Report Infections to Federal Law Enforcement" (Public Service Announcement, I-091516-PSA, 15 September 2016) <https://www.ic3.gov/Media/Y2016/PSA160915>.

The rest of this chapter turns to consider how law deals with cyber-*enabled* offending, before offering some concluding remarks in [5.160] on current and future policy responses to cybercrime.

Cyber-enabled Crimes

[5.80] It should come as no surprise that the internet is used as a tool by offenders who are not typically considered "cybercriminals" in the same way as those perpetrating cyber-dependent crimes. In such cases, the crimes are *enabled* by digital technologies, but are not unique to them. Crimes related to interpersonal violence – including sexual harassment and family violence – are useful examples of this sort of dynamic: perpetrators can use phones, home computers and even smart devices as part of their violence. In trying to understand these kinds of cybercrime, we should recognise the "increasingly embedded and intertwined nature of the physical, digital, and biological", particularly when it involves family violence.[70] In these cases, it is important to treat the use of technology and the internet as fitting within the broader pattern of violence or abuse.

There is no question that the use of the internet to perpetuate interpersonal violence poses some unique challenges: Todhunter notes that online violence deviates from prototypical forms of violence as it is not necessarily a "discrete act of violence against an identifiable target".[71] It can occur across jurisdictions, impact a wide range of victims, involve a range of complex harms and be carried out by people "who would not otherwise be disposed to violence, and who may not even consider their conduct as violence".[72] Despite these differences between online and offline violence, we should treat the conduct as part of a broader pattern of interpersonal and family violence.[73]

There is often resistance to new laws prohibiting online abusive behaviour for both reasons of freedom of speech, and also because there is a failure to appreciate the harm caused by this behaviour; harm which is "often trivialised and minimised in the policies and practices of police, media, the legal profession and other responders to the problem".[74] Assessing the conduct through a wider

---

70 N Henry, A Flynn and A Powell, "Technology-Facilitated Domestic and Sexual Violence: A Review" (2020) 26(15–16) *Violence Against Women* 1828, 1830.

71 O Todhunter, "Logged In and Fed Up: Responding to Gendered Violence in Online Spaces" (2018) 22(4) *Media and Arts Law Review* 420, 422.

72 Todhunter, n 71.

73 Harris and Woodlock, n 3, 532–533.

74 Powell and Henry, n 4, 218.

lens suggests that this failure to appreciate the harm caused by online violence reflects how "offline" forms of harassment are also "trivialised, regarded as part of normal, flirtatious exchanges between men and women in public and private life".[75] Both the online conduct and the broader "offline" pattern it fits within need to be addressed for any legal response to be effective.

This section first considers how abusers use technology to perpetrate family violence[76] online. It provides an overview of the prevalence of such offending before underscoring the fact that the harm caused by online violence is real. Focusing on the technological means of offending risks underestimating the significant impact that it has on the lives of its victims. This section then uses the examples of image-based sexual abuse and online harassment to assess legal responses to cyber-enabled family violence in Australia.

Cyber-enabled family violence

[5.90] How is family violence enabled by digital technology? Perpetrators of family violence use digital technology to achieve the same ends they also seek through other forms of abuse: to control and coerce their intimate partner. This can occur through a variety of methods. The Australian Domestic Violence Bench Book explains that all sorts of technologies – computers, smart phones, GPS navigators, digital cameras and digital recording equipment – are used to stalk and surveil the target victim.[77] These tools are "recognised as easy, accessible and instantaneous methods by which a perpetrator can control, monitor, humiliate and shame the victim, and make it more difficult for the victim to leave the abuse relationship or seek help".[78] The sad reality is that technology has provided abusers with

75 Powell and Henry, n 4.

76 "Family violence" is a broad term used to describe a range of abusive behaviours that "may occur within intimate, immediate and extended family and other communal or extended kinship relationships of mutual obligation and support". Violence includes "physical, sexual, emotional and psychological abuse or injury, as well as conduct designed to exert power by restricting access to financial, familial and cultural resources and limiting social autonomy, sometimes referred to as coercive control": "Terminology" in Australian Institute of Judicial Administration, *National Domestic and Family Violence Bench Book* (6 October 2021) ¶3 <https://www.dfvbenchbook.aija.org.au/contents> (*National Domestic and Family Violence Bench Book*).

77 "Following, harassing and monitoring" in *National Domestic and Family Violence Bench Book*, n 76, ¶3.1.6.

78 *National Domestic and Family Violence Bench Book*, n 76.

"new and more extensive ways to control, coerce, stalk, and harass their victims".[79]

These technological developments have "compounded the severity and complexity of domestic abuse".[80] Similar to cybercriminals who use ransomware to extort companies, perpetrators of family violence do not need to have a great deal of technical expertise to carry out their offending. It often only requires a few keystrokes for perpetrators to be able "harass both their current and former intimate partners without leaving the comfort of their home, instigating fear in an attempt to maintain control".[81]

While some forms of technology-facilitated violence are lo-fi and based on persistent texts, emails or phone calls, others are more sophisticated. To give one of the most troubling examples, spyware and "internet-of-things" devices are increasingly being used by perpetrators.[82] If they can get access to the victim's computers and phones, spyware can be easily purchased and installed without their knowledge.[83] It can allow perpetrators to track the physical location of devices, see every incoming and outgoing message, every web search, listen to live phone calls and turn devices into remote listening devices.[84] The information that is gathered from this activity can be used to "remind victims of their dominion and strength; to remind them that despite their physical absence, their abuser remains in control".[85]

The prevalence of cyber-enabled family violence

[5.100] It is hard to say how often internet tools are used to perpetuate family violence. Research into cyberstalking and other kinds of technology-facilitated family violence is scarce; Essert suggests this might be because it is easier to avoid detection online, and that this sort of conduct is underreported.[86] Much of the research is based on surveys, and the majority of the quantitative

79 H Al-Alosi, "Cyber-Violence: Digital Abuse in the Context of Domestic Violence" (2017) 40(4) *University of New South Wales Law Journal* 1573, 1578.

80 C Essert, "Addressing Imperfect Solutions to Technology-Facilitated Domestic Violence" (2019) 41(3–4) *Women's Rights Law Reporter* 117, 124.

81 Essert, n 80.

82 Essert, n 80, 132–134.

83 Essert, n 80, 133.

84 Essert, n 80.

85 Essert, n 80, 133.

86 Essert, n 80, 125.

research in the field has been on "sexting" among children and adolescents.[87] There has been far less research into non-consensual behaviours related to the use of images between adults, despite the fact there is some research indicating that it is more prevalent.[88]

However, a few things are quite clear. Technology-facilitated abuse repeats the patterns of other forms of family violence. Men are the vast majority of perpetrators.[89] In fact (and unsurprisingly), digital technologies are a very common part of the toolkit of perpetrators of family violence: a 2020 Australian survey with frontline domestic violence workers found that almost all survey respondents (99.3%) had clients who had experienced technology-facilitated stalking and abuse.[90] The most commonly used tool was text messaging, with 60.7% of practitioners seeing it "all the time"; smartphones (36.1%) and Facebook (35.1%) were the next two most commonly used technologies.[91] The use of cameras to covertly or overtly monitor women and children had increased by 182% since the last survey (35% of respondents said they saw them used to perpetrate abuse "all the time"), and GPS tracking was also a common part (16%). This is not a new feature of family violence. Research has consistently demonstrated that technology-facilitated family violence is relatively prevalent. A 2013 study found that 97% of family violence practitioners supported clients whose partners or ex-partners were using mobile technology to track them.[92] The same study found that 78% of victims had been abused or harassed through technology, and 44% said they had been threatened over text, email or social media.[93]

This has also been found in other jurisdictions. A 2016 US survey of people over 15 years of age found that 12% of respondents who had been in a romantic relationship had experienced digital abuse by their current or former

---

87 N Henry, A Flynn and A Powell, "Image-Based Sexual Abuse: Victims and Perpetrators" (*Trends & Issues in Crime and Criminal Justice* No 572, Australian Institute of Criminology, March 2019) 3, 19.

88 Henry, Flynn and Powell, n 87.

89 Al-Alosi, n 79, 1574.

90 D Woodlock et al, *Second National Survey on Technology Abuse and Domestic Violence* (Report, November 2020) 2.

91 Woodlock et al, n 90.

92 D Woodlock, *Technology-Facilitated Stalking: Findings and Recommendations from the SmartSafe Project* (Domestic Violence Resource Centre Victoria, 2013) 15.

93 Woodlock, n 92, 24.

intimate partner.[94] The forms of abuse the survey asked about included "being monitored online or by phone, being purposefully embarrassed online, being called offensive names, and being stalked".[95] It was more prevalent among young people and LGBTQI+ people.[96] Interestingly, the survey reported that men and women experienced intimate partner digital abuse at equal rates.[97] The most common forms of digital abuse were digital monitoring and purposeful embarrassment online.[98] A more recent Australian study found a strikingly high rate of victimisation by image-based sexual abuse: 23% of respondents reported being a victim of at least one form of image-based sexual abuse, including the creation, distribution or threatened distribution of intimate images.[99] Overall, women and men reported similar levels of victimisation by image-based sexual abuse.[100]

The impact of cyber-enabled family violence

[5.110] Online violence can have a very tangible impact. It can affect a person's career and financial livelihood, cause serious psychological harm and fear.[101] It also has the effect of excluding users from online spaces, limiting their autonomy and access.[102] As Powell and Henry explain:

> … technology facilitated sexual violence is an extension of "everyday" forms of sexual violence and a further manifestation of gender inequality. [It] is a form of inequality that further prevents individuals and groups from participating *freely* in public and private life, resulting in a denial of "digital citizenship".[103]

As noted above, online harassment has often failed to be taken seriously, with investigators and prosecutors treating offline, physical violence as being much more problematic and the "real" kind of violent conduct deserving of

94 M Ybarra et al, *Intimate Partner Digital Abuse* (Report No 01.18.17, Data & Society Research Institute, January 2017) 3, 26 <https://datasociety.net/library/intimate-partner-digital-abuse/>.

95 Ybarra et al, n 94.

96 Ybarra et al, n 94.

97 Ybarra et al, n 94, 4.

98 Ybarra et al, n 94, 11.

99 Henry, Flynn and Powell, n 87, 9–10.

100 Henry, Flynn and Powell, n 87, 11.

101 Todhunter, n 71, 425–428.

102 Todhunter, n 71, 428.

103 Powell and Henry, n 4, 201.

a response.[104] Testimony from victims of family violence suggests that they are forced to deal with perceptions that cyber-enabled violence is less serious and distinct from other forms of abuse and stalking.[105] This reflects how the dominant idea that the only kind of "real" violence is physical obscures the impact of non-physical violence.[106] This view of "real" violence is erroneous. There is substantial evidence that cyber-enabled family violence causes real harm to its victims: by overcoming geographic and spatial boundaries, perpetrators are able to continue to contact victims, eroding their perception of safety by "creating a sense of omnipresence".[107] It makes it much more difficult to completely sever ties.[108] A 2020 Australian survey of domestic violence practitioners confirmed this view: the term "fear" was the most commonly used word to describe how technology-facilitated abuse impacted on victims.[109] The Survey Report explained that respondents reported it caused "exhaustion, despair and hopelessness" and that it "increased isolation, and a fear of using technology to keep in contact with friends, family and services".[110]

The difficulty of conceptualising and framing this kind of offending can be seen in the debate about what name to give this kind of offending. Henry, Flynn and Powell and use the phrase "technologically enabled abuse";[111] Douglas, Harris and Dragiewicz use "technology-facilitated domestic and family violence".[112] Harris and Woodlock argue that we should use the phrase "digital coercive control" as it describes the method, the intent and the impact of the conduct, and because the phrase "coercive control" "situates harm within a wider setting of sex-based inequality".[113] This way of describing abusive conduct against intimate partners conducted online is preferable to terms like "cyberbullying" or "cyberstalking". Focusing only on the technology used can miss how the offending fits into this wider pattern.

---

104 See Woodlock et al, n 90, 4.

105 Harris and Woodlock, n 3, 533–534.

106 Powell and Henry, n 4, 50.

107 D Woodluck, "The Abuse of Technology in Domestic Violence and Stalking" (2017) 23(5) *Violence Against Women* 584.

108 Al-Alosi, n 79, 1578.

109 Woodlock et al, n 90, 4.

110 Woodlock et al, n 90.

111 Henry et al, n 70.

112 H Douglas, B A Harris and M Dragiewicz, "Technology-Facilitated Domestic and Family Violence: Women's Experiences" (2019) 59(3) *British Journal of Criminology* 551.

113 Harris and Woodlock, n 3, 533.

This has been an issue with much extant literature on family violence conducted online. It focuses on the medium of abuse – the technology – rather than the actors carrying out the abuse and their relationship to one another, and the arena in which it occurs.[114] While it is possible that some people only experience abuse facilitated by the technology, other studies have "noted the co-occurrence of other forms of abuse and/or traditional stalking".[115] The focus on the medium has curtailed the kinds of conduct that have been studied. There has been much more written on online misogyny and violence associated with online dating than intimate partner and relational violence.[116] This has been observed by other scholars: Powell and Henry note that "studies of virtual or cybercriminality have paid surprisingly little attention to the dynamics of gender, power and inequality".[117] Similarly, Al-Alosi argues that while cybercrimes like "hacking, identity theft, and online fraud" have received considerable attention, "less focus has been given to the issue of technology-facilitated abuse between current and former intimate partners".[118] Instead, by paying proper attention to the nature of the harm rather than just the technology we can help resist the idea that technologically enabled abuse is less serious than other forms of violence.

The next section discusses legal responses to cyber-enabled family violence in the Australian context.

Assessing legal responses to cyber-enabled family violence

[5.120] There are several ways the law can intervene in family violence enabled by the internet. Criminal prosecution is one possible legal response, and there are several potentially relevant criminal offences. Some crimes relate specifically to things that happen via digital means, whereas others can apply to both online and offline conduct. Intervention orders are another legal avenue that may be pursued to protect victims of online family violence. This section provides a brief overview of the type of computer misuse offences found in Australian law that could be applicable to cyber-enabled family violence before turning to assess legal responses to two types of family violence committed online: image-based sexual abuse and online sexual harassment.

114 Harris and Woodlock, n 3, 532.

115 Harris and Woodlock, n 3.

116 Harris and Woodlock, n 3, 532.

117 Powell and Henry, n 4, 50.

118 Al-Alosi, n 79, 1573.

Crimes relating to the improper use of computers

[5.130] As discussed in [5.60], there are nine criminal jurisdictions in Australia: one for each state and territory, and a Commonwealth criminal jurisdiction. The criminal legal framework in each jurisdiction provides for offences that specifically refer to the misuse of computers, with considerable overlap among them. While computer crimes are perhaps more obviously suited to cyber-dependent crimes such as ransomware, there are a number of computer offences that could equally apply to cyber-enabled family violence. For example, s 408E of the *Commonwealth Criminal Code* makes it an offence to "use a restricted computer (password protected) without the consent of the person who controls the computer".[119] While the maximum penalty for this offence is two years imprisonment, this increases to 10 years if the "person causes or intends to cause detriment or damage, or intends to gain a benefit".[120] Such a provision may be applicable to both cyber-dependent and cyber-enabled offending.

There are several Commonwealth offences relating to the improper use of technology that would be suitable for online family violence. For example, s 372.1 of the *Commonwealth Criminal Code* criminalises identity fraud, making it an offence to "make, supply or use" the identification information of another person to pretend to be, or pass oneself off, as another person. This could be relevant where a perpetrator pretends to be an ex-partner and harasses the victim through that impersonation. Other offences refer to the use of a carriage service (which includes telephone and internet services) to make a threat to kill,[121] a threat to cause serious harm,[122] or to menace, harass or cause offence.[123]

Legal responses to image-based sexual abuse

[5.140] One of the most well-known forms of cyber-enabled abuse is the sharing of intimate images without the permission of the subject of the image. This conduct – known as image-based sexual abuse – has been the focus of substantial legislative reform around the world.[124] It is a complex phenomenon, and perpetrators can include family members, friends, acquaintances and unknown people, along with intimate partners.[125] Unlike

---

119 *Criminal Code Act 1995* (Cth), Sch 1 s 408E.

120 *Criminal Code Act 1995* (Cth), Sch 1 s 408E.

121 *Criminal Code Act 1995* (Cth), Sch 1 s 417.15.

122 *Criminal Code Act 1995* (Cth), Sch 1 s 474.15.

123 *Criminal Code Act 1995* (Cth), Sch 1 s 474.17.

124 Powell and Henry, n 4, 203.

125 Henry, Flynn and Powell, n 87, 2.

the forms of cyber-enabled abuse discussed below, while some internet-based sexual abuse "mirrors the dynamic of male-to-female partner abuse, this is far from a gendered issue, with vulnerable and disadvantaged groups most likely to be victimised, and common dynamics of peer-to-peer sexual harassment and abuse also being found to exist".[126]

There is some debate about whether there is a need for specific legislation for image-based sexual abuse (given it is often covered by broad criminal offences or civil wrongs),[127] but Australian jurisdictions have opted to specifically criminalise it. In Queensland, for example, the *Criminal Code Act 1899* (Qld) includes several crimes that are particularly relevant in online contexts. Some offences refer to the creation and distribution of material in breach of a person's privacy. Section 227A makes it an offence to "observe or visually record" another person without their consent and in "circumstances where a reasonable adult would expect to be afforded privacy".[128] In addition, s 227A(2) criminalises the conduct colloquially known as "upskirting", by making it an offence to "observe or visually record another person[s] genital or anal region without [their] consent" where a "reasonable adult would expect to be afforded privacy in relation to that region".[129] It is a further offence to distribute these "prohibited visual recordings" without the consent of the person.[130] The maximum penalty for these offences is imprisonment for two years.

In Victoria, image-based sexual abuse is criminalised by ss 40–41DB of the *Summary Offences Act 1966* (Vic). Similar to Queensland, some of the offences specifically deal with "observing"[131] or "visually capturing"[132] another person's genital or anal region "in circumstances where it would be reasonable for that other person to expect that his or her genital or anal region" could not be observed/visually captured.[133] It is a further offence to distribute images of another person's genital or anal regions (regardless of whether the act of visually capturing the image was in breach of the Act).[134] There are also more general offences dealing with the distribution[135] or the threat to

126 Henry, Flynn and Powell, n 87, 14.

127 Powell and Henry, n 4, 203.

128 *Criminal Code Act 1899* (Qld), s 227A.

129 *Criminal Code Act 1899* (Qld), s 227A(2).

130 *Criminal Code Act 1899* (Qld), s 227B.

131 *Summary Offences Act 1966* (Vic), s 41A.

132 *Summary Offences Act 1966* (Vic), s 41B.

133 *Summary Offences Act 1966* (Vic), ss 41A, 41B.

134 *Summary Offences Act 1966* (Vic), s 41C.

135 *Summary Offences Act 1966* (Vic), s 41DA.

distribute[136] intimate images: the Act provides it is an offence to intentionally distribute an intimate image of another person where the "distribution of the image is contrary to community standards of acceptable conduct".[137] It defines "community standards of acceptable conduct" as including the "nature and content of the image", the circumstances in which the image was captured and distributed, the age and intellectual capacity of the person depicted in the image, and the extent to which the distribution affects their privacy.[138]

While the criminal legislation appears suitable for prosecuting image-based sexual abuse, challenges to combating this type of offending remain. Many victims might be reluctant to report to police because they worry about being blamed for having originally consented to the image, or fear that the images will be accessed by police or others.[139] This is another area where we see the difficulties caused by naming and perceptions of the conduct: the narrow conceptualisation of the conduct as "revenge pornography" carried out as an act of retribution assumes a particular intention on the part of the perpetrator, and it has shaped the legislative response and continues to shape the criminal justice response.[140]

In addition, different people might have different understandings of what amounts to an intimate image. Powell and Henry observe in relation to the Victorian legislation that different people in the community might have different ideas of what amounts to an intimate or sexual image, and that this should be taken into account when interpreting the legislation:

> For instance, would existing laws criminalise the non-consensual distribution of an image of a Muslim woman in her underwear without her hijab on? Would an "intimate" image include women's cleavage or nipples underneath clothing? We contend that interpretations of the meaning of such language should take into account the nature and the content of the image, the degree to which the distribution affects the privacy of the person, as well as the degree to which distribution of images violates that person's community's standards of acceptable conduct.[141]

There are other challenges. Requiring a specific intention to cause emotional harm and distress, or proof of harm or distress, may make prosecution

136 *Summary Offences Act 1966* (Vic), s 41DB.

137 *Summary Offences Act 1966* (Vic), s 41DA.

138 *Summary Offences Act 1966* (Vic), s 41.

139 Powell and Henry, n 4, 203.

140 Powell and Henry, n 4, 203.

141 Powell and Henry, n 4, 208.

difficult.[142] In addition, whether the distribution by third parties of images that they know to be private should be criminalised is contested.[143]

In the background is the challenge of assessing the harm of the distribution. In some cases the subject of the images may suffer limited or no consequences, whereas in others there might be more significant physical, psychological, social and financial consequences, including "risks to personal safety due to stalking, domestic violence, deep shame and humiliation, altered relationships with others, reputational damage, loss of employment prospects, low self-esteem, suicide ideation and withdrawal from social life".[144] The impact might not be felt immediately: one of the ways that the use of digital technologies exacerbates the offending is that online images can remain indefinitely online once they have been distributed.[145]

Investigating cyber-enabled family violence poses real challenges for police and prosecutors. The victim might feel disempowered or may be the only one who can gather relevant evidence of the behaviour.[146] Furthermore – and like other forms of cyber-enabled violence – police and judicial officers might have the perception that the digitally based behaviour is less serious than physical violence, and there may be "a tendency to trivialise the victim's experience and minimise the harm suffered, leading to inadequate legal responses".[147]

Legal responses to stalking and other forms of online sexual harassment

[5.150] The primary way that courts deal with online harassment occurring in the context of family violence is through protection orders (also known as intervention orders). These orders apply to a range of conduct, but regularly cover technologically facilitated abuse like that discussed above: conduct such as persistent messaging or use of recording and tracking devices. The operation of family violence protection orders are quite similar across Australia.[148] Some jurisdictions adopt a model where the order can be made either by the court or

142 Powell and Henry, n 4, 208–209.

143 Powell and Henry, n 4, 209.

144 Powell and Henry, n 4.

145 Powell and Henry, n 4.

146 "Following, harassing and monitoring" in *National Domestic and Family Violence Bench Book*, n 76, ¶3.1.5.

147 "Following, harassing and monitoring" in *National Domestic and Family Violence Bench Book*, n 76, ¶3.1.5.

148 "Purpose" in *National Domestic and Family Violence Bench Book*, n 76, ¶7.1.

the police. For example, in Queensland, a person who is experiencing family violence can apply to the Magistrates Court for a Domestic Violence Protection Order (DVO)[149] or a protection notice can be made by police.[150] A DVO can contain conditions relating to the use of technology, prohibiting the respondent to the order from engaging in domestic violence, contacting the accused or attempting to locate them.[151] If a person breaches a DVO, it can result in a criminal charge.[152] In Tasmania, police are able to make the order without the need to go to court.[153] Other jurisdictions require a court to bring the protection order into effect. For example, in Victoria, police can make a family violence safety notice for temporary protection,[154] but longer-term protection orders can only be made by a court.[155]

After assessing a series of cases of cyber-enabled family violence, Al-Alosi notes that protection orders have some advantages: they allow for those seeking protection to ask the court to include the conditions that address their specific situation and needs.[156] However, getting the conditions right is important. In order to be effective, they need to explicitly include the things that are happening, such as prohibitions on "keeping a protected person under surveillance and distributing, or threatening to distribute, intimate images of the protected person".[157] The legal system – police, courts and lawyers – must also actively ensure that the defendant understands what the order provides and the consequences of breaching it.[158]

Some offences are more specifically targeted to a kind of conduct that can be enabled through digital means. For example, digital technology facilitates stalking behaviour. Some jurisdictions have introduced offences related to stalking,[159] or modified existing offences to apply to these new uses. In Queensland, four elements make up the crime of unlawful stalking. It has to be

---

149 *Domestic and Family Violence Protection Act 2012* (Qld), s 32.

150 *Domestic and Family Violence Protection Act 2012* (Qld), s 101.

151 *Domestic and Family Violence Protection Act 2012* (Qld), s 28.

152 *Domestic and Family Violence Protection Act 2012* (Qld), s 177.

153 *Family Violence Act 2004* (Tas), s 14.

154 *Family Violence Protection Act 2008* (Vic), Pt 3.

155 *Family Violence Protection Act 2008* (Vic), Pt 4.

156 Al-Alosi, n 79, 1592.

157 Al-Alosi, n 79, 1599–1600.

158 Al-Alosi, n 79, 1600.

159 For example, *Crimes (Domestic and Personal Violence) Act 2007* (NSW), s 13; *Criminal Code Act 1899* (Qld), s 359E; *Crimes Act 1958* (Vic), s 21A.

(1) intentionally directed at a person; (2) engaged in on more than one occasion, or "if the conduct lasts for a long time, it is engaged in on any one occasion"; (3) it consists of "stalking" behaviour (which is defined); and (4) it causes the aggrieved person "detriment reasonably arising in the circumstances".[160] Stalking behaviours include conduct that can be facilitated or enabled by technology, including "following" or "watching" a person, contacting them "in any way", posting (or emailing) offensive material, or making threats.[161] While following, harassing and monitoring victims is a feature of intimate partner violence that does not necessarily rely on the digital technologies, the technology does enable it.[162]

There is no consensus on whether there should be cyber-specific offences for online harassment, or if instead we should rely on general offences. There are merits to either approach. For example, specific offences can more precisely communicate that the "new" conduct is considered criminal, or special investigatory powers can attach to assist with prosecutions. It can assist in the administration of justice by allowing for the easier allocation of cyber-enabled offending to specialist investigators, prosecutors and (where appropriate) courts. However, there is a risk that the creation of a subset of offences has the effect of disconnecting the conduct from broader patterns of violence and abuse. Al-Alosi is agnostic about whether further legislation should be introduced, noting that there is a lack of research about the adequacy of existing law to deal with the various types of technology-facilitated abuse.[163] She does note that criminal law can help communicate to the public the boundaries of acceptable behaviour, as well as encouraging police to pursue complaints and victims to report.[164]

Concluding Remarks

[5.160] Legislatures are limited in what they can do to respond to new and emerging cyber-dependent and cyber-enabled crimes. With respect to use of ransomware, for example, there is a patchwork of computer offences and ordinary crimes that could be used to prosecute, but there is no single Australian offence that captures all aspects of this complex incursion. In relation to cyber-enabled family violence, there is no consensus about whether specific or more

---

160 *Criminal Code Act 1899* (Qld), ss 359A–359E.

161 *Criminal Code Act 1899* (Qld).

162 "Following, harassing and monitoring" in *National Domestic and Family Violence Bench Book*, n 76, ¶3.1.5.

163 Al-Alosi, n 79, 1600.

164 Al-Alosi, n 79.

general crimes is preferable for image-based sexual abuse and online sexual harassment.[165] The difficulties of designing the legislation are compounded by challenges in detecting and punishing perpetrators, particularly when they are located in other jurisdictions or have obscured their identity by hiding their IP address.[166]

There are some significant similarities between the shortcomings of the legal responses to cyber-dependent ransomware and cyber-enabled family violence. There is a lack of public awareness about the legal regulation of cybercrime, meaning people do not know what mechanisms are available for them if they have been victims of ransomware or online violence.[167] In addition, it can be difficult to convince police of the seriousness of the conduct and the necessity to respond,[168] and this lack of understanding also exists in other legal institutions, with judges and magistrates not taking cybercrime seriously or not understanding digital evidence.[169] Obtaining relevant admissible evidence may also require agreement among national and international technology providers, website hosts and law enforcement agencies.[170]

Law should not, however, be the only mechanism for addressing cybercrime. Other measures to be explored include policy and structural changes, and a focus on designing computer systems in a way that allows for easier action and prevention strategies.[171] Police must be properly trained to recognise the serious harms caused by cybercrime and better resourced to investigate crimes committed by technological means. The general public should be educated with a particular focus on perpetrator accountability.[172]

Importantly, it should be made clear that "victims are not expected to forsake their use of the internet and digital communication devices simply to avoid cyber-violence".[173] Many policy responses to cybercrime expect individuals to change their online behaviour to better protect themselves. For example, the

---

165 Powell and Henry, n 4, 226.

166 Powell and Henry, n 4.

167 Todhunter, n 71, 431. See also C Cross et al, "Responding to Cybercrime: Results of a Comparison between Community Members and Police Personnel" (Trends & Issues in Crime and Criminal Justice No 635, Australian Institute of Criminology, August 2021).

168 Cross et al, n 167.

169 Todhunter, n 71, 432–433; Peters and Jordan, n 62, 514.

170 Al-Alosi, n 79, 1601.

171 Powell and Henry, n 4, 228; see also J Slupska, "Safe at Home: Towards a Feminist Critique of Cybersecurity" (2019) 15(1) *St Anthony's International Review* 83.

172 Al-Alosi, n 79, 1602.

173 Al-Alosi, n 79.

Australian Government "ReportCyber" website encourages victims to change their security settings to avoid cybercrime.[174] Similarly, state and federal police websites set out ways individuals can be a "tougher target for cybercriminals", including keeping their computer updated, choosing strong passwords and refraining from giving out personal information online.[175] Police advise that businesses can prevent cyberattacks by requiring cumbersome multi-factor authentication and regular staff training to identify potential malware.[176] Police suggest a range of strategies to avoid online harassment, all of which stifle the individual's freedom to use social media in the way that other people do, including things like reducing the amount of personal information online, thinking "carefully" about what they post, closing social media accounts or changing email addresses.[177]

While individuals and businesses can and should implement strategies to minimise their risk of falling victim to cybercrime, attempts to combat cybercrime must be carried out in a way that enables and protects people's capacity to use the internet and digital tools without placing undue burdens and restrictions on users. To that end, the onus to prevent cybercrime should extend to the designers of digital products, databases and electronic communications. The Australian Computer Society has highlighted the fact that "cybercrime almost exclusively leverages the lack of security-focused design in everything from your smartphone and web browser to your credit card and even the electronic systems in your car".[178] We should therefore be encouraging – perhaps mandating – technology and software programmers to design their systems in a way that reduces the risk of the technology being misused. A holistic response that involves users, government, law enforcement, cybersecurity specialists and the technology industry itself, is likely to be the only effective way to respond to cybercrime going forward.

---

174 "Threats", *Australian Cyber Security Centre* <https://cyber.gov.au/acsc/individuals-and-families/threats>.

175 See, for example, "Online Safety", *ACT Policing* <https://police.act.gov.au/safety-and-security/online-safety>; "Online Safety", *NSW Police* <https://police.nsw.gov.au/safety_and_prevention/crime_prevention/online_safety>; "Reporting Cybercrime", *Queensland Police Service* <https://police.qld.gov.au/reporting/reporting-cybercrime>.

176 "Prevent a Cyber Incident", *Victorian Government* <https://vic.gov.au/prevent-cyber-incidents>.

177 "Do Things Securely", *Australian Cyber Security Centre* <https://cyber.gov.au/acsc/individuals-and-families/do-things-securely>; "Cyber Bullying", *Queensland Police Service* <https://police.qld.gov.au/safety-and-preventing-crime/r-u-in-control/cyber-bullying>.

178 Australian Computer Society, *Cybersecurity: Threats, Challenges, Opportunities* (Report, 14 November 2016) 14 <https://acs.org.au/content/dam/acs/acs-publications/ACS_Cybersecurity_Guide.pdf>.

Chapter 6

Protecting Data Privacy in an Evolving Technological Environment

Niloufer Selvadurai*

Introduction

[6.10] From Sherlock Holmes, "it is a capital mistake to theorise before one has data", to Geoffrey Moore, "without big data, you are blind and deaf and in the middle of a freeway", to Clive Humby, "data is the new oil", to Mark Zuckerberg, "we have a responsibility to protect your data", scholars, theorists and entrepreneurs alike have opined lyrical on the value of data.[1] In the contemporary era, data is widely accepted to be society's most valuable economic resource.[2] This high value of data flows both from its potential for commercial monetisation and its capacity to support the self-expression, creativity and well-being of individuals.[3] It is clear that such a valuable and complex resource needs a sophisticated data privacy regulatory framework.

---

* Professor of Technology Law, Macquarie Law School, Macquarie University, BA LLB (Hons I) *USyd*, PhD *Mq*, Program Director, Legal and Ethics of Cyber, Optus Macquarie Cyber Security Hub.

1 P Adediwura, *Big Data – The Raw Material for 4.0 Business* (Interlogica) <https://www.interlogica.it/en/insight-en/without-big-data-analytics-companies-are-blind-and-deaf-wandering-out-onto-the-web-like-deer-freeway-geoffrey-moore/>.

2 B Graham and J Tucker, "The International Political Economy Data Resource" (2019) 14 *Review of International Organisations* 149; N Economides and I Lianos, "Restrictions on Privacy and Exploitation in the Digital Economy: A Competition Law Perspective" (NET Institute Working Paper No 19, NYU Stern School of Business, November 2019); C A Ciocchetti, "E-Commerce and Information Privacy: Privacy Policies as Personal Information Protectors" (2007) 44 *American Business Law Journal* 55.

3 See further V Boehme-Neßler, "Why Democracy Needs Privacy and Data Protection" (2016) 6(3) *International Data Privacy Law* 222; C Brewster and D Hine, "Legibility, Privacy and Creativity" in S Decker, J Hendler and S Kirrane (eds), *Society, Privacy and the Semantic Web – Policy and Technology* (CEUR, 2014).

A governance framework that effectively protects personal privacy, calibrating personal interests in privacy and autonomy with wider societal interests in access to information, economic growth and innovation.[4] However, as privacy laws were largely designed to govern a pre-digitalised world,[5] law and policy in this area have had to be significantly reimaged in order to respond to the challenges and risks generated by the rise of big data.[6] While there have been many waves of law reform to address such technological change,[7] resulting in a variety of reform conversations and statutory amendments,[8] significant regulatory gaps and weaknesses are still evident in our present data privacy laws.

Evolving, fluid technologies generate a variety of challenges for law and policy makers seeking to protect the data privacy of individuals. Constant technological disruptions make it difficult to identify and address potential breaches of personal privacy. It has been observed that the constant and rapid process of technological innovation has amplified threats to personal privacy by enabling personal information to be collected from further away and from multiple locations simultaneously, obfuscating the precise points and portals at which privacy breaches are occurring.[9] Further, evolving technologies shift societal norms on what constitutes appropriate privacy protection, potentially

---

4 See further E Horvitz and D Mulligan, "Data, Privacy, and the Greater Good" (2015) 349(6245) *Science* 253; D Wright et al, "Privacy, Trust and Policy-Making: Challenges and Responses" (2009) 25 *Computer and Security Law Review* 69; S Landau, "Control Use of Data to Protect Privacy" (2015) 347(6221) *Science* 504; M Peek, "The Observer and the Observed: Re-imagining Privacy Dichotomies in Information Privacy" (2009) 8 *Northwestern Journal of Technology and Intellectual Property* 51.

5 For a fascinating insight into early articulations of a right to privacy, see S Warren and L Brandeis, "The Right to Privacy" (1890) 4 *Harvard Law Review* 193; C Fried, "Privacy" (1968) 77 *Yale Law Journal* 475, 482. For a useful historical overview, see D Spar, *Ruling the Waves: Cycles of Discovery, Chaos, and Wealth from the Compass to the Internet* (Houghton Mifflin Harcourt, Boston, MA, 2001).

6 See especially V Torra, *Data Privacy: Foundations, New Developments and the Big Data Challenge* (Springer, 2017); P Jain, M Gyanchandani and N Khare, "Big Data Privacy: A Technological Perspective and Review" (2016) 3 *Journal of Big Data* 25. See further J Reidenberg, "Resolving Conflicting International Data Privacy Rules in Cyberspace" (2000) 52 *Stanford Law Review* 1315; I Rubenstein, "Big Data: The End of Privacy or a New Beginning?" (2013) 57 *International Data Privacy Law* 3, 74–87; A Slane, "Democracy, Social Space and the Internet" (2007) *University of Toronto Law Journal* 81.

7 Australian Law Reform Commission, *For Your Information: Australian Privacy Law and Practice* (Report 108, 2008); Australian Law Reform Commission, *Serious Invasions of Privacy in the Digital Era* (Report 123, September 2014).

8 See Australian Government, *Privacy Act Review – Issues Paper* (October 2020).

9 J Kaivo-oja, "Digital Twin: Current Shifts and Their Future Implications in the Conditions of Technological Disruption" (2020) 15(2) *International Journal of Web Engineering and Technology* 170.

undermining the public policy justification for existing laws and requiring a reassessment of the nature and ambit of legislation.[10] As technologies evolve, coalesce and reshape societal norms, it becomes increasingly complex to delineate the proper ambit of a right to personal privacy. Article 12 of the *Universal Declaration of Human Rights* stipulates that a person should not be the subject of "arbitrary interferences with privacy".[11] The case of *R v Broadcasting Standards Commission*[12] forms an early judicial consideration of the concept of principle. In that case, Lord Mustill famously stated:

> [t]o my mind the privacy of a human being denotes at the same time the personal "space" in which the individual is free to be itself, and also the carapace, or shell, or umbrella, or whatever other metaphor is preferred, which protects that space from intrusion. An infringement of privacy is an affront to the personality, which is damaged both by the violation and by the demonstration that the personal space is not inviolate.[13]

However, delineating the boundaries of this personal protected space and designing laws to effectively protect this space is becoming increasingly complex and challenging.

The notion of "information privacy" forms one aspect of the more broadly defined right to privacy and supports the capacity of an individual to control information as to self. Legal scholars have long held that such information privacy is central to the creation of individual identity, noting that personal identity is dependent upon "particular forms of withholding and disclosure of aspects of the self".[14] Paterson frames the right to information privacy as a right that supports autonomy of the individual,[15] while Fried famously states that the right to information privacy does not merely enable us to maintain "an absence of information about us in the minds of others" but rather enables us "control information about ourselves".[16]

---

10 K Aquilina, "Public Security versus Privacy in Technology Law: A Balancing Act" (2010) 26 *Computer Law & Security Review* 130. See further J Balkin, "The Constitution in the National Surveillance State" (2008) 93 *Minnesota Law Review* 1.

11 General Assembly of the United Nations, *Universal Declaration of Human Rights*, GA Res 217A (III), UN Doc A/Res/810 (1948), Art 12.

12 *R v Broadcasting Standards Commission* [2001] QB 885.

13 *R v Broadcasting Standards Commission* [2001] QB 885, [48].

14 General Assembly of the United Nations, *Universal Declaration of Human Rights*, GA Res 217A (III), UN Doc A/Res/810 (1948), Art 12.

15 G Xu et al, "Data Security Issues in Deep Learning: Attacks, Countermeasures, and Opportunities" (2019) 57(11) *IEEE Communications* 116.

16 C Fried, "Privacy" (1968) 77 *Yale Law Journal* 475, 482.

The potential for internet data collection practices to substantially infringe online information privacy has become a cause of acute concern.[17] While there are a wide variety of potential threats to digital data, a leading cause of infringements of data privacy is the non-secure storage or transmission of personal information.[18] Data that is transmitted as unprotected attachments is, for example, at risk of being intercepted in transit. Similarly, saving files containing personal information in web folders that are accessible online can lead to the data being compromised. Beyond such user enabled infringements of online privacy, cookies[19] stored on the computers of internet user can enable visited websites to access information without the consent or even knowledge of the user.[20] Data relating to a user's search engine use or website visits can also provide powerful information relating to an internet user's consumer preferences, as well as insights into their personal life, including health status, credit history and political and religious affiliations.[21] Additionally, data gathered through spyware, remote access software installed on a user's computer without their knowledge and consent, can substantially infringe online privacy. Web bugs embedded webpages visited by an internet user can also collect data, including data on sites visited, IP addresses and duration of time spent on various areas of a website. In addition to such non-consensual disclosure of data, internet scams and fraudulent practices such as phishing can lead to the voluntarily disclosure of personal information. Moreover, advances in technologies supporting data mining[22] and data matching[23] enable substantial tracts of data from multiple sources to be organised, collated and analysed to reveal valuable identity information as to an individual. Such

---

17 U Kohl, "The Rise and Rise of Online Intermediaries in the Governance of the Internet and Beyond – Connectivity Intermediaries" (2012) 26 *International Review of Law, Computers & Technology* 185; N J King, "Direct Marketing, Mobile Phones, and Consumer Privacy: Ensuring Adequate Disclosure and Consent Mechanisms for Emerging Mobile Advertising Practices" (2008) 60 *Federal Communications Law Journal* 229.

18 A Moens, "Mandatory Data Breach Reporting: Outcomes Since Reporting Began – Part 2" (2019) *GRC Professional* 55.

19 "Cookies" are data transmitted from a computer or website to an internet user's browser.

20 Australian Law Reform Commission, *For Your Information: Australian Privacy Law and Practice* (Report 108, 2008) 9.20; see also Australian Law Reform Commission, *Serious Invasions of Privacy in the Digital Era* (Report 123, September 2014).

21 Y Fen Lim, *Cyberspace Law: Commentaries and Materials* (Thomson Reuters, Melbourne, 2017) 127–128.

22 "Data mining" refers to the practice of using a set of automated techniques used to extract buried or previously unknown pieces of information from large databases.

23 "Data matching" involves the large-scale comparison of records or files in order to identify matters of interest.

cross-matching can involve both voluntarily proffered data, such as on social media sites, and non-consensual data, such as that extracted using cookies. Valuable identity data, such as full name, date of birth and nationality, can be generated using such data mining and data matching technologies.

In such a complex and fluid context, the purpose of this chapter is to consider the nature, operation, ambit and adequacy of Australian digital privacy laws, focusing in detail on the provisions of the *Privacy Act 1988* (Cth),[24] the *Australian Privacy Principles* (APPs), relevant case law, literature and law reform discourse in the field.

The Legal Framework Governing Data Privacy

Common law

[6.20] Australian law does not recognise a general common law right to privacy. In *Victoria Park Racing & Recreation Grounds Co Ltd v Taylor*,[25] in obiter comments, the High Court noted that an action for unauthorised disclosure or use of information should be based on an established basis of liability such as the infringement of a duty of confidentiality or a repudiation of a contract, with Latham CJ noting:

> With regard to the question of privacy, no doubt the owner of a house would prefer that a neighbour should not have the right of looking into his windows or yard, but neither this court nor a court of law will interfere on the mere ground of invasion of privacy; and a party has a right even to open new windows, although he is thereby enabled to overlook his neighbour's premises, and so interfering, perhaps, with his comfort.[26]

However, in the subsequent case of *Australian Broadcasting Corporation v Lenah Game Meats Pty Ltd*, the High Court commented that *Victoria Park* did not preclude the future development of an "enforceable right to privacy". Despite these promising words, a general common law right to privacy has not been developed in Australia.[27] In the absence of judicial recognition of a

---

24 *Privacy Act 1988* (Cth).

25 *Victoria Park Racing & Recreation Grounds Co Ltd v Taylor* (1937) 58 CLR 479.

26 *Victoria Park Racing & Recreation Grounds Co Ltd v Taylor* (1937) 58 CLR 479, 540; see further D Stewart, "Protecting Privacy, Property, and Possums: Australian Broadcasting Corporation v Lenah Game Meats Pty Ltd" (2002) 30 *Federal Law Review* 177.

27 See further D Butler, "A Tort of Invasion of Privacy in Australia?" (2005) 29 *Melbourne University Law Review* 339; S Ludington, "Reining in the Data Traders: A Tort for the Misuse of Personal Information" (2006) 66 *Maryland Law Review* 140; M Oswald, "Twitter Forces Rethink on English Privacy Law" (2011) 210 *New Scientist* 4; M Oswald, "Facebook Group Implies Consent to Disclosure of Personal Data" (2013) 3 *International Data Privacy Law* 61.

right to privacy, the 1988 enactment of the federal *Privacy Act* formed a seminal moment in Australian privacy law.

The federal Privacy Act

[6.30] The *Privacy Act 1988* (Cth) and APPs create a regulatory framework for the protection of personal information that is administered by the Office of the Australian Information Commissioner (OAIC). The primary objective of the *Privacy Act* is to promote the protection of the privacy of individuals. The Act seeks to create a foundation for a nationally consistent regulation of privacy and the handling of personal information in order promote the responsible and transparent handling of personal information. However, the Act recognises that individual privacy needs to be collaborated with competing interests. For instance, s 2A(b) expressly stipulates the need to balance the protection of individual privacy of individuals with the broader interests of entities in carrying out their functions or activities.[28] Similarly, s 2A(f) stipulates that the objective of the Act is to facilitate the free flow of information across national borders while also ensuring that the privacy of individuals is respected.[29] Beyond these overarching objectives, in the specific area of credit reporting, the objective of the Act is to facilitate an efficient credit reporting system that also respects the privacy of individuals. Further to these substantive aims, the act seeks to create an effective institutional structure and provide a process that enables individuals to complain about alleged interferences with privacy.

Regulated entities

[6.40] The *Privacy Act* is not of general application but is limited to certain prescribed entities. The Act applies to federal government "agencies" and "organisations" with an annual turnover more than $3 million.[30] "Organisation" is defined in s 6C to encompass individuals, body corporates, partnerships, other unincorporated association and trusts. However, under s 6D(4) certain designated small business operators with an annual turnover of *less* than $3 million per year are also subject to the Act, including most notably, private sector health service provider, a business that sells or purchases personal information, a credit reporting body or a contracted service provider for an Australian Government contract.[31] Parties outside the definition of

28 *Privacy Act 1988* (Cth), s 2A(b).

29 *Privacy Act 1988* (Cth), s 2A(f).

30 The Act also has a prescribed application to the Norfolk Island administration.

31 See s 6D definition of a "small business operator" for the full list of bodies.

"organisations" include registered political parties and state or territory authorities.[32] "Agencies" are defined to include a federal government Minister, Department or body established under a Commonwealth enactment.[33] Federal courts and the federal Police are excluded from the definition.[34]

A principles-based approach to privacy governance

[6.50] The APPs form Sch 1 of the federal *Privacy Act* and outline the fundamental legal principles that form the basis for the APP entities obligation to ensure the privacy of individuals' personal information.[35] This has been described as a "principle-based" approach to privacy governance as it is premised on fundamental principles rather than mere prescriptive directives. The objective of such an approach is to create overarching principles of good governance that are not technology-specific and can remain relevant in a context of rapid and constant technological change. The *Explanatory Memorandum* notes that this principles-based approach is designed to regulate in a "flexible way".[36] Instead of connecting information privacy obligations to specific technologies or activities, the APPs describe the "situations" in which privacy obligations arise, focusing on the circumstances relating to the creation, collection, use and dissemination of information. APP entities are required to manage personal information in an open and transparent way and adopt such measures as are reasonable in the circumstances to support compliance with the APPs.[37]

Similar to the imposition of privacy obligations, exceptions to privacy obligations are also triggered by designated "situations". The exceptions framework is based on two fundamental concepts, a "permitted general

32 See s 6 definition of "organisation" for the full list of bodies.

33 Section 6(c). An incorporated company, society or association or an organisation that is registered under the *Fair Work (Registered Organisations) Act 2009* (Cth) or a branch of such an organisation are excluded from this provision.

34 Section 6(g) and 6(h). See s 6 definition of "agency" for the full list of bodies.

35 It is relevant to note that the present APPs have now replaced the former 11 *Information Privacy Principles* (IPPs) that applied to the handling of personal information by government agencies and the 10 former *National Privacy Principles* (NPPs) that applied to the handling of personal information in the private sector including large businesses and certain small businesses and non-government organisations. See further N Selvadurai, "Protecting Online Information Privacy in a Converged Digital Environment – The Merits of the New Australian Privacy Principles" (2013) 22(3) *Information & Communications Technology Law* 299.

36 Explanatory Memorandum, *Privacy Amendment (Enhancing Privacy Protection) Bill 2012* (Cth) 52.

37 Australian Privacy Principle 1, cl 1.1.

situation"[38] and a "permitted health situation".[39] The existence of either of these situations create exceptions to the general obligations imposed on APP entities. Section 16A outlines situations where the collection, use or disclosure by an APP entity is permitted. An APP entity may disclose personal information or a government related identifier where it is unreasonable or impracticable to obtain the person's consent to the collection, use or disclosure, *and* the APP entity reasonably believes that the collection, use or disclosure is necessary to lessen or prevent a serious threat to the life, health or safety of any person or public health or safety.

What constitutes "personal information"?

[6.60] Central to the application of the *Privacy Act* is the concept of "personal information". "Personal information" is defined by s 6 of the Act, in technologically neutral terms, to be "information or an opinion about an identified individual, or an individual who is reasonably identifiable".[40] The truth or falsity of such information or opinion and the form in which it is recorded, are not relevant to this assessment of personal information.[41] A determination as to whether information is personal information needs to be made on a case-by-case basis in the context and particular circumstances of the case. As noted in the *Explanatory Memorandum to the Privacy Bill 2012*,[42] this critical definition seeks to be flexible and technology-neutral to encompass new and evolving forms of information collection and use. It is also consistent with international standards and precedents. The concept of "reasonably identifiable" further ensures that the concept is applied in the relevant context and circumstances in which the information is collected and held.[43] Within this broad category of personal information, the Act delineates a variety of specific

38 *Privacy Act 1988* (Cth), s 16A describes permitted general situations, where the collection, use or disclosure by an APP entity of personal information about an individual, or of a government related identifier, will not be a breach of certain APP obligations.

39 *Privacy Act 1988* (Cth), s 16B describes permitted health situations, where the collection, use or disclosure of certain health information or genetic information will not be a breach of certain APP obligations.

40 This definition of personal information is extended by s 187LA of the *Telecommunications (Interception and Access) Act 1979* (Cth) to encompass information kept under Pt 5-1A of that Act.

41 *Privacy Act 1988* (Cth), s 6.

42 Explanatory Memorandum, *Privacy Amendment (Enhancing Privacy Protection) Bill 2012* (Cth) 53.

43 Explanatory Memorandum, *Privacy Amendment (Enhancing Privacy Protection) Bill 2012* (Cth) 53.

types of information. This includes "sensitive information" which includes health information, as well as information about an individual's racial or ethnic origin, political opinion, religious beliefs, sexual orientation or criminal record,[44] credit information[45] and tax file number information.[46]

It is important to understand that personal information encompasses both confidential information and information which is publicly available. The critical test of whether information is "personal" is that it is information or opinion about the individual from which the individual is reasonably identifiable. Hence, personal information is not confined to information as to an individual's personal or private life. It encompasses any information or opinion about an individual from which they can be reasonably identified. Accordingly, while an individual's name, address, email address, date of birth, bank account details and medical records are clearly personal information, so too is information about an individual's working life, including their job title, work address and work practices. Further, an opinion as to a person which is premised on other information relating to them, for example, an opinion as to an individual's race which is based on information as their name, falls within the ambit of personal information about the individual.[47]

What constitutes "information about an individual"?

[6.70] In *Privacy Commissioner v Telstra Corporation Ltd*, Justices Kenny and Edelman held that information is information is "about" an individual where there is a connection between the information and the individual.[48] This holding was consistent with the earlier 2015 case of *Telstra Corporation Ltd v Privacy Commissioner*.[49] As there have been relatively few published decisions on critical terms in the *Privacy Act*, it is useful to examine in some detail the Full Federal Court case of *Privacy Commissioner v Telstra Corporation Ltd*.[50] While the factual relevance of decision in relation to mobile phone

44 *Privacy Act 1988* (Cth), s 6(1).

45 *Privacy Act 1988* (Cth), s 6N.

46 *Privacy Act 1988* (Cth), s 6(1), and more generally the *Privacy (Tax File Number) Rule 2015* (Cth).

47 Information which is not expressly defined to be personal information under the *Privacy Act* may be recognised as personal information under other legislation. For example, under the *Telecommunications (Interceptions and Access) Act 1979* (Cth), certain telecommunications data (sometimes referred to as "metadata") is taken to be personal information for the purposes of the *Privacy Act*.

48 *Privacy Commissioner v Telstra Corporation Ltd* [2017] FCAFC 4, [43], [64].

49 *Telstra Corporation Ltd v Privacy Commissioner* [2015] AATA 991, [112].

50 *Privacy Commissioner v Telstra Corporation Ltd* [2017] FCAFC 4.

data is limited, due to subsequent legislative amendment, the Court's consideration of critical concept of what constitutes information relating to an individual remains instructive.[51] In the case, the applicant, Grubb, requested the metadata information which Telstra had stored about his mobile phone service. Telstra refused, asserting it was not personal information under the *Privacy Act* and that Telstra was therefore not obliged to provide access to such information under NPP 6.1 (now APP 12, cl 12.1). To address the central issue, the Full Federal Court first considered the meaning and scope of the words "about an individual" noting that "[t]he words 'about an individual' direct attention to the need for an individual to be a subject matter of the information or opinion".[52] The Federal Court rejected the decision of the Privacy Commissioner that information from which an individual's identity is apparent or could reasonably be ascertained is necessarily information about that individual. The Federal Court stated that such an interpretation would render the words "about an individual" to be obsolete[53] and argued that such an approach was consistent with the principle of statutory interpretation that stipulates that no word, clause or sentence should be held to be superfluous if by an alternative construction it could be provided a substantive operation.[54] *Privacy Commissioner v Telstra Corporation Ltd*[55] further held that the issue of whether information is about an individual is a "question of fact" that is shaped by the context and circumstances of the case.[56]

Who is a "reasonably identifiable" individual?

[6.80] Critical to the definition of personal information, and hence the application of the *Privacy Act*, is the concept of a "reasonably identifiable" individual. Significant in the context of digital data is the fact that certain information which may not, on its own, reasonably identify an individual, it may do so when it is matched or combined with other data or data sets held or

---

51 It is relevant to note that the former wording of s 6 of the *Privacy Act* defined "personal information" as "information or an opinion (including information or an opinion forming part of a database), whether true or not, and whether recorded in a material form or not, about an individual whose identity is apparent, or can reasonably be ascertained, from the information or opinion". While not identical to the present above definition, it is similar and past judicial discussion in this regard is still broadly useful.

52 *Privacy Commissioner v Telstra Corporation Ltd* [2017] FCAFC 4, [63].

53 *Privacy Commissioner v Telstra Corporation Ltd* [2017] FCAFC 4, [62].

54 See further *Project Blue Sky Inc v Australian Broadcasting Authority* (1998) 194 CLR 355, [71].

55 *Privacy Commissioner v Telstra Corporation Ltd* [2017] FCAFC 4.

56 *Privacy Commissioner v Telstra Corporation Ltd* [2017] FCAFC 4, [63]–[64] (Kenny and Edelman JJ).

accessible to an entity. Moreover, as data sets can evolve, coalesce and change over time, the concept of reasonably identifiable is fluid and can also change over time. In considering whether an individual is reasonably identifiable it is hence necessary to consider the nature and extent of information relating to an individual, the parties who have or have access to the relevant information, any additional data sets available to the person having access to the primary data and the practicability and likelihood of such information being used to identify an individual.[57] As the s 6 definition contains the word "reasonably", it would also seem relevant to consider the existence or absence of motivations for an attempted re-identification and the like hood of such re-identification occurring. Hence, in order for an individual to reasonably identifiable it is likely that there will be two criteria to be fulfilled. First, it must be technically possible for re-identification to occur. This could be from the primary information or through a combination of such information with other accessible data sets. Second, there must be reasonable likelihood of such re-identification occurring.[58]

De-identification and re-identification of personal information

[6.90] The corollary of the *Privacy Act* governing personal information relating to an individual is that it does not govern de-identified information. Such information is not personal information as it does not relate to an identifiable individual or an individual who is reasonably identifiable. The *OAIC De-identification Guide*[59] provides important guidance on when information can be thought to be de-identified. It notes that information is likely to be "de-identified" for the purposes of the *Privacy Act* where two distinct steps have been followed.[60] First, it is necessary to remove any direct identifies. Examples of direct identifiers include a person's name, date of birth

57 Office of the Australian Information Commissioner, *De-identification and the Privacy Act* (March 2018) 8 <https://www.oaic.gov.au/privacy/guidance-and-advice/de-identification-and-the-privacy-act/>; see further Office of the Australian Information Commissioner, *De-identification Decision-Making Framework* (September 2017) <https://www.oaic.gov.au/privacy/guidance-and-advice/de-identification-decision-making-framework/>.

58 See relevant criteria in Office of the Australian Information Commissioner, *De-identification Decision-Making Framework* (September 2017). The criteria are extrapolated from C M O'Keefe et al, *The De-identification Decision-Making Framework* (CSIRO Reports EP173122 and EP175702, 2017).

59 Office of the Australian Information Commissioner, *De-identification and the Privacy Act* (March 2018).

60 Office of the Australian Information Commissioner, *De-identification and the Privacy Act* (March 2018) 8–9.

or address.[61] Once this preliminary step is complete, it is necessary to adopt safeguards and controls in the data environment to mitigate the risk of re-identification. Such additional techniques can encrypt the data, obfuscate the data or arrange or aggregate it in some manner to manner to minimise the risk of re-identification. Examples of such techniques could include the imposition of restriction on access to data and the signing of non-disclosure agreements by relevant individuals.

It is important to note that standard of de-identification required by the *Privacy Act* is not impossibility of identification (which would in any event be difficult to determine or enforce) but rather the achievement of a very low risk of re-identification, having regard to all the circumstances of the particular situation. Hence, the standard for de-identification varies according to context. For example, if a research institution with sophisticated data safeguards and a high level of ethical compliance discloses de-identified research to a prescribed set of researchers who are legally required (eg, through signing relevant contracts) to ensure the information is not re-identified, such information is not likely to constitute personal information. In comparison, if the identical de-identified information was released to the general public on a website, it is likely to constitute personal information as such disclosure would be associated with a higher likelihood of re-identification. Finally, it is relevant to note that any purported de-identified information which is subsequently re-identified will constitute personal information and be subject to the obligations imposed by the *Privacy Act*.[62]

Credit information

[6.100] While credit information is a type of personal information, it is governed separately pursuant to Pt IIIA of the Act. Part IIIA is supported by the *Privacy Regulation 2013* (Cth) and the *Privacy (Credit Reporting) Code 2014* (Cth) (*CR Code*). Together these instruments seek to calibrate the need to support efficient credit reporting and the need to protect personal privacy. The

---

61 See further A Cavoukian and K El Emam, *Dispelling the Myths Surrounding De-identification: Anonymisation Remains a Strong Tool for Protecting Privacy* (Information & Privacy Commissioner of Ontario, June 2011) 4; I Rubinstein and W Hartzog, "Anonymization and Risk" (New York University Public Law and Legal Theory Working Papers, Paper 530, 2015); I Rubinstein and W Hartzog, "Anonymization and Risk" (2016) 91 *Washington Law Review* 703.

62 Further, it is relevant to note that de-identification is not only a legal concept but a technical concept. In this respect it is useful to examine the CSIRO and Data61, *The De-identification Decision-Making Framework* (18 September 2017).

need for credit providers to have sufficient personal information to make an informed decision as to the provision of credit needs is balanced with the need for individuals to protect their personal information. Part IIIA stipulates the nature and types of personal information that a credit provider can disclose to a credit reporting body for the purpose of preparing a credit report, as well as the entities who can access such information and the purposes for which such information can be accessed, used and handled. Supporting Pt IIIA of the *Privacy Act* and *Privacy Regulation 2013* is the *CR Code* that applies to both credit providers and credit reporting bodies. The *CR Code* supplements the provisions contained in Pt IIIA of the *Privacy Act* and the *Privacy Regulation 2013*. It is relevant to note that the *CR Code* is mandatory and that any infringement of the *CR Code* is deemed to be an infringement of the *Privacy Act*.[63]

Health information

[6.110] As health information is considered to be one of the most sensitive types of personal information, it is the subject of a variety of additional privacy protections. Organisations providing a health service and holding health information are subject to the *Privacy Act*. Pursuant to the Act a "health service" includes any activity that involves assessing, maintaining or improving a person's physical or psychological health, managing a person's physical or psychological health, diagnosing or treating a person's illness, disability or injury, recording a person's physical or psychological health for the purposes of assessing, maintaining, improving or managing the person's health and dispensing a prescription drug or medicinal preparation by a pharmacist. Health information held in a person's *My Health Record*[64] and healthcare identifiers are regulated by the federal OAIC. Where it is impracticable for medical researchers to obtain a person's consent, the *Privacy Act* permits the handling of health information and personal information for health and medical research purposes in certain prescribed circumstances. The *National Health and Medical Research Council Guidelines*, produced pursuant to ss 95 and 95A of the *Privacy Act*, govern the handling of health information for research purposes without individuals' consent.

---

63 Following a 2017 independent review of the *CR Code*, conducted by PricewaterhouseCoopers, the Australian Information Commissioner approved a variation to the *CR Code* on 13 December 2019. The amended *CR Code* commenced operation on 14 February 2020.

64 *My Health Record* is an online summary of key health information relating to Australian citizens and residents <https://www.myhealthrecord.gov.au/>.

State and territory privacy legislation

[6.120] As the above discussed *Privacy Act 1988* is a federal law, it does not cover local, state or territory government agencies.[65] It is important to note that Australian states and territories have equivalent legislation which govern their public sector agencies.[66]

Sector-specific and data-specific laws

[6.130] It is important to note that in addition to privacy legislation, certain sections of state, territory and federal legislation govern specific types of activities and specific types of data. In addition to the above discussed enactments in relation to health and health records, other examples include the *Telecommunications Act 1997* (Cth), the *Banking Act 1953* (Cth) and the *Insurance Act 1973* (Cth). Further, the *Do Not Call Register Act 2006* (Cth) limits unsolicited phone calls while the *Spam Act 2003* (Cth) limits commercial emails. Two recent developments in this area are of particular note. In 2018, the *Telecommunications and Other Legislation Amendment (Assistance and Access) Act 2018* (Cth) created a legal framework to enable law enforcement agencies to access encrypted data for serious criminal investigation and imposed certain access obligations on designated communications providers. It is also relevant to note that in 2017, following a number of policy reviews, including the *Data Availability and Use* report by the Productivity Commission, the *Review into Open Banking in Australia* report by the federal Treasury and the Commonwealth Government introduced a consumer data right (CDR). The CDR enables consumers to access certain data relating to them which is held by a third party. The CDR has first been applied to the banking sector, to be followed by the energy sector and the telecommunications sector. As the CDR encompasses matters relating to privacy and confidentiality, it will be regulated by both the Australian Competition and Consumer Commission and the OAIC.

---

65 It is relevant to note that certain acts and practices of State and Territory entities which relate to *My Health Records* and individual healthcare identifiers are covered by the federal *Privacy Act*. Certain state and territory entities may also be prescribed by the *Privacy Regulation 2013* (Cth) and come within the ambit of the federal *Privacy Act*.

66 *Privacy and Personal Information Protection Act 1998* (NSW); *Privacy and Data Protection Act 2014* (Vic); *Information Privacy Act 2009* (Qld); *Freedom of Information Act 1992* (WA); *Personal Information and Protection Act 2004* (Tas); *Information Act 2002* (NT); *Information Privacy Act 2014* (ACT). It is also relevant to note that States and Territories have their own privacy regulators, such as the New South Wales Information and Privacy Commission and the Victorian Office of the Information Commissioner.

International dimensions

[6.140] The *Privacy Act* applies to entities established in jurisdictions other than Australia if the relevant APP entity has an "Australian link", as defined by s 5B(2) and (3) of the *Privacy Act*. For example, such a link is established if the relevant entity "carries on business in Australia". Moreover, from May 2018, Australian businesses of any size who have an establishment in the European Union or offer goods and services in the European Union need to comply with the data protection requirements in the European Union *General Data Protection Regulation* (*GDPR*).[67] While the *GDPR* and the Australian *Privacy Act* have a variety of common requirements, including a privacy by design approach to privacy protection, compliance with prescribed privacy principles and transparent information handling processes, there are also a variety of significant differences. Certain *GDPR* rights, such as the right to be forgotten, are not replicated in Australian privacy law. Hence, Australian businesses conducting business with entities in the European Union need to ensure that their personal data handling practices comply with the *GDPR*.

The Australian Privacy Principles

[6.150] Schedule 1 of the *Privacy Act* consists of 13 APPs,[68] and it is useful to consider each in some detail.

Open and transparent management of personal information: Critical to the obligations created by the *Privacy Act* is APP 1 which mandates the open and transparent management of personal information. Clause 1.2 stipulates that an:

> APP entity must take such steps as are reasonable in the circumstances to implement practices, procedures and systems relating to the entity's functions or activities that:
>
> (a) will ensure that the entity complies with the Australian Privacy Principles and a registered APP code (if any) that binds the entity; and
> (b) will enable the entity to deal with inquiries or complaints from individuals about the entity's compliance with the Australian Privacy Principles or such a code.

67 *Regulation (EU) 2016/679 of the European Parliament and of the Council of 27 April 2016 on the Protection of Natural Persons with Regard to the Processing of Personal Data and on the Free Movement of Such Data, and Repealing Directive 95/46/EC (General Data Protection Regulation)* [2016] OJ L 119/1, 1–88.

68 The APPs are available at <https://www.oaic.gov.au/privacy/australian-privacy-principles>.

Clause 1.3 further requires an APP entity to have a clearly expressed and up to date policy, termed the "APP privacy policy", that articulates policies for the management of personal information. Pursuant to cl 1.4, and without limiting the generality of cl 1.3, such an APP privacy policy of the APP entity must contain information as to:

(a) the kinds of personal information that the entity collects and holds;
(b) how the entity collects and holds personal information;
(c) the purposes for which the entity collects, holds, uses and discloses personal information;
(d) how an individual may access personal information about the individual that is held by the entity and seek the correction of such information;
(e) how an individual may complain about a breach of the Australian Privacy Principles, or a registered APP code (if any) that binds the entity, and how the entity will deal with such a complaint;
(f) whether the entity is likely to disclose personal information to overseas recipients;
(g) if the entity is likely to disclose personal information to overseas recipients – the countries in which such recipients are likely to be located if it is practicable to specify those countries in the policy.

The APP entity must further take reasonable steps to make the privacy policy available free of charge and in such form as is appropriate, including publishing the policy on its website.[69]

Anonymity and pseudonymity: APP 2 imposes obligations as to anonymity and pseudonymity. Pursuant to cl 2.2, when dealing with APP entities, individuals must be provided with an option of not identifying themselves, or of using a pseudonym. However, this wide obligation is constrained by the exceptions outlined in cl 2.2. Such exceptions include where:

(a) the APP entity is required or authorised by or under an Australian law, or a court/tribunal order, to deal with individuals who have identified themselves; or
(b) it is impracticable for the APP entity to deal with individuals who have not identified themselves or who have used a pseudonym.

Collection of personal information: Building on APPs 1 and 2, APPs 3 and 4 focus on the maintenance of privacy during the process of collecting personal information. Importantly, the governance of solicited personal information is dealt separately from the governance of unsolicited personal information. If an APP entity is an agency, the entity must not collect personal information (other than sensitive information) unless the information is reasonably necessary for, or directly related to, one or more of the entity's functions or activities.

69 *Privacy Act 1988* (Cth), [1.5].

Clause 3.2 further stipulates that if an APP entity is an organisation, the entity must not collect personal information (other than sensitive information) unless the information is reasonably necessary for one or more of the entity's functions or activities.

Importantly, cll 3.1 and 3.2 do not apply to sensitive information. "Sensitive information" is defined by s 6 to include information or an opinion about an individual's racial or ethnic origin, political opinions, political affiliations, religious beliefs or affiliations, sexual orientation or practices, philosophical beliefs and membership of a professional or trade association or trade union. Health information, genetic information, biometric information and criminal records are also deemed to be sensitive information. If the entity is an agency, such information must be reasonably necessary for or directly related to the entity's functions or activities. If the entity is an organisation, such information must be reasonably necessary for or related to the entity's functions or activities. Grounds of exception for the collection of sensitive information in certain prescribed circumstances is provided in cl 3.4, including where the information is required or authorised under Australian law, the APP entity is an organisation and a permitted health situation[70] exists in relation to the collection of information, the APP entity is an enforcement body, the entity is the Immigration Department and the information is reasonably necessary for enforcement related activities, the APP entity is a non-profit organisation and the information relates to the activities or members of the organisation.

The means of collection of such personal information is governed by cll 3.5 and 3.6. Clause 3.5 stipulating that APP entities must collect personal information only by lawful and fair means. Clause 3.6 further stipulates that APP entities must collect personal information about an individual only from the individual. A variety of exceptions are enumerated in cl 3.6. If it is unreasonable or impracticable to do so, then an APP entity may collect personal information about an individual from someone other than the individual. In contrast, if the entity is an APP agency and the individual consents to the collection of the information from someone other than the individual, then the agency may collect personal information about an individual from someone other than the individual. Further, if the entity is required or authorised by or under an Australian law, or a court/tribunal order, to collect the information from someone other than the individual, they may collect personal information about an individual from someone other than the individual.

70 "Permitted general situation" – see s 16A; "Permitted health situation" – see s 16B.

The collection of unsolicited personal information, being the situation where an APP entity receives personal information which they did not solicit, is separately governed by APP 4. In such a circumstance, the APP entity is required, within a reasonable period after receiving the information, to determine whether the entity could have lawfully collected such information under APP 3 relating to solicited the information. If the APP entity determines that it could have lawfully collected the unsolicited personal information, it is required to destroy such information or ensure that it is de-identified. Such actions must be taken as soon as is practicable to do so. An exception is made, under cl 4.3, if it is not lawful and reasonable to do so. In contrast, if the APP entity determines that it could have lawfully collected the unsolicited personal information, it is required to comply with APPs 5–13 with respect to the information in the same way as if the entity had collected the information under APP 3.

Notification: APP 5 imposes obligations in relation to the notification of the collection of personal information. As soon as practicable after the collection of personal information, an APP entity is required to take reasonable steps in the circumstances to notify the relevant individual of the identity and contact details of the APP entity or otherwise make them aware of these matters.

Additionally, the APP entity is required to notify the individual of the purposes for which it has collected the personal information and the primary consequences for the individual if the APP entity fails to collect all or some of the personal information. Further the individual must be notified by the APP entity of any other parties to which the APP entity usually discloses such personal information. In circumstances where the entity has collected the information from a third party and the individual may not be aware of the collection of such information, the entity is required to notify of the collection and the circumstances of that collection. Where the collecting entity is likely to disclose such personal information to an overseas party, the entity is required to notify of this matter and inform the individual of the countries where such overseas parties are located. The nature and ambit of APP 5 was considered by the Privacy Commissioner in *Tenants' Union of Queensland Inc, Tenants' Union of NSW Co-op Ltd v TICA Default Tenancy Control Pty Ltd*.[71] In that instance, the Privacy Commissioner held that "if an organisation provides the information required to meet its obligations on different forms or in different locations it would generally need to alert individuals to the fact the other information was

71 *Tenants Unions v TICA (Complaint Determinations 1-4 of 2004)*, Privacy Commissioner ACD 4 (16 April 2004).

available ... it should [also] seek to ensure that there are appropriate references to that information in the primary form".[72]

Use and disclosure of personal information: Central to the regulatory framework created by the *Privacy Act* is APP 6 on the use or disclosure of personal information. In this regard, cl 6.1 stipulates that if an APP entity "holds personal information about an individual that was collected for a particular purpose (the primary purpose), the entity must not use or disclose the information for another purpose (the secondary purpose)". This obligation is subject to two enumerated exceptions. First, the cl 6.1 obligation does not apply in circumstances where the individual has consented to the use or disclosure of the information. Second, the cl 6.1 obligation does not apply if the individual would reasonably expect the APP entity to use or disclose the information for the secondary purpose and the secondary purpose related to the primary purpose. If the information in question is sensitive information, the information must be "directly" related to the primary purpose. If the information does not constitute sensitive information, it is sufficient that it merely "related" to the primary purpose. Additional exceptions to cl 6.1 include if the use or disclosure of the information is authorised by an Australian law or if the APP entity reasonably believes that the disclosure is reasonably necessary for enforcement related activities by an enforcement body.

Direct marketing: APP 7 governs the use of personal information in direct marketing. Clause 7.1 stipulates that if an organisation holds personal information about an individual, the organisation must not use or disclose the information for the purpose of direct marketing. However, pursuant to cl 7.2, such use and disclosure may be permitted if the individual would reasonably expect the organisation to use or disclose the information for that purpose, and the organisation provides a simple means by which the individual may easily request not to receive direct marketing communications from the organisation, and the individual has not made such a request to the organisation.

Cross-border disclosure of personal information: Beyond the general use and disclosure obligations imposed by APP 6, the cross-border disclosure of personal information is governed by APP 8. Pursuant to cl 8.1, prior to an APP entity disclosing personal information about an individual to an overseas third party (termed the overseas recipient), the entity is required to take reasonable in the circumstances to ensure that the overseas recipient upholds APPs 2–13, with respect to such information. In this situation, any act done by the overseas

72 *Tenants Unions v TICA (Complaint Determinations 1-4 of 2004)*, Privacy Commissioner ACD 4 (16 April 2004) [80], [82]. See also Explanatory Memorandum, *Privacy Amendment (Enhancing Privacy Protection) Bill 2012* (Cth) 83.

recipient is deemed to have been done by the APP entity. However, this provision does not apply if the APP entity reasonably believes that the overseas recipient is subject to a law that "has the effect of protecting the information in a way that, overall, is at least substantially similar to the way in which the *Australian Privacy Principles* protect the information" (cl 8.2). Additionally, the APP entity must reasonably believe that "there are mechanisms that the individual can access to take action to enforce that protection of the law or binding scheme" (cl 8.2). Alternatively, if the individual expressly consents to the disclosure of personal information to the overseas recipient, cl 8.1 will not apply. An exception to cl 8.1 also arises where the disclosure of the information is required or authorised under an Australian law, a permitted general situation, where the APP entity is an agency and the disclosure of the information is required or authorised under an international agreement relating to information sharing to which Australia is a party. An exception also exists if the entity is an agency who reasonably believes that the disclosure of the information is reasonably necessary for enforcement activities.

The use of government related identifiers: APP 9 creates a regulatory framework for the adoption, use and disclosure of government related identifiers.

Maintaining the quality and security of personal information: Privacy Principle 10 imposes obligations on APP entities to maintain the quality of personal information. Pursuant to cl 10.1, an APP entity must take such steps as are reasonable in the circumstances to ensure that the personal information that the entity collects is "accurate, up-to-date and complete". Central to the data privacy regime is APP 11 which imposes obligations on entities to take reasonable steps to support the "security" of personal information. Principle 11 requires entities to adopt "such steps as are reasonable in the circumstances" in order to secure personal information from misuse, interference, loss and unauthorised access, modification or disclosure. In this regard, Moens argues that multi-factor authentication forms a "reasonable step to take to secure personal information" and that failure to do would constitute an infringement of the *Privacy Act*.[73]

Access to personal information: APP 12 creates a regulatory framework for accessing personal information stored with an APP entity. Subject to the exceptions created in cll 12.2 and 12.3, cl 12.1 an APP entity which holds personal information about an individual, must, on request by an individual, give the individual access to the information.[74]

---

73 Moens, n 18, 56. In support of her view, Moens reproduces an exchange between the Australian Information and Privacy Commissioner and Senators in the course of the 22 October 2018 Senate Estimates hearings, pp 56–57.

74 *Privacy Act 1988* (Cth), Sch 1 cl 12.1.

Correction of personal information: Finally, APP 13 imposes duties on APP entities in relation to the correction and updating of personal information to support the accuracy and reliability of information held.

Evolving law reform discourse

[6.160] As discussed, developing effective data privacy laws is an ongoing process that is characterised by successive waves of law reform. In October 2021, the Australian Attorney-General's Office introduced an Exposure Draft of the *Privacy Legislative Amendment (Online Privacy and Other Measures) Bill*. If enacted, the legislation would create a mandatory *Online Privacy Code* governing the activities of social media services, data brokers and digital online platforms operating in Australia.

Notifiable Data Breaches Regulation

Rationale and ambit of operation

[6.170] Part IIIC of the *Privacy Act* makes it compulsory for organisations to notify affected individuals if they suspect or know of the occurrence of a data breach. A IBM study called "What Is Big Data?" estimates that the amount of data generated worldwide in 2002 (5 billion GB) is presently being created approximately every two days.[75] In its report entitled "Data Availability and Use", the Australian Productivity Commission noted the prevalence of big data in modern society, and noted that it is characterised by high volume, high velocity and high variety (ie, a high level of diversity in the sources from which the data is collected and the formats in which the data is presented).[76] These features make modern databases vulnerable to attack. Further, a variety of studies have found that breaches of data security are increasing in both magnitude and frequency. The *Telstra Cyber Security Report* found that an IT security breach had been experienced by approximately a quarter of Australian businesses in the previous 12 months, with 60% having experienced a data breach in the preceding five years.[77] Moreover, while the threat of data breach is escalating, there is evidence to suggest that a significant proportion of organisations have not invested in adequate measures to

---

75 IBM, "What Is Big Data?" <https://developer.ibm.com/blogs/what-is-big-data-more-than-volume-velocity-and-variety/>.

76 Australian Productivity Commission, *Data Availability and Use* (Report, November 2016). The final report was handed to the Australian Government on 31 March 2017 and publicly released on 8 May 2017 (draft report in 2016).

77 Telstra Corporation Limited, *Telstra Cyber Security Report* (Report, 2014).

protect themselves from cyberattacks. The *Telstra Cyber Security Report* found that 36% of organisations were inadequately prepared for a cybersecurity incident. In such a context, a strong public policy case can be advanced for such laws. Smyth, for example, argues that data breach notification laws can "minimise the economic loses that flows from an unauthorised access to personal information".[78] She notes that in order to avoid the negative publicity necessarily generated by a public data breach notification, organisations can be motivated to strengthen their information security practices. In its report *For Your Information: Australian Privacy Law and Practice*, the Australian Law Reform Commission notes that such laws can reduce identity theft an identity fraud.[79]

What constitutes an "eligible data breach"?

[6.180] An eligible data breach occurs if: (a) there is unauthorised access to, unauthorised disclosure of, or loss of, personal information held by an entity; and (b) a reasonable person would conclude that the access or disclosure would be likely to result in serious harm to any of the individuals to whom the information relates.[80] If an entity is aware that there are *reasonable* grounds to believe that there has been an eligible data breach, they must provide a statement to the Information Commissioner as soon as practicable after the entity becomes so aware.

The nature and ambit of the notification requirement

[6.190] The statement must set out a description of the eligible data breach that the entity has reasonable grounds to believe has happened, the kind or kinds of information concerned and recommendations about the steps that individuals should take in response to the eligible data breach that the entity has reasonable grounds to believe has happened. The Act outlines two distinct categories of parties to be notified. However, unlike the absolute duty to notify the Commissioner, this obligation to notify affected parties is contingent upon notification being practicable. The first category is individuals to whom the

---

78 S Smyth, "Does Australia Really Need Mandatory Data Breach Notification Laws – And If So, What Kind?" (2012) 22(2) *Journal of Law, Information & Science* 159; see also earlier discussion in S Smyth and J Winn, "Are Better Security Breach Notification Laws Possible?" (2009) 24(3) *Berkley Technology Law Journal* 1133.

79 Australian Law Reform Commission, *For Your Information: Australian Privacy Law and Practice* (Report 108, 2008).

80 See further N Selvadurai, N Kisswani and Y Khalaileh, "Strengthening Data Privacy: The Obligation of Organisations to Notify Affected Individuals of Data Breaches" (2019) 33(3) *International Review of Law, Computers & Technology* 271, 277.

information relates. The second category is individuals who "are at risk from the eligible data breach". No elaboration is provided in legislation as to what is meant by "if it is practicable". While this limitation has been defended on the basis that it reduces the burden of regulatory compliance, the inclusion of this phrase significantly weakens the law as organisations could potentially present compelling cost concerns and commercial efficiency considerations to escape the notification obligation. If it is practicable to do so, the APP entity must publish a copy of the statement on the entity's website (if any) and take "reasonable steps" to publicise the contents of the statement. Again, the addition of the words "reasonable steps" weakens the notification obligation. It could, for example, enable party to publish a notice in an industry publication with a small circulation and argue that it is reasonable in the circumstances.

Likely to result in serious harm

[6.200] The *Privacy Act* outlines the relevant considerations to be taken into account when determining whether a reasonable person would conclude that the data breach would be "likely to result in serious harm". Relevant factors to be taken into considerations include the kind or kinds of information that may or have been accessed, the sensitivity of the information and the likely nature of the harm.[81]

Relevance of the level of security and encryption

[6.210] Significantly, it is also necessary to consider the security technology or methodology which was used in relation to the information and the extent to which it was designed to make the information unintelligible or meaningless to unauthorised persons. The extent to which the chosen technology or methodology could be circumvented is also deemed a relevant consideration. This embedding of security measures within the regulatory scheme is highly useful and forms a significant incentive for organisations to implement and maintain effective encryption and security measures to protect personal data. The ability to avoid bad publicity by implementing appropriate security measures can form a powerful reason to invest in security and help minimise data breaches.

Third parties

[6.220] An important question that arises is what happens if the access, disclosure or loss that constituted the data breach of the organisation is also a data breach of one or more *other* entities? For example, what happen if the

81 See further Selvadurai, Kisswani and Khalaileh, n 80, 278–279.

organisation experiencing the data breach has data sharing arrangement with related companies or uses a cloud service provider. In such a context the legislation stipulates that the primary organisation is not responsible for the data breaches of those other entities, effectively limiting the organisations obligations to matters within its direct control.

Conclusion

[6.230] The *Privacy Act* imposes civil penalties on organisations who fail to comply with the notification obligations in cases of serious or repeated interference with privacy.[82] The Australian Information Commissioner can also impose enforceable undertakings[83] and the Federal Court can issue injunctions[84] to uphold the provisions of the *Privacy Act*. Despite these provisions, there is ongoing discussion of the need to strengthen the enforcement framework of the *Privacy Act*.[85]

In our current society, where the online environment is becoming the norm for both work and leisure, it is imperative that privacy laws remain effective and evolve to address new technological threats to data privacy.

82 *Privacy Act 1988* (Cth), s 80U.

83 *Privacy Act 1988* (Cth), s 80V.

84 *Privacy Act 1988* (Cth), s 80W.

85 See further G Greenleaf, "Privacy Enforcement in Australia Is Strengthened: Gaps Remain" (2014) 128 *Privacy Laws & Business International Report* 1.

Chapter 7
Social Media and Social Influences

Melissa de Zwart*

Introduction

[7.10] The COVID-19 pandemic brought into stark relief the complicated evolution of social media, from its role in bringing joy to millions confined in their houses, by presenting us with mood-lifting celebrity videos on "how to make your own lockdown sour dough"[1] to the facilitation of a raid on the US Capitol building by Trump supporters in early 2021.[2] If Mark Zuckerberg thought he had a difficult year in 2018 when the Cambridge Analytica furore broke, 2020 was certainly worse. Recent months have also witnessed the banning of (then) President Trump first from Twitter, which has long been his communication medium of choice, even prior to the 2016 election, and then his consequent banning from a cascading number of other social media platforms.[3]

What then is the legacy of social media at the beginning of this new decade and how has it evolved from its early beginnings as a mechanism to bring friends together and share news updates? The nature of social media platforms themselves has evolved radically from the early days of MySpace and Facebook and their role in shaping social and political beliefs as well as discourse has been revealed via a number of scandals. And yet, the use of social media as a daily communication tool has not diminished. Social media has become an addictive and powerful source of propaganda, as well as a banal platform for

---

* Professor (Digital Technology, Security & Governance), Jeff Bleich Centre for the US Alliance in Digital Technology, Security & Governance, Flinders University, Adelaide, South Australia.

1 Facebook, "The Great Kiwi Lockdown Sourdough Bakeoff" (2020) <https://www.facebook.com/groups/877136139391060/>.

2 E Dwoskin, "Facebook's Sandberg Deflected Blame for Capitol Riot, but New Evidence Shows How Platform Played Role", *The Washington Post* (14 January 2021) <https://www.washingtonpost.com/technology/2021/01/13/facebook-role-in-capitol-protest/>.

3 E Douek, "Trump Is Banned. Who Is Next?", *The Atlantic* (10 January 2021) <https://www.theatlantic.com/ideas/archive/2021/01/trump-is-banned-who-is-next/617622/>.

the co-ordination of local sporting and community groups, social functions, fundraising and personal highlights and lowlights. It is a mega-billion dollar advertising platform which has radically changed and challenged mainstream media and it is an unaccountable private industry which is remaining recalcitrant to attempts to regulate and control it.

This chapter will briefly outline what the key characteristics of social media are and then outline and analyse a number of milestones which have caused us to revaluate our relationship with social media. In particular, it will address the following issues which have given rise to some specific regulatory responses and which, as we will see, are all inherently connected:

- user-generated content and social influencers;
- content regulation; and
- disinformation and fake news.

This chapter cannot be a complete examination of all of the legal issues to which social media has given rise, as we are only at the beginning of understanding the profound changes which social media platforms have wrought to how we receive and understand news and content. What we are beginning to understand however is that some regulation has now become necessary as the millennial child of the internet has grown up to be a troublesome and problematic influence on society. Indeed, as the developments of the last five years have demonstrated there are real questions regarding the use and misuse of social media platforms in a democratic system and whether their lack of transparency and facilitation of echo chambers make them a threat to open democracy.

This chapter will conclude that lessons learned from the interrogations of Facebook's practices over the last few years point towards the need to review decisions taken regarding regulation in the early days of the internet. They also point to the need to understand changes in society itself, and the way it interacts with its online manifestation. Documentaries such as Netflix's expose *The Social Dilemma*,[4] have brought to our attention the fact that such platforms are not neutral, that they do not simply host our content and present the feeds of our friends in a consistent way, but rather they curate, promote and exploit that content to capture our attention and keep us coming back for more, with our attention being a product for sale to the highest bidder.

4 *The Social Dilemma* (Directed by Jeff Orlowski, Netflix, 2020) <https://www.netflix.com/au/title/81254224>.

What is Social Media?

[7.20] "Social media" is a term encompassing a range of platforms and practices which have evolved from the narrower concept of "social networking", a practice facilitated through social network sites, such as Facebook and Instagram. The classic definition of a social network site was provided by boyd and Ellison in 2007:

> ... web-based services that allow individuals to (1) construct a public or semi-public profile within a bounded system, (2) articulate a list of other users with whom they share a connection, and (3) view and traverse their list of connections and those made by others within the system.[5]

This definition suggests that the key activity facilitated by these sites is indeed social networking: the making, sharing and expanding of contacts. As anyone who has watched the movie *The Social Network* would know, Facebook was created as a means for Harvard students to connect up.[6] This same story is told from another perspective by Zadie Smith, who explores the question of the nature, value and depth of such "connections", questions which continue to plague our relationship with social media.[7] From there the service rapidly expanded out to other users, and grew as a platform for providing news, messaging and even as a portal to the broader internet itself.[8] Since that time, the platform has continued to evolve.[9] Writing in a later piece, boyd identified that the affordances provided by online social networks create a unique form of networked publics. The very attributes of the platforms themselves "reorganise how information flows and how people interact with information and each other".[10] She identified the four key features which created the conditions for social networks to act as networked publics: profiles, friends'

5 d boyd and N Ellison, "Social Network Sites: Definition, History, and Scholarship" (2007) 13 *Journal of Computer-Mediated Communication* 210, 211.

6 *The Social Network* (Directed by David Fincher, Columbia Pictures, 2010).

7 Z Smith, "Generation Why?", *The New York Review of Books* (25 November 2010) <https://www.nybooks.com/articles/2010/11/25/generation-why/>.

8 N Thompson and F Vogelstein, "Inside the Two Years that Shook Facebook – And the World", *Wired* (12 February 2018) <https://www.wired.com/story/inside-facebook-mark-zuckerberg-2-years-of-hell/?utm_source=onsite-share&utm_medium=email&utm_campaign=onsite-share&utm_brand=wired>.

9 I Lapowsky, "15 Moments that Defined Facebook's First 15 Years", *Wired* (4 February 2019) <https://www.wired.com/story/facebook-15-defining-moments/>.

10 d boyd, "Social Network Sites as Networked Publics: Affordances, Dynamics and Implications" in Z Papacharissi (ed), *A Networked Self-Identity, Community and Culture on Social Network Sites* (Routledge, New York, 2011) 41.

lists, public commenting tools and stream-based updates.[11] While the precise nature and manifestation of these features of social media vary across the different platforms and have evolved across the years, it is these very features which have also created distortions and dangers within those networked publics. Importantly, boyd reinforced the concept that the very specific digital architecture of an online platform is itself the environment that shapes and determines how people will behave and interact within that space.[12] In other words, the rules and features of the online platform, what may be uploaded, how it is accessed and seen, the rules of attribution and interaction, all determine the shape of user engagement. These architectural or coded rules take the place of the laws of that space.

One of the most obvious concepts which is shaped by those rules is privacy. As Smith and others have recounted, Zuckerberg's own drive to use Facebook as a tool for connection, results in software and platform design choices that create "weak, superficial connections" and deprioritise privacy.[13] These design choices in turn have created new issues for regulators and society at large, creating scope for cyberbullying, surveillance, identity theft and the issues discussed below.

Facebook was not the first social media platform. As Facebook was preceded by the now unknown MySpace, the appeal of Facebook is largely being resisted by Generation Z, who prefer briefer, faster and more transient media via Snapchat, Instagram, WhatsApp and TikTok. However, some of the fundamentals remain the same. The development of the ubiquitous smart phone created a platform shift for access to and use of social media. While Facebook, Twitter and other platforms started off as web-based platforms, they have now almost entirely migrated to apps. The embedding of social media in a portable device with a built-in camera facilitated a turn to image sharing, encouraging a shift from "how am I feeling?" to "how am I looking?" Like most internet businesses it has adapted and grown over the years in response to threats and opportunities. As internet speeds increased, users had moved from PC platforms to smart phones, and as connectivity become cheaper and more ubiquitous, Facebook has moved from text-based interface, to highly graphic, including full video, and acquiring a number of other

---

11 boyd, n 10, 43.

12 boyd, n 10, 42, citing the earlier work of N Negroponte, *Being Digital* (Vintage Books, New York, 1995); L Lessig, *Code 2.0* (Basic Books, New York, 2006); W J Mitchell, *City of Bits, Space, Place and the Infobahn* (MIT Press, Cambridge, MA, 1995); J Grimmelmann, "Regulation by Software" (2005) 114 *Yale Law Journal* 1719.

13 Smith, n 7.

platforms along the way, including Instagram and WhatsApp. Users became creators of content, making them both consumers and producers of culture, in turn to be consumed by others for the benefit of the platform owner.[14] It also created an "always on" sense of being able to share content at all hours of the day. Suddenly, platform owners had at their disposal a vast community of users, who not only provided content for monetisation via advertising, but who were also generating highly accurate databases of user activities, location, profiles and preferences. These databases have created new opportunities for marketers, scammers, political parties, governments and influencers, as well as the social media platforms themselves. They can be accessed and manipulated with sophisticated and highly targeted marketing as well as the more ambivalent and unpredictable use of algorithms.

Fundamentally therefore, social media still involves the connection and sharing of content between lists of contacts, as well as increasingly content curated for you by an algorithm built upon your expressed and implicit preferences. The constantly refreshed feed consists of content, which is predominantly "user-generated content" although in recent years increasingly this has been reposts of news and other stories, and the capacity to "like" and further share such content with a single click.

Facebook is a private platform, participation in which may only be achieved by agreeing to the Terms of Service and other policies by clicking through and accepting the relevant provisions. These Terms of Service are amended from time to time, and users are sent reminders to review and update their privacy settings. In theory, users can decide if they want to use the platform and consent to those Terms of Service which provide the default rules and standards of the platform. In other word, Facebook is a contractual community which can set and enforce its own rules and any dissatisfied member can then opt-out via exit from the platform. However, increasingly community organisations, groups, schools, businesses and individuals are using Facebook

---

14 S Hinton and L Hjorth, *Understanding Social Media* (Sage Publications, London, 2013) 2, citing the work of H Jenkins, *Convergence Culture* (NYU Press, New York, 2006); A Bruns, "Produsage: Towards a Broader Framework for User-Led Content Creation" in B Schneiderman (ed), *Proceedings of the 6th ACM SIGHI Conference on Creativity and Cognition* (Association for Computing Machinery, United States, 2007) 99–105; M Andrejevic, "Social Network Exploitation" in Z Papacharissi (ed), *A Networked Self-Identity, Community and Culture on Social Network Sites* (Routledge, New York, 2011). In this, there is discussion of the role of participatory culture, where users both create and consume content, repackaging it in such a way as to express their own identity. This free labour is in turn exploited by the platform owners who use the attention garnered by such content to sell advertising associated with such "user-generated" content, shifting the labour from the platform provider to the users.

as their default method of communication. If you are not on Facebook you run the risk of being left out of a range of activities, markets and updates.

Mark Zuckerberg repeatedly asserts that Facebook is a community and one which should be responsive to community interests.[15] Globally, as at March 2021, there are 2.8 billion registered users of Facebook. Instagram users number 1 billion, Twitter 187 million, Snapchat 265 million, TikTok 100 million and LinkedIn 738 million.[16] How do you agree "community standards" among this many people, people who are likely to have a broad diversity of interests and opinions, let alone cultural backgrounds, living conditions and demographics? Despite the rhetoric, these community standards are not consensual but are developed and enforced by Facebook and determined in order to satisfy commercial rather than individual interests. As a private platform it is not governed by the requirements of the US First Amendment law which requires that Congress "shall make no law … abridging the freedom of speech, or of the press". It may enforce its own standards of communication and speech as it sees fit and yet, by its own admission, it is a powerful platform with global reach.

Social media platforms have largely resisted regulatory intervention on the basis that it would be impossible for them to monitor and pre-approve content, due to the sheer volume of content being uploaded at any one time. This autonomy was created by s 230 of the *Communications Decency Act* (US),[17] which provides: "No provider or user of an interactive computer service shall be treated as the publisher or speaker of any information provided by another information content provider."[18] Unlike traditional media providers who are accountable for the content that they publish, whether it is obscene, defamatory, hate speech or infringing, user-generated content platforms, including social media, have thus largely avoided liability with respect to content posted by their users. Similar immunity exists in the United States with respect to copyright on the basis of the "notice and take down" regime which limits liability of service providers to removal of content in response to notification of infringement.[19] These laws require the platform provider to investigate

15 Thompson and Vogelstein, n 8.

16 B Barnhart, "Social Media Demographics to Inform Your Brand's Strategy in 2021", *Sprout Social* (9 March 2021) <https://sproutsocial.com/insights/new-social-media-demographics/>.

17 *Communications Decency Act*, 47 USC § 230 (1996).

18 For a discussion of the sweeping effects of 47 USC § 230 (1996), see M A Franks, "How the Internet Unmakes Law" (2020) 16(1) *Ohio State Law Journal* 10.

19 *Digital Millennium Copyright Act*, 17 USC § 512 (1998).

content only following a notification or flag that the content is infringing, obscene, defamatory or otherwise unsuitable. The Australian copyright "safe harbour" provisions are considerably narrower than the US equivalents and apply to carriage service providers.[20] The Australian equivalent with respect to harmful content is found in Schs 5 and 7 of the *Broadcasting Services Act 1992* (Cth).[21]

The "safe harbour" laws have required action to be taken in response to the "flagging" of content, however the actual rules and practices surrounding removal of content have remained opaque and are certainly not standard across platforms. The very practice of "flagging" of content has evolved into a specialist practice of its own, with various methodologies used on different platforms. Users are given various options to vote, like, unlike and report content, with very little clarity or accountability regarding these practices. Users can report and block content for a variety of reasons, ranging from the simple fact that they disagree with it, to the belief that it is offensive or illegal. Many users report that they simply do not understand why their content has been removed or their accounts blocked and there is little redress in the event that they believe that they have been wrongly treated by such actions. And yet, these practices can have significant impact on users' ability to express themselves, to communicate and participate in civil society. Due to the realisation that much of the material now appearing on social media is "fake news" there is increasing pressure to block and remove such content. However, even the recent decision to "de-platform" Donald Trump was not met with enthusiasm. Commentators have observed that that the power to remove the former President from various social media platforms is one that may be exercised with respect to any user for any reason. While it may appear that these decisions may be taken to avoid insurrection and protection of public safety, they can also be viewed as arbitrary and made for political and commercial reasons.[22]

User-Generated Content and Social Influencers

[7.30] As is well known, unlike other traditional media outlets which must pay journalists and others to create the content they distribute, platforms such as Facebook, YouTube, Twitter and Instagram provide a platform upon which users can upload content. Relying upon the laws enacted in the early years

20 *Copyright Act 1968* (Cth), Pt V Div 2AA; see also *Copyright Act 1968* (Cth), s 115A.

21 *Broadcasting Services Act 1992* (Cth).

22 Douek, n 3.

of the Internet to encourage the development of e-commerce and internet service providers, the "safe harbour" business model evolved whereby internet platforms were classified as distributors or hosts of third-party content rather than publishers of that content. This means that while users can – and frequently do – upload their own original creative content, it has also manifested in a "copy and paste" culture, where users feel at liberty to simply repost third party and other people's content without permission.[23]

The "always on show" capability of combining a camera with social media has resulted in a number of new facets for media platforms, the emergence of the "influencer" and the blurring of work and private lives, with *Insta-famous* personalities creating a visual smorgasbord of beautiful breakfasts, perfect workouts and contented families.[24]

Instagram first entered the "applications" market in October 2010, initially requiring nothing more than posting an image. In 2016, the platform expanded to include daily "stories", consisting of several updates from users across the day, and videos, facilitating expanded amounts of content delivery. Users can scroll through a rapidly updated timeline of posts from people they follow, likely a mixture of friends, celebrities, and suggested content such as advertising. Being a largely visual medium, Instagram has naturally appealed to visual artists of all kinds, especially professional and amateur photographers, allowing immediate sharing of work with followers. It has, however, expanded to a vast range of content, including food, travel, clothing and fashion trends generally.

While offering a platform for sharing daily updates, Instagram is now increasingly used for marketing, including a significant cross-promotion with mainstream media. This has led to the emergence of a new group of social media marketers called "influencers".[25] These people are paid for advertising and product placement, able to charge fees according to numbers of followers. Akin to a lifestyle magazine, much of the content they post is ghosted by professional photographers reflecting hours of work, rather than the casual lifestyle portrayed. Like glossy magazines, these accounts suggest a glamorous and idealised lifestyle, reflecting an imagined persona rather than

---

23 M de Zwart, "Repost This: Instagram and the Art of Re-photography" in L Edwards, B Schafer and E Harbinja (eds), *Future Law: Emerging Technology, Regulation and Ethics* (Edinburgh University Press, 2020) 380.

24 For further analysis of the issues discussed in this section, see de Zwart, n 23.

25 M Chafkin, "Confessions of an Instagram Influencer", *Bloomberg Businessweek* (30 November 2016) <https://www.bloomberg.com/news/features/2016-11-30/confessions-of-an-instagram-influencer>.

a real person (ironically given the very common tag given on such accounts to attract followers #liveauthentic).[26] Images posted to the account link to daily "reels" on the account holders' story which may invite user interaction, such as liking and voting.

Clearly the key issue with this type of content is copyright. How do the users ensure that they have the right to post their chosen image and how is infringement dealt with by the platform? Again, in this regard platforms have chosen to take a hands-off response, allocating all of the responsibility for avoiding, reporting and dealing with potential copyright infringements to content posters, via the relevant terms of service. In accordance with the United States § 230 model outlined above, platforms claim merely to host the content, with no capacity to monitor or enforce infringement of copyright. There remains, of course, the fact that most platforms also claim an irrevocable, royalty-free right to use such content as is posted to their feed. Again, the social media model insulates the platform from liability while giving them the capacity to monetise their feed.

Content Regulation

[7.40] As noted above, with respect to copyright infringement social media and other internet platforms have resisted regulation on the basis that they are merely hosts, rather than publishers, of content. Therefore, not only should they not be held liable under laws related to defamation or obscenity because the sheer volume of such content is impossible to monitor or filter, but also that they should not pay for such content, as they are not responsible for the choice of posting (or more benignly "sharing") such content.

However, the attitude to this hands-off approach to regulation and responsibility has begun to change. This commenced with enhanced calls for regulation, monitoring and filtering of unsuitable, obscene or confronting content. Until recently there has been little transparency regarding how content is classified and reviewed, nor how decisions were made with respect to vetting, approving, blocking or removing content. What was known was that content review was a complex interplay between user feedback and reporting, monitoring by the platform, human review and intervention and the use of algorithms to detect and block certain content.[27] Importantly, it is clear that this is all done by a combination of computers and people (many of

26 Chafkin, n 25.

27 K Crawford and T Gillespie, "What Is a Flag for? Social Media Reporting Tools and the Vocabulary of Complaint" (2016) 18(3) *New Media & Society* 410, 411.

whom are outsourced workers remote from the linguistic and cultural context of the users, employed to do basic moderation according to a rule book).[28] Much depends upon the detection of predetermined "unsuitable content" by algorithms, programmed to identify certain words and phrases or images, what Google Chairman Eric Schmidt describes as "spell checkers ... for hate and harassment".[29] While it may seem more consistent and potentially objective to rely upon such algorithmic filters, it is also clear that despite this technological determinism, that a human decision-maker is still required, take for example, the furore over removal of images of breast feeding. Content is clearly context dependent.

In the face of increasing scrutiny of Facebook practices (largely relating to allegations of manipulation of US Election results in the wake of the Cambridge Analytica revelations which will be discussed below) it has undertaken to be more responsive and accountable. In April 2018, Facebook released its revised community standards, including internal guidelines for the application of those standards. At the same time, it announced that it would be seeking further input into those standards via "events" with users. This was a major reversal of policy as, until that point, Facebook's internal guidelines on content moderation and training material for moderators had been kept confidential, known only through leaks to the media. Such confidential documents were criticised for their lack of internal consistency as well as apparent lack of rigorous and impartial application. Practices allowed content to remain on Facebook (or not) dependent upon the identity of the speaker, for example, claims that "white people are racist" would be deleted while equivalent claims about other ethnic groups would be permitted.[30]

Facebook claims that its community standards are based on a recognition of three key principles: safety, voice and equity.[31] In particular, the community standards assert that "it is important for Facebook to be a place where people feel empowered to communicate" recognising the cultural diversity that

28 T Gillespie, "Don't Ignore Facebook's Silly-Sounding Policies", *Salon* (22 February 2012) <https://www.salon.com/2012/02/22/dont_ignore_facebooks_silly_sounding_policies/>; A Chen, "The Laborers Who Keep Dick Pics and Beheadings Out of Your Facebook Feed", *Wired* (23 October 2014) <https://www.wired.com/2014/10/content-moderation/>.

29 E Schmidt, "Eric Schmidt on How to Build a Better Web", *New York Times* (7 December 2015) <https://www.nytimes.com/2015/12/07/opinion/eric-schmidt-on-how-to-build-a-better-web.html>.

30 J Angwin and H Grassegger, "Facebook's Secret Censorship Rules Protect White Men from Hate Speech but Not Black Children", *Pro Publica* (28 June 2017) <https://www.propublica.org/article/facebook-hate-speech-censorship-internal-documents-algorithms>.

31 Facebook, *Community Standards* (2018) <https://www.facebook.com/communitystandards>.

exists within its massive user group. With respect to diversity, the overarching principles note that "at times we will allow content that might otherwise breach our standards if we feel that it is newsworthy, significant or important to the public interest". The categories identified in the community standards are violence and criminal behaviour, safety, objectionable content, integrity and authenticity, respecting intellectual property and content-related requests.[32] Each of these categories addresses a different category of user content and behaviour and the Standards provide overarching principles regarding how the Standards may be applied.

In response to concerns regarding Facebook's continuing hands-off approach to content moderation, a Civil Rights Audit was commenced in 2018, a project led by civil rights experts and lawyers Laura Murphy and Megan Cacace, with the support of Facebook. The Final Report of that Civil Rights Audit, issued in July 2020, expressed major concerns regarding the "particular definition of free expression" espoused by Zuckerberg and Facebook.[33] In particular, the Report noted, "the prioritization of free expression over all other values, such as equality and non-discrimination, is deeply troubling".[34] The Auditors focused especially on Zuckerberg's speech to Georgetown University in 2019 and three posts by President Trump in 2020, in the context of nationwide protests regarding police violence against the Black community. Including the notorious statement by Trump "when the looting starts, the shooting starts". It concludes that "Facebook has been far too reluctant to adopt strong rules to limit misinformation and voter suppression".[35] Facebook moved to create an Oversight Board in May 2020, with the purpose of providing greater authority to decisions made by the platform with respect to content. The Board is intended to provide independent and high level guidance regarding matters of freedom of expression and decisions to remove material.[36]

It should be noted that, following the public and political outcry regarding the streaming of the murderous attack on Christchurch Mosques in 2019 the Australian Governments passed laws to insert provisions in the *Criminal Code*

---

32 For further analysis of the issues discussed in this section, see M de Zwart, "Keeping the Neighbourhood Safe: How Does Social Media Moderation Control What We See (and Think)?" (2018) 43(4) *Alternative Law Journal* 283.

33 Facebook, "Facebook's Civil Rights Audit-Final Report" (8 July 2020) 9.

34 Facebook, n 33.

35 Facebook, n 33; M Isaac, "Facebook's Decisions Were 'Setbacks for Civil Rights' Audit Finds", *New York Times* (8 July 2020) <https://www.nytimes.com/2020/07/08/technology/facebook-civil-rights-audit.html>.

36 Facebook, *Oversight Board* (2021) <https://oversightboard.com/>.

Act 1995 (Cth) to require the "expeditious removal" of "abhorrent violent material" hosted by an online platform.[37] Abhorrent violent material is sound, images or other footage of conduct such as terrorism, murder, rape, torture and related material that in the circumstances would be regarded as offensive.[38]

Further to this concern regarding the hosting of unsuitable content and lack of accountability for hosted content, Facebook encountered increasing pressure from traditional news media regarding its role as a primary source of news. Mainstream publishers consider that Facebook threatens their future by capturing the majority of online advertising, much of it placed in conjunction with content produced by traditional media.[39] This dispute manifested in Facebook implementing a ban on all news content on its platform in Australia in February 2021. Rather than shaking up the news providers, Facebook found itself at odds with many facets of Australian society who suddenly found that their Facebook site had been shut down, including charities, not-for-profits and governments. The Australian Government has proposed the News Media and Digital Platforms Code, which would require Facebook and other "market-dominating" platforms, including Google, to negotiate revenue-sharing arrangements with the providers of the news displayed via their platform. In the face of political and public pressure the ban was reversed but there now remains a bad feeling within much of the Australian public that Facebook is less like a trusted community and more like a corporate behemoth.[40] It remains to be seen if this experience will drive more users to subscribe to news service providers to obtain their online updates or if Facebook will continue to be the easy "one stop shop" for users.

The Rise of Disinformation and Fake News

[7.50] As discussed above, social media relies upon networks of contacts. This particular feature of social media, which makes it the ideal platform to distribute news and updates among friends regarding births, deaths, successes, graduations, sporting timetables, bakesales, cute videos and marriages, also makes it useful for targeted marketing. It therefore also provides a useful breeding ground for the dissemination of news, both real and fake. The overwhelming amount of content, which is now available for consumption,

37 *Criminal Code Amendment (Sharing of Abhorrent Violent Material) Act 2019* (Cth).

38 *Criminal Code Amendment (Sharing of Abhorrent Violent Material) Act 2019* (Cth), ss 474.31, 474.32.

39 Thompson and Vogelstein, n 8.

40 J Slezak, "Facebook's Petty Unfriending of Australia", *Wired* (23 February 2021) <https://www.wired.com/story/opinion-facebooks-petty-unfriending-of-australia/>.

means that attention is in short supply. The platform of voluntarily sorted consumers provided by social media platforms make them a ready audience for advertisers. As Menczer and Hills explain: "We prefer information from people we trust, our in-group."[41] Further, it turns out, we are more likely to pay attention to and share negative information which confirms our pre-existing fears and biases. As information supply becomes overwhelming "we let our cognitive biases decide what we should pay attention to".[42] This sense of overwhelm, combined with the deployment of sophisticated algorithms, means that as we share more information, even further information repeating and confirming the same biases will be served to us, creating an ever-narrower "echo chamber" of opinion.[43]

While considered a somewhat benign aspect of social media the potential for this capacity to be weaponised was brought into stark relief initially by the Cambridge Analytica scandal and more recently, by activities such as the QAnon conspiracy movement.

In 2013 Dr Alexsander Kogan, a Cambridge Professor of Psychology, had developed an app offering users a personality quiz called "thisisyourdigitallife". That app was accessible via Facebook and was downloaded by some 300,000 users. Once downloaded it collected user activity, including "likes" and profile information. It was also configured to obtain the same information from the friends of those who had downloaded the app, which resulted in the collection of information from approximately 87 million people. The collected information was then passed from Kogan to Strategic Communications Laboratories, the owner of Cambridge Analytica, which used the data to target conservation political advertising campaigns, including the Trump 2016 Presidential campaign. While the collection of data from Facebook users and their friends was permitted by their consent to the terms of use, the transfer of that data to a third party was a breach of Facebook's Terms of Service. The use of this data was revealed by a whistleblower.[44] It remains unclear how effective

41 F Menczer and T Hills, "The Attention Economy" (2020) 323(6) *Scientific American* 54.

42 Menczer and Hills, n 41.

43 Y Yiu, "Visualizing Twitter Echo Chambers", *Inside Science* (18 March 2020) <https://www.insidescience.org/news/visualizing-twitter-echo-chambers>; M Conover et al, "Predicting the Political Alignment of Twitter Users" (Conference Paper, 2011 IEEE Third International Conference on Privacy, Security, Risk and Trust and 2011 IEEE Third International Conference on Social Computing, 9–11 October 2011) 192–199.

44 C Cadwalladr and E Graham-Harrison, "Revealed: 50 Million Facebook Profiles Harvested for Cambridge Analytica in Major Data Breach", *The Guardian* (18 March 2018) <https://www.theguardian.com/news/2018/mar/17/cambridge-analytica-facebook-influence-us-election>.

the strategies of Cambridge Analytica actually were in terms of influencing the election outcome, but it did bring to the public attention that, far from being benign, the simple and enjoyable tests, quizzes and games available via Facebook and other online platforms were highly effective at harvesting their user data. That data was willingly disclosed by the users in pursuit of entertainment, but little did they understand the value of that data to marketers and pollsters. While the consequence of the activities of Cambridge Analytica resulted in that entity being shut down, the potential for the weaponisation of social media data and the capacity to uses such data to influence political outcomes had been brought to the public attention. At this time, allegations of foreign interference in the election outcomes through the involvement of Russian troll farms and entities such as the Internet Research Agency in distributing news and propaganda through fake social media accounts began to surface. Again, the exact impact of these activities is difficult to measure, but the sheer volume of activities gives rise to concerns regarding the impact on democratic process.[45] The actions of Cambridge Analytica are believed to have impacted directly on the 2016 US Presidential Election and the Brexit Referendum.[46]

Following the Trump victory in the 2016 US Presidential Election, Zuckerberg was aware of allegations that fake news distributed via Facebook had been decisive in Trump's victory. Two days after the election Zuckerberg announced at a conference:

> The idea that fake news on Facebook – of which, you know, it's a very small amount of the content – influenced the election in any way, I think, is a pretty crazy idea.[47]

Yet, aware of continued allegations regarding the impact of fake news, Facebook moved to recruit external fact checkers. There remain concerns regarding what Facebook is prepared to do to address the vulnerabilities and exploits revealed by the Cambridge Analytica example.

More recently, concerns have focused on the online activities of QAnon, a far right conspiracy theory based around a central belief that that US is secretly run by a group of Satan-worshipping paedophiles, against whom former President Trump was undertaking a struggle to win America back to democracy. Q is said to be the deep state agent who is releasing information about the Satanist

---

45 N Thompson and I Lapowsky, "How Russian Trolls Used Meme Warfare to Divide America", *Wired* (17 December 2018) <https://www.wired.com/story/russia-ira-propaganda-senate-report/>.

46 Cadwalladr and Graham-Harrison, n 44.

47 Thompson and Vogelstein, n 8.

conspiracy. Various beliefs are associated with the movement, including anti-vaxxing and disbelief in the reality of COVID-19, however some of these beliefs have moved over from the domain of online rumour to near fatalities in real life. One such event was "Pizzagate" where the distribution via social media of an online meme that Hillary Clinton was operating a paedophile ring from the basement of a Washington DC pizza shop, resulted in a man driving from North Carolina to DC and entering the pizza bar armed with an AR-15 semiautomatic rifle, a .38 handgun and a folding knife, determined to free the children (who were of course not found in the restaurant nor in the non-existent basement at the centre of the rumours).[48] A similar example of the reposting of malicious messages on social media, which took place in the small town of Forks, best known for its role in the Twilight saga, almost resulted in the murder of a family passing through the town in a repurposed school bus.[49]

Facebook has now moved to block QAnon content and to ban groups and pages that self-identify with the QAnon movement.[50] However, as noted above, there is some concern that simple steps such as blocking and removing content does little to address the factors causing that content to be distributed in the first place. These examples are unlikely to be the last instances of the viral spread of fake news on social media nor of the manipulation of such stories by bad actors for their own advantage.

Conclusions

[7.60] Menczer and Hills remind us:

> Free communication is not free. By decreasing the cost of information, we have decreased its value and invited its adulteration. To restore the health of our information ecosystem, we must understand the vulnerabilities of our own overwhelmed minds and how the economics of information can be leveraged to protect us from being misled.[51]

48 A Robb, "Anatomy of a Fake News Scandal", *Rolling Stone* (16 November 2017) <https://www.rollingstone.com/feature/anatomy-of-a-fake-news-scandal-125877/>.

49 L Smiley, "The True Story of the Antifa Invasion of Forks, Washington", *Wired* (8 October 2020) <https://www.wired.com/story/antifa-social-media-rumor-forks-washington/>.

50 S Satterley, "Facebook Is Removing QAnon Pages and Groups from Its Sites, but Critical Thinking Is Still the Best Way to Fight Conspiracy Theories", *The Conversation* (8 October 2020) <https://theconversation.com/facebook-is-removing-qanon-pages-and-groups-from-its-sites-but-critical-thinking-is-still-the-best-way-to-fight-conspiracy-theories-147668>.

51 Menczer and Hills, n 41.

The brief overview of a range of examples of use of social media in this chapter should serve to highlight the pressing need for consideration of the role of social media as potentially the most influential communications medium of our time. This fact should be considered in stark opposition to the fact that, unlike every other preceding communications platform, social media platforms are subject to very little regulation. In fact, social media was born from a very deliberate choice to insulate such online platforms from regulation. It is time that this regulatory decision is revisited.

That review will need to be conducted in the knowledge that Facebook, as the largest of these services in the English-speaking world, has a population much larger than many nation states and that it has already proven to be quite resistant to regulatory oversight. As has been discussed above, a platform that so strongly reflects the personality of its creator, has taken on a great number of personality traits that make it impervious to greater scrutiny and accountability. It will require reform of national laws that impact the financial bottom line of social media platforms, such as the requirement to pay licensing fees for content to truly create an avenue for change.

While social media can be a wonderful platform for sharing connections with our friends, it also leaves us vulnerable to sharing our data with algorithms and people with less benign intent. In all the areas outlined above, from content creation and monetisation to the regulation of offensive content and the dissemination of fake news, more could be done to empower and educate the users of such platforms. If they are truly a community, then they need to be held to a higher standard of accountability to that community.

Chapter 8

Technologies and the Future

Heather Forrest and Mark Perry*

Laggardly Reputations, High Expectations, Cataclysmic Predictions

[8.10] Pivot. This was the buzzword of 2020.[1] It singly, crisply, concisely captures the zeitgeist of a year that rocked every corner of the globe – utterly and completely. It is fair to argue that if 2020 failed to provide the catalyst to at last bring the law and legal profession into the digital era, nothing ever would. Looking ahead to the future, then, is perhaps best initiated by first quickly looking backwards over the accomplishments of these first two decades of the 20th century and culminating in 2020. What were the predictions and expectations for law and technology as the new century approached? How many of these have been realised and how many remain unfulfilled, despite the urgencies of the global pandemic that came to be named SARS COVID-19? Have the law and legal profession at last embraced the digital era, and what does 2020 portend for the future of technology and the law?

The legal profession's reputation: "Tradition-bound and notoriously slow"

[8.20] Around 25 years ago an author wrote:

> Cyberjargon litters the media. It is virtually impossible to read a serial publication or watch a television news report without coming across some mention of computers and the Internet. Behind this media phenomenon is more than just a passing fad of Batmanesque proportions. On a micro scale, chips are ubiquitous and for the most part so commonplace that we do not even notice that we are using them. On the

* Heather Forrest is an Associate Professor in the School of Law at the University of Tasmania, Hobart, Tasmania; and Mark Perry is a Professor of Law in the School of Law at the University of New England, Armidale, New South Wales.

1 E Keller, "'Pivot' – 2020 Word of the Year" (20 May 2020) <https://www.linkedin.com/pulse/pivot-word-year-elaine-keller?articleId=6668913054329253888#:~:text=The%20word%20'pivot'%20has%20become,the%20end%20of%20the%20year>.

> macro scale there has been a transilience in the way that information is gathered, managed, processed and promulgated. ... The challenge for legal education is to use communications and information technologies to best advantage, and accommodate changes in the legal paradigm.[2]

The previous chapters of this book contribute to an enigmatic tale of the relationship between law, legal professionals and technology, but illustrate that despite the decades passing, and the huge societal changes, law and lawyering have not really kept pace. Each chapter evidences advances made in how we communicate and interact in commercial and non-commercial settings, how we approach legal rights acquisition and enforcement, and how technology facilitates this. Some may argue that these advances happened in spite of, rather than because of, the law and the professionals who work in and with it. Certainly, the internet's engineers were quite suspicious of the imposition of legal concepts upon their creation and did what they could to keep the lawyers at bay.[3]

Arguably, the intersections of law and technology have changed around lawyers, rather than through them, with assessments such as these quite commonplace: "At close to $1T globally, the legal services market is one of the largest in the world. At the same time, it remains profoundly underdigitised. For better or worse, the field of law is tradition-bound and notoriously slow to adopt new technologies and tools."[4] Such remarks perpetuate the lawyer-as-luddite[5] trope, failing to fully acknowledge the past, and perhaps in so doing, influencing the future of law and technology.

Few would be quick to highlight, for example, that the legal profession was an early adopter of database technologies: dial-up terminals were introduced into law libraries in the early 1970s.[6] The two major global legal database providers trace their surprisingly grass roots-type origins to this era,[7] LexisNexis

---

2 M Perry, "Creating Cyberlawyers – Net Dreams or Facing the Inevitable" (September 1997) *New Zealand Law Journal* 309.

3 See, for example, T Denton, "RE: [gnso-rn-wg] Comments on ICANN/IANA Reserved Names Reports", *ICANN* (28 February 2007) <http://forum.icann.org/lists/gnso-rn-wg/msg00169.html>. See generally, H A Forrest, *Protection of Geographic Names in International Law and Domain Name System* (Wolters Kluwer, 2nd ed, 2017) 13–14.

4 R Toews, "AI Will Transform the Field of Law" (19 December 2019) <https://www.forbes.com/sites/robtoews/2019/12/19/ai-will-transform-the-field-of-law/?sh=7a40321f7f01>.

5 N P Miller and D S White, "Helping Law Firm Luddites Cross the Digital Divide – Arguments for Mastering Law Practice Technology" (2009) 12(2) *SMU Science and Technology Law Review* 113.

6 M Fraas, "Legal Databases: Comparative Analysis", *Center for Research Libraries Global Resources Network* <https://www.crl.edu/collections/topics/legal-databases-comparative-analysis>.

7 LexisNexis, "About LexisNexis®" <http://www2.lexisnexis.com.au/en-au/about-us/about-us.page#:~:text=Reed%20Elsevier%20acquired%20LexisNexis.,research%20and%20analysis%20was%20conducted>.

launching in 1973 as a "'free-text' search and retrieval system" developed for one of the American state bar associations[8] and its competitor Westlaw two years later based on a small-scale Canadian system.[9] As the 21st century approached, Lexis would be seen as the largest database in the world.[10] It and Westlaw ushered the law into the internet age well ahead of other fields with the launch of their first web-based services early in the dot-com boom.[11]

The utility of digital legal research platforms of course depended upon, and thus evolved hand-in-hand with, courts' ability to digitise. Jurisdictions quicker to embrace digitisation logically made correspondingly quicker and greater advancements in digitised legal research capabilities. The sheer scale of the task of transforming centuries of paper-based precedent – so critical to common law legal systems in particular – was (and in some jurisdictions, remains) enormous.[12] "Most decisions issued before the mid-90s were only preserved in printed form even if they were initially prepared electronically."[13] In the early days, the digitisation process relied heavily upon manual labour and a sort of translation-like effort:

> Digitizing decisions directly from the court record is, not surprisingly, a most challenging endeavor. Even where the court's file system is organized so that reasons for decision can be sorted easily, the decisions' identifying data might be difficult to extract. Even an element as important as the date of decision could be missing from the paper version kept in the file, as it was often stamped only on the printed versions distributed to parties. In appellate courts where reasons are issued by a bench of more than one judge, the "opinions" from the different judges might be scattered in the paper record and mistaken as constituting standalone decisions where they should be read together. Many times these different opinions do not bear the same date, which may add to the confusion. Finally, as these documents were not intended for online publication at the time they were issued, they might be subject to legal publication restrictions or to the application of a court's policy which minimizes online publication of personal information.[14]

---

8 LexisNexis, n 7.

9 R Ambrogi, "Westlaw's Days Are Numbered", *LawSites* (26 May 2015) <https://www.lawsitesblog.com/2015/05/westlaws-days-are-numbered.html#:~:text=Westlaw%20originally%20launched%20in%201975,operated%20from%201968%20to%201973>.

10 R Susskind, *The Future of Law: Facing the Challenges of Information Technology* (Oxford University Press, 1998) 57.

11 See Fraas, n 6; and LexisNexis, n 7.

12 F Pelletier, "Making Old Cases New: The Digitization of Case Law", *Lexum* (13 May 2015) <https://lexum.com/en/blog/making-old-cases-new-the-digitization-of-case-law/>.

13 Pelletier, n 12.

14 Pelletier, n 12.

North American innovators helped to overcome these challenges by facilitating the implementation of courtroom technology. For example, Professor Fredric I Lederer's Courtroom 21 Project, based at the College of William and Mary in Virginia, supported the systemic[15] initiative to install technology in American state and federal courts from the late 1990s.[16] By 2003, a significant proportion of US federal district courts had "access to primary forms of advanced technology-either via a permanent installation in one or more courtrooms or equipment that is shared among courtrooms".[17] Canadian courts were likewise leaders in becoming technology-enabled.[18]

In other jurisdictions, lower internet penetration rates, familiarity with technology, political will, infrastructure and funding have been barriers. The COVID-19 pandemic unavoidably exposed the gaps between legal technology-enabled and legal technology-unenabled jurisdictions. The weaknesses of South Africa's fully paper-based court system, for example, were suddenly magnified and multiplied.[19] Kenyan courts, meanwhile, leveraged the pandemic and existing guidelines enabling digital proceedings to hastily launch an e-filing system in March 2020.[20]

Some but not all of these stories follow traditional north/south or western/non-western lines. Living up to its self-appointed reputation as the "lucky country",[21] Australia's courts only narrowly avoided chaos when the pandemic closed borders and forced lockdowns in early 2020: the High Court of Australia

---

15 Judge H B Dixon Jr, "The Basics of a Technology-Enhanced Courtroom", *American Bar Association* (1 November 2017) <https://www.americanbar.org/groups/judicial/publications/judges_journal/2017/fall/basics-technologyenhanced-courtroom/>.

16 "Center for Legal & Court Technology", *William and Mary Law School* <https://law.wm.edu/academics/intellectuallife/researchcenters/clct/>.

17 F I Lederer, "The Courtroom 21 Project: Creating the Courtroom of the Twenty-First Century" (2004) *Popular Media* 42.

18 A Salyzyn, "A New Lens: Reframing the Conversation about the Use of Videoconferencing in Civil Trials in Ontario" (2012) 50(2) *Osgoode Hall Law Journal* 431.

19 R Baboolal-Frank, "Revolutionising the Civil Courts in South Africa through Information Technology" (22 August 2015) <https://papers.ssrn.com/sol3/papers.cfm?abstract_id=2648638>.

20 See M Ketchell, "Kenya Is Struggling to Deliver Justice Online: What Needs to Be Done", *The Conversation* (9 August 2020) <https://theconversation.com/kenya-is-struggling-to-deliver-justice-online-what-needs-to-be-done-139675>; Chief Justice D Maraga, "Launch of Judiciary E-Filing System" (Speech, Republic of Kenya Judiciary, 1 July 2020) <https://www.judiciary.go.ke/download/speech-by-cj-david-maraga-at-launch-of-judiciary-e-filing-system/>.

21 S Cousins, "Contemporary Australia – The Lucky Country", *Australian Broadcasting Corporation* <http://www.abc.net.au/ra/australia/pdf/lucky_country.pdf>.

had only just mandated electronic lodgment in cases commenced after 1 January 2020.[22] Various Australian State courts had adopted electronic lodgment portals a mere year or two earlier.[23] It was not until the implementation in 2014 of the National Court Framework, which at last harmonised the functions of the various State registries, that a single digital platform for e-filing even became possible.[24] China, by contrast, was more prepared to weather the limitations wrought by the pandemic: as of late 2019, an estimated 90%+ of Chinese courts employed online tools, while an Internet Court in Hangzhou had been resolving disputes with virtual, artificial intelligence (AI)-powered "judges" since 2017, and a mobile court offered through social media platform WeChat had "handled more than three million proceedings since its introduction in March 2019".[25]

In exposing the gaps between prepared and unprepared jurisdictions, the COVID-19 pandemic also brought to light the reasons for varying rates of speed and success in the legal profession's embrace of technology around the globe. These manifestly extend well beyond the luddite lawyer stereotype, which has always viewed the legal profession through an unabashedly wealthy, privileged, western lens. Glib attributions of the profession's rate of technological adaptation to those whose "e-mail and instant messaging, if any, comes all in lower case", and who "believe that the computer gods (or the firm's IT personnel) are conspiring against them"[26] profoundly demean and disrespect the millions of legal professionals practicing outside of the wealthy, privileged western bubble.

The year 2020 more than any other – more even than the dot-com boom of the late 1990s or bust of the early 2000s and the much-feared Y2K "disaster" in between those two major technology milestones – would test the legal profession and its overly simplistic, western-centric luddite lawyer stereotype. Long anticipated to be an important milestone year for law and technology, it would be a crucible – welcome or not – for testing so many of the expectations

22 "Digital Lodgment System Information", *High Court of Australia* <https://www.hcourt.gov.au/digital-lodgment-system/information>.

23 Chief Justice Allsop AO, "Technology and the Future of the Courts" (Speech, TC Beirne School of Law, University of Queensland, 26 March 2019) <https://www.fedcourt.gov.au/digital-law-library/judges-speeches/chief-justice-allsop/allsop-cj-20190326>.

24 Allsop, n 23.

25 B Lynn, "Robot Justice: The Rise of China's 'Internet Courts'", *VOA Learning English* (11 December 2019) <https://learningenglish.voanews.com/a/robot-justice-the-rise-of-china-s-internet-courts-/5201677.html>.

26 See Toews, n 4.

and predictions of the two preceding decades about the law and legal profession's future and their ability to evolve and survive. This chapter revisits those earlier predictions and re-evaluates them against the realities of the challenges of 2020, before moving on to identify future milestones and their potential to change the legal system.

The predictions (or, they "died off or clung on by their fingernails")

[8.30] Cataclysmic predictions about legal professionals being rendered obsolete and the law being completely reformed or replaced by technology are so commonplace today that they have a certain white noise quality about them. "What is the law but a series of algorithms? Codified instructions proscribing dos and don'ts – ifs and thens. Sounds a lot like computer programming, right?" So the story goes, under headlines that paint a bleak picture for aspiring and current legal professionals: "Experts say 23% of lawyers' work can be automated",[27] "Future court rooms to look different; tech may replace fresh-out-of-college lawyers at entry level"[28] and "Analyse this: AI faster at evaluating contracts than human lawyers in Alibaba contest".[29] Such predictions about the law being revolutionised and legal professionals being rendered obsolete by technology are as old if not older than the luddite lawyer stereotype itself. Modernise or perish, the lawyers are told, just as for publishers who, "[b]y in large … didn't adjust. Instead, a cadre of up-and-comers ate their lunch and most of the stodgy publishers died off or clung on by their fingernails with herculean effort".[30]

---

27 A J Hess, "Experts Say 23% of Lawyers' Work Can Be Automated – Law Schools Are Trying to Stay Ahead of the Curve", *CNBC* (7 February 2020) <https://www.cnbc.com/2020/02/06/technology-is-changing-the-legal-profession-and-law-schools.html>.

28 A P Handfinger and R M Drover, "Is My Lawyer a Robot? Technology's Impact on Professional Services", *Law.com* (14 May 2020) <https://economictimes.indiatimes.com/magazines/panache/future-court-rooms-to-look-different-tech-may-replace-fresh-out-of-college-lawyers-at-entry-level/articleshow/77124133.cms>.

29 M Borak, "Analyse This: AI Faster at Evaluating Contracts than Human Lawyers in Alibaba Contest", *South China Morning Post* (9 December 2020) <https://www.scmp.com/tech/innovation/article/3113058/analyse-ai-faster-evaluating-contracts-human-lawyers-alibaba>.

30 D Fagella, "AI in Law and Legal Practice – A Comprehensive View of 35 Current Applications", *Emerj* (14 March 2020) <https://emerj.com/ai-sector-overviews/ai-in-law-legal-practice-current-applications/#:~:text=In%20the%20legal%20profession%2C%20AI,%2C%20legal%20researchers%2C%20and%20litigators.&text=Helping%20lawyers%20perform%20due%20diligence%20and%20research>.

In 1996, during the so-called dot-com boom, British lawyer and legal technologist Richard Susskind cast a new and – to many – deeply disturbing light on the legal profession in *The Future of Law: Facing the Challenges of Information Technology*.[31] As his work in this field has continued, he has come to be known as "the world's most cited author on the future of legal services".[32] The conclusion in *The Future of Law*, his bestseller,[33] shook lawyers to their very core: "that there is no future for the traditional legal profession if it cannot adapt to the challenge of information technology".[34] This was a fitting capstone to the 10 almost heretical predictions the book proffered about what and how would change. Technology bounded ahead in the mere two-year gap between the publication of the hardcover and softcover editions, only reinforcing his view that "[t]he legal marketplace … will change beyond recognition as we progress into the information society".[35]

Looking over the first 20 years of the new century, which ended so dramatically with the events of 2020, it feels timely to ask whether the legal marketplace has indeed "changed beyond recognition". Susskind's expectations of a "global telecommunications infrastructure which, for practical purposes, will enable the instantaneous transmission of seemingly limitless amounts of digital information at negligible cost"[36] have undoubtedly been borne out, and indeed exceeded, in most jurisdictions. "Electronic mail", a term which Susskind had to define at the time for his readers,[37] has almost certainly become "more widely used than the telephone"[38] in legal services. Hardware convergence of desktop computer and telephone has also come to pass, and perhaps even more radically than anticipated through the pocket-sized, hand-held smartphone, a critical milestone achieved at a truly mass market level with the launch of the first iPhone in 2007.[39] Although his predictions of the late 1990s "assume[d]

---

31 See Ambrogi, n 9.

32 B Marr, "The Future of Lawyers: Legal Tech, AI, Big Data and Online Courts", *Forbes* (17 January 2020) <https://www.forbes.com/sites/bernardmarr/2020/01/17/the-future-of-lawyers-legal-tech-ai-big-data-and-online-courts/?sh=49cef305f8c4>.

33 See Ambrogi, n 9.

34 D Bausor, "Review of Susskind, R, The Future of Law: Facing the Challenges of Information Technology" (1999) 1(1) *Digital Technology Law Journal* 2.

35 See Susskind, n 10, x.

36 Susskind, n 10, xiii.

37 Susskind, n 10, 152.

38 Susskind, n 10, xiv.

39 A Montgomery and K Mingis, "The Evolution of Apple's iPhone", *ComputerWorld* (16 October 2020) <https://www.computerworld.com/article/2604020/the-evolution-of-apples-iphone.html>.

no major step changes"[40] such as the iPhone, Susskind did foresee higher level seismic shifts, including the "convergence of information and entertainment – the television and the personal computer".[41]

So axiomatic have these technologies become that it is difficult to appreciate the disbelief and apprehension that arose from Susskind's predictions of their impacts on the law and the legal profession. But has the legal marketplace "changed beyond recognition"? No doubt e-government, digital publication of legislation and virtual legal libraries have had profound impacts. Nevertheless, legal education in the first two decades of the 21st century was singularly geared to preparing graduates for what Susskind termed the "traditional legal service".[42] Legal accreditation bodies, which oversee law school curricula, take relatively little account of what Susskind termed the "commoditised legal service",[43] and even less of the "latent legal market" of "multi-disciplinary systems and services"[44] aimed at providing no- or low-cost, easily accessible quasi-legal guidance (as distinguished from formal lawyer-to-client personalised legal advice – the enduring focus of legal education). Law students are certainly being prepared for a profession in which they will be expected to draft documents and correspond without the support of a typing pool or secretary, but they are not being trained to anticipate more than these low impact automations. Meanwhile, social media use in a lawyer's personal and professional life, outsourcing and commoditising transactional work through the "gig economy" and project management tools and skills are attention-grabbing topics for one-off continuing legal education courses, not law school curricula.

If nothing else, the COVID-19 pandemic told us that the law and legal profession remain mostly reactive, not proactive, to technological advancement. This conclusion is more nuanced than those who so blithely propagate the lawyer luddite stereotype would have us believe. Has the upset of 2020 provided a turning point? Is this year of disruption the catalyst for convergence of law and technology in a proactive way?

---

40 Susskind, n 10, xii.

41 Susskind, n 10, xvi–xvii.

42 Susskind, n 10, xlvi.

43 Susskind, n 10, xlvii–l.

44 Susskind, n 10, l.

Law and technology in 2020: COVID-19 changes (nearly) everything

[8.40] With time, the full extent of the changes wrought by COVID-19 on law and the legal profession will be revealed. No single chapter in a book published as many countries' borders remain shut and vaccination programs struggle launch could fully cover this topic. Jurisdictions around the world responded through laws and regulations to the sudden demands of fighting a global pandemic through such unprecedented actions as suspending legal documentation requirements on migrants seeking medical or other social services, eligibility requirements for employment benefits, and licensing requirements on medical professionals from foreign jurisdictions.[45] Assessing the changes brought about in the relationship between law and technology is blurred by complexity: there are the substantive changes to the law (new laws created, extant laws amended or repealed) to integrate technological needs and expectations, procedural changes to the way laws are enforced and the way the legal profession operates, and the substantive laws and technological processes that encourage or facilitate the sort of innovation (eg, air flow systems, personal protective equipment, vaccines, barriers and screens) that overcoming a pandemic inspires.

This section of the chapter carves out the most immediately felt and seen impacts of 2020 and the COVID-19 pandemic on the relationship between law and technology. In doing so, it primarily analyses the way technology changed the legal profession, rather than identify the substance of new laws created to manage and overcome the pandemic. Laws change with time and circumstances – that is their nature. Processes, procedures and norms of the legal system and legal profession, however, are in ordinary times far slower to change (hence the lawyer-as-luddite stereotype), so it is here that the greatest potential for lasting effect lies.

The COVID-19 pandemic pushed life online, and with it, at last, in the face of decades of apparent resistance, the legal profession. No longer simply a showcase project of wealthy, developed nations, easeful online accessibility to the law and legal system became a universal necessity from March 2020. This

45 "What Is the Impact of the COVID-19 Pandemic on Immigrants and Their Children?", *OECD* (Report, 19 October 2020) <http://www.oecd.org/coronavirus/policy-responses/what-is-the-impact-of-the-covid-19-pandemic-on-immigrants-and-their-children-e7cbb7de/>.

was the year that brought online dispute resolution (ODR) and other aspects of virtual and automated lawyering squarely into mainstream legal practice.

Online dispute resolution

[8.50] ODR[46] admittedly falls within the broader umbrella of "virtual lawyering", which is taken up in the next subsection of this chapter. It is, however, such a significant component of virtual lawyering that it demands individualised attention. ODR featured far more prominently in the realm of, or as a minor subset of, alternative dispute resolution prior to 2020, through for example specific dispute resolution policies such as the Uniform Domain Name Dispute Resolution Procedure[47] in specified, inherently online fields such as domain name dispute resolution. The COVID-19 pandemic brought ODR into previously untapped areas of traditional face-to-face litigation and related proceedings, suddenly overcoming decades of latent confidence issues with electronic transactions.[48] Across the globe, laws and regulations were passed, processes and procedures were updated, and technology was implemented to allow dispute-relevant documents to be filed via email or through dedicated electronic portals[49] and signed electronically.[50] Changes in rules to permit remote appearances by parties, their legal representatives, witnesses and others[51] tore down, seemingly overnight, longstanding obstacles to accessing dispute resolution services.

With these developments came corresponding expectations of the conduct of the parties to online litigation:

> The courts have strongly encouraged practitioners to cooperate more than ever with their colleagues and court personnel to ensure the efficient conduct and integrity of any proceeding in the virtual courtroom. There is an obligation on practitioners to

---

46 "When You Can't Meet in Court: Pros and Cons of Online Dispute Resolution Alternative Dispute Resolution during the Coronavirus Crisis", *LexisNexis* <https://www.lexisnexis.com.au/en/COVID19/blogs-and-articles/when-you-cant-meet-in-court-online-alternative-dispute-resolution-during-coronavirus-covid19>; R Dori, "75% of Lawsuits Will Be Handled Online Within a Decade, Says Law Professor", *CTech* (27 October 2019) <https://www.calcalistech.com/ctech/articles/0,7340,L-3772500,00.html>.

47 See "Uniform Domain-Name Dispute-Resolution Policy", *ICANN* <https://www.icann.org/resources/pages/help/dndr/udrp-en>.

48 G Kaufmann-Kohler and T Schultz, "Online Dispute Resolution: Challenges for Contemporary Justice" (2004) *Kluwer Law International* 76.

49 Judicial College of Victoria, "Coronavirus and the Courts" <https://www.judicialcollege.vic.edu.au/resources/coronavirus-and-courts>.

50 Judicial College of Victoria, n 49.

51 Judicial College of Victoria, n 49.

> familiarise themselves with e-court technology and to adequately prepare for any challenges that may arise, including dealing with technological issues, determining how and when to provide materials to the court before a hearing, tendering evidence electronically during a hearing, and how to handle commercial-in-confidential material.[52]

Such profound shifts immediately brought to light challenges, even at the most fundamental level of ensuring natural justice and the right to a fair trial.[53] Following a well-worn developed vs developing argument path, socially, economically and technologically better prepared jurisdictions could transition to ODR more quickly. Even with that infrastructure in place, however, some struggled with pressure on longstanding professional and cultural norms. Susskind's eerily prescient *Online Courts and the Future of Justice*,[54] published in late 2019, predicted just such challenges and warned of deep-rooted extant obstacles for all legal systems, not just in developing nations. Transformation, he argued, continuing a theme developed in 1996 with the publication of *Technology and the Law*, rather than automation, would be key:

> Transformation applies to the use of technology, not to automate the previous ways of working but to allow one to do things that previously weren't possible. I have not been saying that these tools are meant to help lawyers work better. Rather, my position is that we have the ability through technology to allow individuals who are not lawyers to gain access to legal guidance and documentation. My message has always been one of transformation through technology rather than straightforward automation.

In due course, in-depth investigation may reveal whether the changes motivated by the COVID-19 pandemic in 2020 were more transformational or automational in nature. Comments from judges, for example, expressing their commitment to maintaining "business as usual",[55] although well-meaning, hint at the latter rather than lasting systemic transformation.

---

52 T Boys, "COVID-19 and the Virtual Courtroom: Is Technology a Friend or Foe?", *Holding Redlich* (14 October 2020) <https://www.holdingredlich.com/covid-19-and-the-virtual-courtroom-is-technology-a-friend-or-foe>.

53 *R v Macdonald; R v Edward Obeid; R v Moses Obeid (No 11)* [2020] NSWSC 382, [29] ("The accused are entitled to a fair trial which includes, necessarily, fair process and procedures. I am of the view that a trial in a virtual courtroom is impractical. I have further resolved to the view that the accused's right to a fair trial would be at risk were I to order that it continue at this time.").

54 R Susskind, *Online Courts and the Future of Justice* (Oxford University Press, 2019).

55 *Australian Securities and Investments Commission v GetSwift Limited* [2020] FCA 504, [7] ("Just because one cannot have a hearing conducted in accordance with traditional practices and procedures, does not mean that the Court's judicial function cannot be performed effectively where it is necessary to do so. As Voltaire observed, one must ensure the perfect does not become the enemy of the good.").

Virtual lawyering

[8.60] In 1998, Susskind predicted that "[w]ith a global information infrastructure in place, it will be far easier than ever before for lawyers to collaborate and maintain contact on a genuinely international basis".[56] Few would deny that this had come to fruition well before the COVID-19 pandemic disrupted the world in 2020. Email, law firm virtual private networks and teleconferencing platforms have all increasingly facilitated cross-border legal collaboration and lawyering since the late 1990s.

Cloud computing has changed the hardware, software and support service needs of lawyers worldwide by eliminating the need for on-site equipment, machines or systems. Through cloud computing, data and information are stored in offsite machines and storage devices made accessible on demand through a secure internet connection rather than large, costly onsite machines and storage devices.[57] Many legal firms, courts and professionals had already migrated to "the cloud" prior to the pandemic; by late 2019, an estimated 75% of UK businesses were using the cloud in some way and storing "an average of 29 per cent of their data" that way.[58] Long seen as obvious risks (and therefore impediments) to cloud computing, in reality data protection, information security, confidentiality and business continuity issues are no less (and likely more so) risky when law firms and legal bodies store data and offer services through their own systems and teams.

According to consultancy firm Price Waterhouse Cooper, global spending on cloud computing "rose 37% to $29 billion during the first quarter of 2020", a trend it believed would continue throughout the year even as overall IT spending would fall.[59] Competitor consultancy firms Gartner and McKinsey similarly saw 2020 as a turning point for cloud computing, advising business "[l]eaders ... to accelerate their journey to the cloud in order to digitize quickly and effectively in the wake of COVID-19"[60] while acknowledging

---

56 Susskind, n 10, xxvii.

57 S Ranger, "What Is Cloud Computing? Everything You Need to Know about the Cloud Explained", ZDNet (13 December 2018) <https://www.zdnet.com/article/what-is-cloud-computing-everything-you-need-to-know-about-the-cloud/>.

58 Ranger, n 57.

59 "Can You Meet Customer Demand for Cloud-Based Computing? For Tech Infrastructure Companies, COVID-19 Has Accelerated Customer Demand for Cloud-Based Offerings", *PwC United States* <https://www.pwc.com/us/en/industries/tmt/library/covid19-cloud-infrastructure.html>.

60 "Three Actions CEOs Can Take to Get Value from Cloud Computing", *McKinsey Digital* (21 July 2020) <https://www.mckinsey.com/business-functions/mckinsey-digital/our-insights/three-actions-ceos-can-take-to-get-value-from-cloud-computing#>.

the pressures that increased demand for cloud services would put on service providers.[61] More cloud infrastructure, in the form of regional data centres, will alleviate this problem in both developed[62] and developing[63] parts of the world. Meeting the demand for and expectations of virtual lawyering post-pandemic absolutely depends on the sorts of transmission speeds and data storage volumes that such localised data centres can bring. This is discussed further in [8.80].

Another aspect of virtual lawyering propelled forward by the COVID-19 pandemic is the virtual conference. In recent years, remote participation technology in international conferences has become both more commonplace and more user-friendly, bringing legal professionals together without the cost and inconvenience of long-haul travel even in jurisdictions with lower local internet penetration rates. The first ever virtual Annual Conference and General Meeting of the East Africa Law Society, for example, was held in December 2020.[64] Once the pandemic hit and travel restrictions were imposed, international legal conferences such as the International Trademark Association's Annual Meeting, originally scheduled to occur in-person in Singapore in April 2020 with some remote participation facilities, were rescheduled in a fully virtual mode.[65]

While virtual meetings and conferences existed prior to 2020, some viewed them as a "novelty".[66] By mid-year, polls were already suggesting that the novelty had worn off, and the absence of face-to-face interaction was already being acutely

---

61 "When Cloud Meets COVID-19: Threats and Opportunities", *Gartner* <https://www.gartner.com/en/conferences/hub/cloud-conferences/insights/when-cloud-meets-covid-19-threats-opportunities>.

62 See, for example, C Niesche, "Big Data Centres on Regional Areas", *Australian Financial Review* (2019) <https://www.afr.com/companies/professional-services/big-data-centres-on-regional-areas-20190811-p52g0m>.

63 M Ketchell, "Cloud Computing Could Be Key to Speeding Up Africa's Development", *The Conversation* (28 August 2019) <https://theconversation.com/cloud-computing-could-be-key-to-speeding-up-africas-development-121344>.

64 East Africa Law Society, "25th East Africa Law Society Annual Conference and General Assembly" (Facebook, 3 December 2020) <https://www.facebook.com/ealawsociety/posts/the-first-ever-virtual-annual-conference-and-general-meeting-of-the-east-africa-/3547938481941625/>.

65 "International Trademark Association Working to Reschedule Annual Meeting in Singapore; Will Hold 2020 Event in the United States", *INTA* (Press Release, 14 February 2020) <https://www.inta.org/2020_annual_meeting_0220/>.

66 "Don't Let Zoom Fatigue Affect Attendance for Your Virtual Events", *WBT Systems* <https://www.wbtsystems.com/learning-hub/blogs/zoom-fatigue-virtual-events>.

felt.[67] New terms were quickly coined for the fatigue associated with long days spent engaging with colleagues in front of a screen.[68] Simply replicating offline conferences in an online format was quickly deemed insufficient to maintain pre- or even early-pandemic attendance figures: discussions in the CREO (Corona Response for Event Organisers) online community pointed to "a decline in virtual event attendance. One respondent said, 'As we went into lockdown at the end of March and early April [2020], you could expect 70%+ attendance rate from register > attend. However, now in June [2020], that seems to have slid a lot to more like 30%–50%.'" While much had been made of the opportunities, little thought had apparently been given prior to 2020 of the potential impacts of a world in which online participation was the only conference participation option for a sustained period of time. These things point to two questions for virtual conferences going forward: are these merely a temporary automation (to return to Susskind's pre-2000 terminology[69]) of what existed before, or a lasting catalyst for innovation and systemic change?

The same questions can of course be asked of other developments in virtual lawyering in 2000, including how the world trains and examines new lawyers. Law schools that had resisted online learning had no choice but to pivot as universities closed their campuses in implementing public health and safety protocols. While fully or near-fully online law degrees are a well-travelled path in Australia,[70] in the United States, where more than 130,000 are enrolled each year in accredited law study,[71] "[la]w schools have staunchly resisted online learning until COVID-19 rendered it a necessity. The tech-enabled, crisis-created shift from classroom to online learning occurred with astonishing speed, pervasiveness, and seamlessness".[72] The changes now seen as inevitable

---

67 R Holmes, "2 Million Professionals Polled on How to Make Virtual Conferences Better – Here Are Their Top 10 Hacks", *Forbes* (11 June 2020) <https://www.forbes.com/sites/ryanholmes/2020/06/11/i-asked-2-million-professionals-how-to-make-virtual-conferences-better--here-are-their-top-10-hacks/?sh=63c3b6593132>.

68 See "Don't Let Zoom Fatigue Affect Attendance for Your Virtual Events", n 66.

69 See Susskind, n 10, xxi.

70 See, for example, M Kirby, "Online Legal Education in Australia: The New CQU Law Degree" (2011) 34 *Australian Bar Review* 237.

71 D Lederman, "Number of New Law Students Dipped in 2019", *Inside Higher Ed* (13 December 2019) <https://www.insidehighered.com/quicktakes/2019/12/13/number-new-law-students-dipped-2019#:~:text=Overall%20enrollment%20in%20the%20country's,rose%20by%201.2%20percent%20also>.

72 M A Cohen, "Post-Pandemic Legal Education", *Forbes* (13 August 2020) <https://www.forbes.com/sites/markcohen1/2020/08/13/post-pandemic-legal-education/?sh=6fd5e59575d2>.

("In the new paradigm, legal education will morph from a place to a process; appointed time to on-time and in real-time learning; and an artisanal delivery model to a tech-enabled, scalable one. Legal education will be more affordable, data-enhanced, results-driven, and accountable"[73]) are at last the changes needed to bring Susskind's pre-2000 predictions about the future of the legal profession to fruition.

The endurance of seemingly irreplaceable elements of the "old" model of legal education is unclear. In a profession so embedded with professional and ethical obligations, assessing law students and graduates in the online environment is a sensitive matter. On the one hand are studies showing a correlative increase in cheating with the shift to online education.[74] On the other hand are student assertions of privacy rights and expressions of personal indignation at the perceived lack of trust, with some even taking shape as legal action[75] against the universities tasked with assessing them. American state bars were forced to move bar examinations online out of necessity in 2020;[76] while the experience is not one usually described as pleasant, characterisations of "avoidable disaster" and "cruel vindictiveness" are sufficiently extreme to force either sweeping innovation or a hasty retreat to the pre-pandemic status quo. There too, integrity and ethical standards were tested and found wanting.[77]

Last, though no less significantly, is the impact that the pandemic had on lawyers, judges and other legal professionals themselves, and the physical environments in which they practice. Lawyers in countries with pre-pandemic high internet penetration rates, relatively low-cost high-speed data, and some experience with digital storage and communications tools were well placed to

---

73 Cohen, n 72.

74 D Newton, "Another Problem with Shifting Education Online: A Rise in Cheating", *Washington Post* (8 August 2020) <https://www.washingtonpost.com/local/education/another-problem-with-shifting-education-online-a-rise-in-cheating/2020/08/07/1284c9f6-d762-11ea-aff6-220dd3a14741_story.html>.

75 Hoger Onderwijs Persbureau, "Students Sue University over Webcam-Monitored Exams", *Erasmus Magazine* (4 June 2020) <https://www.erasmusmagazine.nl/en/2020/06/04/students-sue-university-over-webcam-monitored-exams/>.

76 B Ambrogi, "20 for 2020: The Legal Tech Trends that Defined the Year", *LawSites* (30 December 2020) <https://www.lawsitesblog.com/2020/12/20-for-2020-the-legal-tech-trends-that-defined-the-year.html>.

77 S F Ward and L Moran, "Thousands of California Bar Exam Takers Have Video Files Flagged for Review", *ABA Journal* (18 December 2020) <https://www.abajournal.com/web/article/thousands-of-california-bar-exam-takers-have-video-files-flagged-for-review>.

transition to working from home in 2020.[78] As a demographic, the lawyers in these jurisdictions may have been some of the least affected by the pandemic. The population centres surrounding firms' physical premises have, by contrast, unquestionably suffered.

> Rent is a law firm's second-biggest expense, after salaries. Estimates say it generally eats up 6–15 percent of gross revenue, depending on the size of the firm and the location of its offices. Well before the pandemic, many firms were already looking to reduce their physical footprints as a way of cutting expenses, and technology increasingly made that possible.[79]

While post-pandemic physical presence will in large part be dictated by local conditions and government responses to those conditions, in Australia (where the risk and rate of infection is relatively low but vaccine rollout lags behind other Organisation for Economic Co-operation and Development (OECD) partners[80]), for example, some firms' managers moved quickly to return to the "old" normal before a "new normal" could cement itself in firm culture.[81] For many, the longer term prospects for changes to the dependency on a physical location in the legal profession hinge on vaccination rates but also more time to reflect on the impacts of working remotely on wellbeing, training and retention.[82]

Automated lawyering

[8.70] Given all the fuss made over the first two decades of the 21st century about the inevitable usurpation of legal jobs by automated technology, one could be forgiven for wondering whether concerns about the impacts on

78 See Ambrogi, n 76.

79 Ambrogi, n 76.

80 I Ting, K Shatoba and A Palmer, "Tracking Australia's COVID Vaccine Rollout Numbers", *ABC News* (19 March 2021) <https://www.abc.net.au/news/2021-03-02/charting-australias-covid-vaccine-rollout/13197518?nw=0>.

81 M Pelly, "We Want You Back in the Office, Law Firm Tells Partners", *Australian Financial Review* (24 May 2020) <https://www.afr.com/companies/professional-services/we-want-you-back-in-the-office-law-firm-tells-partners-20200524-p54vv6>; M Pelly and H Wootton, "Law Firms Set Work from Home Limits", *Australian Financial Review* (3 December 2020) <https://www.afr.com/companies/professional-services/lawyers-to-be-in-the-office-more-often-than-not-20201130-p56izz>.

82 C Simmons et al, "Get Comfortable at Home: Big Firms Plan to Allow Remote Work for Rest of Year", *Law.com* (3 September 2020) <https://www.law.com/americanlawyer/2020/09/03/get-comfortable-at-home-big-firms-plan-to-allow-remote-work-for-rest-of-year/?slreturn=20210201202203>.

lawyers of working remotely are overblown. Surely the bigger concern here is how to cushion the blow from the loss of legal jobs to robots, right?

While 2020 proved a catalyst for much change in the legal profession, by the end of the year pundits were still asking "Is it time to embrace automated decision-making?" rather than remarking on an automated revolution having taken place. Here is an area where the full force of Susskind's pre-2000 predictions have not yet borne out, and even the pandemic did not provoke obvious change in the same way that law schools suddenly moved classes online, bar exams went digital, and courts and law firms closed and told everyone to work from home. Nevertheless, as 2020 drew to a close, automation was said to be "both closer and further away than most lawyers think".[83] "Inevitable"[84] remains the catchphrase; as the next part of this chapter will discuss in detail, virtual legal assistants and AI-powered chatbots are gaining traction, but have not revolutionised the profession at a systemic, global scale just yet. Perhaps this is the next big frontier.

The innovators were already out there prior to 2020. The DoNotPay app, which markets itself as "the world's first robot lawyer",[85] initially launched in 2015 in the United States as an "AI-based app to fight parking tickets".[86] Its scope quickly expanded to cover a broad range of legal challenges.[87] The year 2020 brought legal troubles for the app's creators when a class action lawsuit was filed alleging unsolicited advertising text messages in violation of the *Telephone Consumer Protection Act*.[88] Other market notables Robot Lawyer LISA (Legal Intelligence Support Assistant)[89] and Billy Bot[90] merged in mid-2017 with an "initial focus on the 'retail' market segment".[91] Billy "is [LISA's] first relationship", the company cheekily claims, "but it won't be

83 K Schwarz, "Is It Time to Embrace Automated Decision-Making?", *LSJ Online* (12 October 2020) <https://lsj.com.au/articles/is-it-time-to-embrace-automated-decision-making/>.

84 Schwarz, n 83.

85 "DoNotPay Community", *DoNotPay* <https://donotpay.com/learn/>.

86 R Adhikari, "Robot Lawyer Faces Legal Troubles of Its Own", *TechNews World* (18 December 2020) <https://www.technewsworld.com/story/86956.html>.

87 Adhikari, n 86.

88 Adhikari, n 86.

89 *Robot Lawyer LISA* <https://www.f6s.com/robotlawyerlisa>.

90 N Hilborne, "Love Is in the Air as Robot Lawyer LISA Partners with Junior Clerk Billy Bot", *legalfutures* (30 August 2017) <https://www.legalfutures.co.uk/latest-news/love-air-robot-lawyer-lisa-partners-junior-clerk-billy-bot>.

91 "The Latest Legal Delivery Collaboration: LISA and Billy: They're Robots", *Legal Mosaic* <https://www.legalmosaic.com/the-latest-legal-delivery-collaboration-lisa-and-billy-theyre-robots/>.

exclusive for long".[92] These developments may not have revolutionised the profession in 2020, but they have set the stage for change in the coming decade.

Beyond 2020, "Beyond Recognition"?

[8.80] What lies ahead? Was 2020 truly a pivot point for technology in the law, or simply an aberrant year when things were uncomfortably very different for as short a time as possible? Was the COVID-19 pandemic the long-anticipated springboard to Susskind's portended "change beyond recognition"? It remains impossible, as Susskind found pre-2000, to generalise about a profession with so many different stakeholders with different (and at times competing) needs, resources and priorities. Building on the narrowed focus of the previous section of this chapter, which identified some of the most immediately felt and seen impacts of the COVID-19 pandemic on the relationship between law and technology, this final section of the chapter seizes upon three of the most commonly featured technologies in post-pandemic predictions: AI, applications of blockchain technology and the future internet which will underpin them both.

Core themes cut across these three topics. First, access. AI promises to make legal services and the many functions attendant to them cheaper and easier. Centuries-old barriers between lawyers and non-lawyers will be broken down as increasingly complex legal functions are automated by AI or perhaps even replaced by blockchains. The future of the internet is equally a story about access as more devices go online. Accuracy is another theme: the sweet spots for both AI and blockchain technology lie in areas of high potential for human error. Meanwhile, at a deeply technical level, the ability of today's internet to support the many devices of tomorrow is questioned in terms of the accuracy of transmitting data packets; the latency that makes our internet-enabled phone calls choppy is bad news for virtual surgery. Third, security and privacy. The automation of traditional legal functions gives rise to questions about the privacy and security of transacting with machines. The very foundation of blockchain technology, by contrast, is its offer of an enduring, unalterable record, while the freedom of today's open architecture internet is offset by the lack of security (and loss of privacy) that centralised control could bring.

92 "The Latest Legal Delivery Collaboration", n 91.

Artificial intelligence

AI for lawyers

[8.90] Rare are the predictions on law and technology that do not include, if not focus intensely on, AI. Years before the COVID-19 pandemic, Susskind[93] predicted that 2020 would prove a sort of milestone year for the role of AI in the law. Continuing a recurrent theme in this chapter, this potential can be characterised twofold: the potential for substantive change (eg, laws regulating liability of driverless vehicles) and the potential for procedural changes wrought by the introduction of AI (eg, services predicting a juror's verdict). A short introduction to the concept of AI and its potential application to the law serves as context for tackling big-picture questions of whether AI will replace lawyers and what the future may hold.

Driving much of the fear, anticipation and speculation about the potential impacts of AI on the law and legal system is a less-than-perfect non-scientific person's understanding of what AI is. Broadly speaking, the "artificial" in the term "artificial intelligence" signals non-human; AI at its heart thus encompasses "the entire universe of computing technology that exhibits anything remotely resembling human intelligence".[94] While for many the term "AI" conjures up science fiction films featuring robots enslaving humans, this deeply humanised story tends to overlook the very mechanical, non-human way in which AI works. To the extent that we can characterise computers' activity as thinking, this is not "thinking" as we would describe the average human day-to-day experience, even though there are distinct similarities. While logic is unquestionably part of the human decision-making process, few people are driven solely by logical formulae when they decide to buy a red car rather than a blue car, eat ice cream for dinner rather than a healthy salad, or holiday at the beach rather than the mountains.

AI entails problem-solving by machines. Machines solve problems by following algorithms, which are step-by-step procedures or formulae. In the early days of computer science education, students would be tasked with, for example, making certain words appear on a computer screen. The student would input

---

93 I Lopez, "But What about Lawyers? A Q&A with Richard Susskind on AI in Law", *LAW.COM* (25 July 2016) <https://www.law.com/legaltechnews/almID/1202763509782/?slreturn=20210102204441>.

94 "Artificial Intelligence", *IBM* (Educational Module, 3 June 2020) <https://www.ibm.com/cloud/learn/what-is-artificial-intelligence>.

step-by-step instructions and, if done correctly, the desired end result would be achieved. Engineering students who grappled with graphing calculators are equally familiar with this sort of task, but so, too, are primary students when learning that adding two and two gives the result of four. Lawyers are certainly no strangers to algorithms: much of the purpose of law school is to teach logical thinking skills based on if/then logic. Certainly, the value of precedent is derived from if/then logic: if these facts occurred and court A decided X on the basis of those particular facts, then Y court faced with the same set of facts should also decide X. Herein lies the inherent link between AI and the law: "both look to historical examples in order to infer rules to apply to new situations".[95]

The "intelligence" aspect of "artificial intelligence" provokes questions of machines just as of humans about how they "learn". The related term "machine learning" signifies a more complex "network of algorithmic calculations";[96] data is inputted, calculations are made, conclusions are drawn from those calculations, which then impact the conclusions of subsequent calculations. The "solution", so to speak, to the problem becomes more refined with each further calculation. As the volume of data and volume of calculations grow, so too the confidence in the derived conclusions. This occurs without human intervention, as the machine runs its equations over and over again. For example, a machine can "learn" to make a medical diagnosis after identifying patterns in symptoms or medical imaging. These sorts of predictive abilities have obvious applications in the law.

Will AI replace lawyers?

[8.100] The idea that machines will replace humans has moved from science fiction thriller to everyday headline. Will AI replace the lawyers, judges and other legal professionals that populate the legal system? Not entirely, but some degree of replacing human labour with machine labour in the future seems inevitable. Yet components or aspects of machine-based lawyering (in the broadest sense, including the provision of formal or informal legal advice, the resolution of disputes, drafting documents, billing clients, marketing and client development, etc) can be adopted by existing legal service providers, courts, dispute resolution bodies and other organisations without existential disruption. Even some of the gloomiest predictions bear this out: McKinsey estimates that 22% of a lawyer's job and 35% of a law clerk's job can be

95 Toews, n 4.

96 "Artificial Intelligence", n 94.

automated,[97] but few are the headlines that announce the corresponding 78% and 65% that are not so conducive to automation. Even the leading innovators in the field concede that the future of AI in the law is not an all-or-nothing game: "for some legal matters there may be little choice but to leverage human expertise, but other processes and services will be augmented heavily by AI, and the field itself will eventually have to shift".[98] What this likely means is some major changes to some aspects of the law and lawyering; how much consequential change to the profession overall will ripple from this is ripe for speculation.

Some expect AI adoption in the law and legal profession to follow the standard "technology adoption curve",[99] which looks like this:

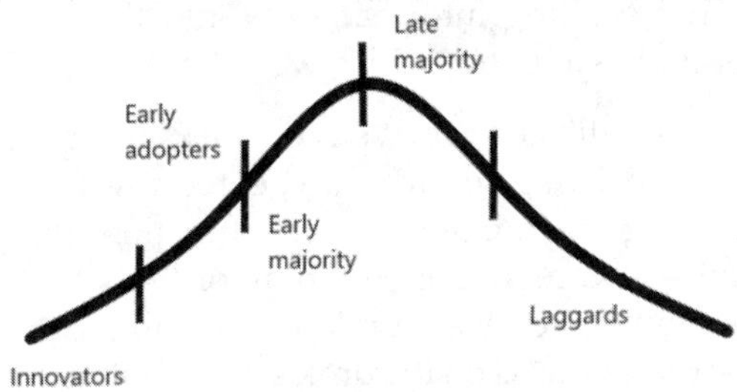

Under such thinking, 2020 might be the line between innovation and early adoption. From a non-lawyers' perspective one possible manifestation of this transition could take shape as the first "retail" customers of the merged Robot Lawyer LISA and Billy Bot.[100] On the lawyers' side, Daniel Faggella, CEO of AI market research firm Emerj, sees AI's early adopter lawyers as being "small, nimble legal firms ... focused from day one on maximal automation and efficiency ... to leverage technology to garner large profit-per-employee numbers. This won't be done through massively high rates for their billable hours, but by charging low rates and scaling their services with automation".[101]

97 E Winick, "Lawyer-Bots Are Shaking Up Jobs", *MIT Technology Review* (12 December 2017) <https://www.technologyreview.com/s/609556/lawyer-bots-are-shaking-up-jobs>.

98 Fagella, n 30.

99 G Mirthinti, "Technology Adoption Curve: Traits of Adopters at Each Stage of the Lifecycle", *WhatFix* (9 June 2020) <https://whatfix.com/blog/technology-adoption-curve/>.

100 See Hilborne, n 89.

101 Fagella, n 30.

Logical inroads for AI in the law and legal profession are areas with high human error risk, which may be sufficient to offset the risks associated with computerisation. With this in mind, investigative services, which take the form in law of legal research but also due diligence, contract/document review and discovery, are a likely early growth area in the AI adoption trajectory. Natural language processing and machine learning can be utilised in these activities not necessarily to replace but to improve human involvement, for example by identifying and extracting relevant text from documents and highlighting this to the lawyer's attention. The lawyer is not gone, but his/her touchpoints are more targeted, refined and efficient: at the initiation of such a project, "[a] lawyer would have to customize the type of information that needs to be extracted from scanned documents, and the software will then convert it to searchable text". The resulting information would then be compiled by the machine and generated as a report, which would be interpreted by the lawyer.

Another potential growth area driven by risk mitigation is prediction technology. Here, too, existing services are geared towards enhancing rather that totally supplanting the human lawyer's function. Early movers in this field have patented software systems with algorithms that work to identify litigation risk.[102] Another service predicts opposing counsel's arguments. Turning the microscope inwards on the profession, another innovation predicts a litigator's success rate on the basis of past cases.[103]

Cost cutting is a natural driver, particularly in a challenging post-pandemic global economy with clients exerting greater downwards pressure on legal services fees. AI systems can, for a start, facilitate better billing practices by automating time recording.[104] More existentially, such systems can facilitate a very significant reduction in human resources by identifying efficiencies and redundancies. One AI-enabled project management system boasts enabling a law firm client to "cut down on redundant workers from 100 lawyers down to 5 … . The software was able to perform the e-Discovery tasks of the lawyers at a 95 percent cost savings according to the law firm".[105] Another competing system claims to be "able to reduce the time spent to 48 hours from 255 days

102 See, for example, "Want to Find the Risks in Your Ocean of Data?", *Intraspexion* <https://intraspexion.com/>. See also G M Lee et al, "Predicting Litigation Risk via Machine Learning" (1 December 2020) <http://dx.doi.org/10.2139/ssrn.3740954>.

103 "Have CARA AI Find You the Most On-Point Authorities", *casetext* <https://casetext.com/cara-ai/>.

104 "What Is Automatic Time Tracking?", *Timely* (14 October 2020) <https://memory.ai/timely-blog/what-is-automatic-time-tracking>.

105 Fagella, n 30.

by a utility company by searching for thousands of contracts with specific clauses".[106] Not all cost cutting comes at the expense of jobs: speed is an equally attractive benefit of AI implementation. One system on the market today is purportedly capable of analysing "more than 50 documents in less than a minute, 10 percent more accurate than a manual review process".[107]

A notable corollary of this transition into early adoption of AI technologies in the legal profession is the growing recognition that a lawyer's professional and ethical competence must now take account of these technologies. This may ultimately be the single biggest driver of the transition from innovation to early adoption in this area. For example, the California State Bar has since 2015 required lawyers to have a working knowledge of the use of the state's e-Discovery system. Further, "if a lawyer is incompetent on the facility, he should learn the skill, hire someone who's knowledgeable, or just simply decline representation".[108] To this is added the pressure arising from different tools yielding different results, seemingly expanding the attorney's professional obligations while potentially pouring labour cost savings into the new cost of acquiring and maintaining multiple software packages or services.[109]

The challenges arising from this intersection of professional ethics and competence with the introduction of new technologies should not be underestimated. It would be easy to dismiss a slow transition from innovation to early adoption as typical, lawyerly old-fashionedness, but this would not take account of the significant transfer of risk from client to legal service provider that early adoption of AI in the law involves. Client services – both at the formal, traditional lawyer-client level and the informal "retail" market level, can improve (access, cost, speed, accuracy), but the early adopters who offer those advantages to their clients must be willing to take on and manage their own heightened legal, ethical and financial liability.

Blockchain

Blockchain for lawyers

[8.110] Less understood than AI but equally if not more likely to impact the law and legal profession is blockchain technology. Algorithmic calculations lie

106 Fagella, n 30.

107 Fagella, n 30.

108 *The State Bar of California Standing Committee on Professional Responsibility and Conduct*, Formal Opinion No 2015-193 <https://www.calbar.ca.gov/Portals/0/documents/ethics/Opinions/CAL%202015-193%20%5B11-0004%5D%20(06-30-15)%20-%20FINAL.pdf>.

109 Fagella, n 30.

at the heart of blockchain technology. These calculations serve validation and authentication functions, which tap into core concepts in the law and legal system around ownership and proof. Fundamental to blockchain's application to the law and legal system is its creation of an immutable ledger that is stored in a distributed way, meaning it dispenses with the need of a central repository or authority. That central authority, for so many transactions in society, is currently provided by government and the legal system that underpins its laws. That said, blockchain "is not magical; it will not solve all problems".[110]

Consider as an introductory example a land register: a single central authority (often a government) maintains a record of all interests and transactions in land (such as ownership, transfers, mortgages, easements, caveats). The record is deemed authoritative because it is the single comprehensive source of this data; trust flows from the perceived authority of the register's maintainer and from the rules (laws) that govern entries in the register. Without such a register, transactions involving land could be called into question: when person A purports to sell a parcel to person B, how does person B know that the land belongs to person A? What if person B takes occupation of the property only to discover that person C has been granted permission to live there or use the land in a particular way? What if person A enters into two separate transactions, one with person B, one with person D, to transfer the exact same parcel of land?

The register functions to document these transactions. It is a ledger. For generations, land registers were recorded by hand on paper. Increasingly today, land registers, like other ledgers, are "stored digitally, often in large databases owned and operated solely by centralized 'trusted' third parties on behalf of a community of users (ie, the third party is the owner of the ledger)".[111] Irrespective of its storage format, because it is maintained by a single centralised authority, it falls on that one central authority to protect the register against loss, tampering and destruction and to validate all transactions. "Of course, it is in the best interest of any centralized ledger to backup data, validate transactions, include all valid transactions, and not to alter history."[112]

Blockchain technology solves the age-old weaknesses of ledgers by distributing the record across a network. Each participant in the network has a copy of the record, thus eliminating the single possible point of failure. Participants add to

---

110 D Yaga et al, "NISTIR 8202 Blockchain Technology Overview" (National Institute of Standards and Technology, 2018) <https://nvlpubs.nist.gov/nistpubs/ir/2018/NIST.IR.8202.pdf>.

111 Yaga et al, n 110, 15.

112 Yaga et al, n 110.

the ledger and validate each other's additions using cryptographic algorithms. Historical entries into the record cannot be altered unless all agree to do so, as altering one copy on one participant's computer will yield an output different to all others. In a "permission" blockchain there is a known set of participants in the network, while in "permissionless" blockchain, anyone can join the network and participate in these authentication and validation functions. In this way, blockchain technology may solve legal problems more neatly and efficiently than the law itself has done for hundreds of years, which of course gives rise to notions of existential threat. Before discussing these, however, a non-technologist lawyer's basic understanding of blockchain is needed.

Blockchains encrypt data and store them in a ledger. Each entry in the ledger forms another "block"; in other words, each "block" records transactions affecting that data. The stored data could be as inconsequential as a single typed character or as voluminous as the digitised contents of an entire national library. Irrespective of the volume of data captured in a block, it is run through an algorithmic formula that assigns it a unique identifier referred to as a "hash" (while the activity of doing so takes the verb form, ie, "to hash" data). The "hash" then uniquely identifies that exact data. One benefit of hashing data is that the process takes any size input (eg, the single character "a", or the entire contents of a library) and reduces it into a fixed-size output. For larger bodies of data, this compression into a fixed-size identifier has obvious advantages both in terms of storage and workability, making even enormous bodies of data more manipulable and tamper resistant.

Hashing the contents of a block into that single, fixed-size identifier essentially hides the data itself. Multiple levels of hashing offer multiple layers of cryptographic protection. Consider the example of hashing a street address: Consider the hash of data x as Hash(x). Hashing Hash(x) – in other words, running the identifier Hash(x) through the hash algorithm – yields a new result, a new hash (identifier). In this example, depicted in Figure 8.1, the original data is hidden behind two layers of algorithmic computation (the "hash" function, represented by the arrow).

Hashes only work one-way,[113] so that one cannot derive x from Hash(x) (at least that is the intention in their deployment). In other words, in Figure 8.1, the arrows

Figure 8.1: Multiple layers of hashing offer multiple layers of cryptographic security

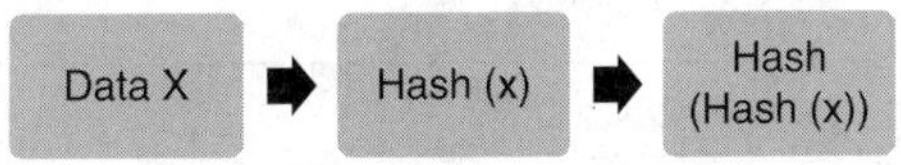

113 Yaga et al, n 110, 19–22.

can only point to the right; they cannot be reversed. Even knowing Hash(x) and part of x, it is still very hard to arrive at the entirety of x. More precisely, it is computationally possible but practically not feasible to find the input that maps to a particular hash: "If a particular output is desired, many inputs must be tried by passing them through the hash function until an input is found that produces the desired result."[114] So, although not impossible, this would require far greater computing power than is readily available today, but one that may be an issue when quantum computing with high q-bits becomes a reality.

Similarly, it is not entirely accurate to describe each hash as unique, but for most non-technical people's purposes, it is safe to think of hashes as unique identifiers. At its most basic, this nuance again comes down to the fact that there is an infinite number of possible inputs (in other words, the "x" in Figure 8.1 can be absolutely anything, from a single typographical character to a film, image, document or collections of any or all of these arranged in any order or way) and a finite number of possible output values (rendered finite by the fact that the algorithm is programmed to yield a fixed length result). It is computationally possible but "infeasible to find two or more inputs that produce the same output".[115] The rarity with which this might occur make it very unlikely to cause disruption.[116] In this way, hashes are considered "collision resistant".

Data x will always render the same hash when the algorithm is applied; in Figure 8.1, this means that the exact same x (irrespective of what "x" is, whether a single typographical character to a film, image, document or collections of any or all of these arranged in any order or way) will always produce exactly the same hash. Thus, while hash functions are computations that are difficult to solve, their solutions, once computed, are easy to verify as correct. If two hashes are the same, pragmatically speaking, the data underpinning those hashes is identical. This means that any differences are immediately apparent, because any change, no matter how consequential, to x, will yield a different hash. Even deleting one single word from a 300-page long book or changing one number in a decade's worth of financial records would yield a different hash. Returning to the land register example offered at the start of this section, suppose an error occurs in manually recording the transfer of a particular parcel of land. In early records, the parcel is recorded as comprising 20.02 hectares. At a subsequent point in the chain of title, a typographical error is made depicting the area as 20.20. Graphically, the problem looks like this, with the dotted line representing the point of error:

---

114 Yaga et al, n 110, 12.

115 Yaga et al, n 110.

116 Yaga et al, n 110.

Figure 8.2: Sample property transfer chain

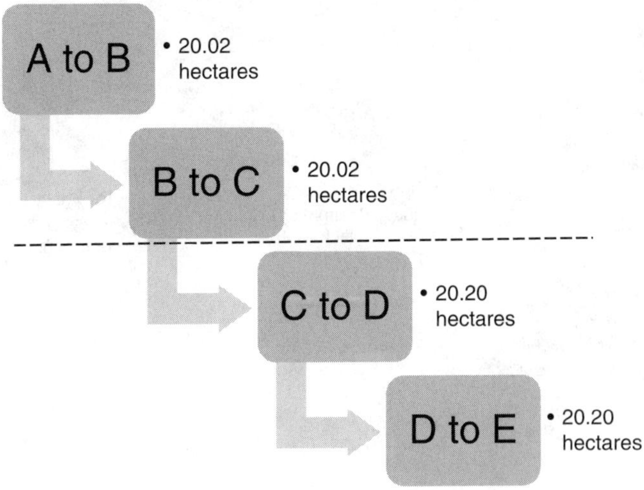

Figure 8.2 illustrates the "chain" aspect of blockchains, which "are comprised of blocks, each block being a group of transactions". A "transaction" records "a transfer of assets (digital currency, units of inventory, etc) between parties".[117] For each block, the hash serves as a "fingerprint".[118] Each block contains the cryptographic hash of the previous block. A new hash is created for and recorded in the current block; this hash will be recorded within the next block in the chain. "Over time, each block is then chained to the previous block in the chain by adding the hash of the previous block to the header of the current block."[119] This is illustrated in Figure 8.3.

"Anyone with the same list of transactions can generate the exact same 'fingerprint'."[120] In other words, anyone with the record of Transactions 1, 2 and 3 can generate the same "fingerprint" needed to create the next block, Transaction 4, in the chain of Figure 8.3. "New blocks are replicated across all copies of the ledger within the network, and any conflicts are resolved automatically using established rules."[121] These multiple copies give the distributed nature of blockchain technology, eliminating the need for one single authority to maintain one single, authoritative ledger.

117 Yaga et al, n 110, 13.

118 Yaga et al, n 110.

119 Yaga et al, n 110, 9.

120 Yaga et al, n 110, 13.

121 Yaga et al, n 110, 50.

Figure 8.3: Blockchain is a series of blocks linked together in a chain

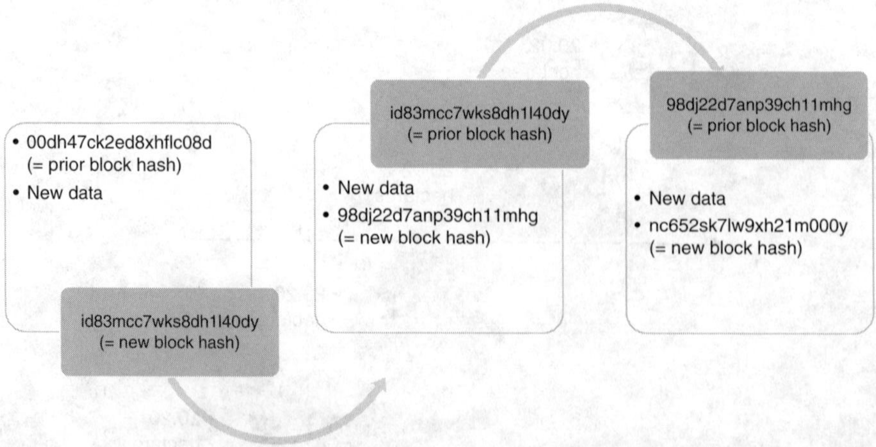

The integration of the previous block's hash, its digital fingerprint, so to speak, into each new block makes it extremely difficult to change historical data in a blockchain system because a change in one block does not simply change that block, but rather assigns a new hash to every block after it. Suppose in Figure 8.1 the ledger above Party B's name were later changed. In a hard copy ledger, such a change would have no impact on subsequent entries mentioning B's name. In a blockchain system, retrospectively changing B's name in the first transaction between A and B would yield a different hash. That differing hash would not then match up with the original hash's use at the header of the block of data documenting the transaction from B to C. The change to the historical record breaks, or invalidates, the chain from the point of change.[122]

While a single centralised authority (the government that manages the land register, for example) can make a one-off change to the single, authoritative record book or database, blockchain's distributed nature means that the participants in the network must agree that such a change is valid, and all of the distributed copies of the ledger must be updated to match. Thus, "[a]t its most basic level, [blockchains] enable a community of users to record transactions in a ledger public to that community such that no transaction can be changed once published".[123]

122 Yaga et al, n 110, 23.

123 Yaga et al, n 110, ii.

The most common present usage of blockchain technology is in cryptocurrency, the most popular of which at this time is Bitcoin. The very first application of blockchain technology was not, however, in a monetary context, but a legal one, in the form of an "electronic ledger for digitally signing documents in a way that could easily show none of the signed documents in the collection had been changed".[124] The disrupting potential of blockchain in the law and legal system is evident from its authentication capabilities. The risk of human error is almost entirely mitigated, and blockchain's distributed nature adds far more security, reliability and accessibility than human-managed central systems can offer. This gives rise to deeply philosophical questions as to the merits of perpetuating existing, inefficient, error-prone legal mechanisms and systems versus devising an entirely new construct (such as property rights) from scratch. Nick Szabo, the originator of the "smart contract" concept,[125] acknowledged the high cost of replacing such ancient systems as contract and property law and rather saw blockchain's potential in leveraging common law's longstanding norms and principles.[126] This still begs the question of the role of human lawyers in such a paradigm.

Will blockchain replace lawyers?

What about a short definition of blockchain?

[8.120] Blockchain is the technology that sits behind a new kind of database called a distributed ledger. It gives us a much more secure way to store and manage data. Data is shared across a network, and everyone in the network has their own identical copy of it. If anyone changes the data, it shows up in all the copies within minutes, or even seconds. That makes it more difficult to attack a blockchain database than a single one, where the data is all in one place. It's also harder to tamper with the data, because the members of the blockchain network will immediately spot a change to one part of the database.[127] Blockchain – a peer-to-peer network that sits on top of the internet – was introduced in October 2008 as part of a proposal for bitcoin, a virtual currency system that eschewed a central authority for issuing currency,

124 Yaga et al, n 110, 9.

125 N Szabo, "Smart Contracts: Building Blocks for Digital Markets" (25 January 1996) <http://www.truevaluemetrics.org/DBpdfs/BlockChain/Nick-Szabo-Smart-Contracts-Building-Blocks-for-Digital-Markets-1996-14591.pdf>.

126 Szabo, n 125.

127 See <https://www.pwc.co.uk/industries/entertainment-media/insights/blockchain-recording-music-industry.html>.

transferring ownership and confirming transactions. Bitcoin is the first application of blockchain technology.[128] A distributed database that maintains a continuously growing list of ordered records, called "blocks".[129]

Foundational to blockchain technology is the absence of a trusted, centralised authority. In financial transactions, as in legal transactions, the elimination of a middleman can save both time and money. This has undeniable attraction in a global economy recovering from a pandemic. In theory, anywhere the legal system operates as a single source of verification, authentication or validation could be supplanted by blockchain technology; in some, but not all, areas of the law, this transition obviate the need for human involvement entirely or nearly entirely. Stock exchanges,[130] energy exchanges[131] and intellectual property rights registers[132] are prime examples of early adopters in this field. Here, each transfer of a legal right from one party to another is recorded in a block; reliability comes from the record being fully transparent, replicated and dispersed across a network.

The possibilities for industries plagued by counterfeits are likewise significant. Some analysts predict that the music industry will be run entirely on blockchain technology.[133] Recall that hash functions compress data into a set-size identifier: each transfer of a song, or a collection of songs (what might be released as an album, or an entire catalogue) can be recorded in a blockchain, giving artists or producers greater control in policing the integrity and authenticity of their work. The film industry similarly stands to benefit as it too shifts to the internet as a primary mode of distribution. Blockchain is not a silver bullet against piracy, but it can be used to manage the distribution chain – in the same way that it can record the transfer of physical goods in a logistics chain from producer to transporters to retail store. Further, and

---

128 See <https://hbr.org/2017/01/the-truth-about-blockchain/>.

129 See <https://hbr.org/2017/02/a-brief-history-of-blockchain?ab=at_art_art_1x1>.

130 See, for example, "About CHESS Replacement", *ASX* <https://www2.asx.com.au/markets/clearing-and-settlement-services/chess-replacement/about-chess-replacement>.

131 See, for example, M Andoni et al, "Blockchain Technology in the Energy Sector: A Systematic Review of Challenges and Opportunities" (2019) 100 *Renewable and Sustainable Energy Reviews* 143.

132 See, for example, M Burn, "CWS/6 IP Australia's Blockchain Initiatives", *World Intellectual Property Organization* (2018) <https://www.wipo.int/edocs/mdocs/classifications/en/cws_6/cws_6_item_5b_ip_australia.pdf>.

133 "Blockchain: Recording the Music Industry", *PWC* <https://www.pwc.co.uk/industries/entertainment-media/insights/blockchain-recording-music-industry.html>.

perhaps more valuable in the fight against pirates, the presence or absence of a blockchain can help service providers to quickly distinguish authorised from unauthorised content.

Such applications of blockchain technology enhance the legal service offering rather than supplant the lawyer's function, but a natural consequence of increased accuracy, transparency and reliability in transactions is ultimately fewer legal disputes. Herein lies the existential threat to lawyers and the legal profession. So-called smart contracts automate both the creation and execution of obligations: computer code stored in a blockchain system automatically executes all or parts of an agreement on the satisfaction of specified terms (eg, triggering payment of funds after a particular action, or exacting a penalty if a particular action is not done by a designated time).[134] The code may constitute the entirety of the agreement between the parties, or it may be used in conjunction with a traditional contract to execute certain of its terms. In this paradigm, contract drafting work can be subsumed in computer programming, while downstream dispute resolution work is minimised by the automated nature of contract execution. Human lawyering is not rendered obsolete, but rather more specialised, much as Susskind predicted[135] at the turn of the 21st century when he wrote: "Getting contracts right at the outset will become more important than recovery when things go wrong, and lawyers will be a vital part of that process."[136] Rather than read documents, tomorrow's lawyers may spend their days reading code. Perhaps much greater than replacing lawyers, therefore, is the potential for blockchain to replace legal infrastructure, as in the mechanics of contract enforcement.

Blockchain may also soon replace the infrastructure that underpins the provision of legal services, such as records management and billing systems. Some lawyers and law firms even accept cryptocurrencies as payment, prompting at least one US state bar to develop ethics guidance on the topic.[137] The tax and trust-based accounting implications of cryptocurrencies must also

---

134 S D Levi and A B Lipton, "An Introduction to Smart Contracts and Their Potential and Inherent Limitations", *Harvard Law School Forum on Corporate Governance* (26 May 2018) <https://corpgov.law.harvard.edu/2018/05/26/an-introduction-to-smart-contracts-and-their-potential-and-inherent-limitations/>.

135 See Susskind, n 10, 274–276.

136 Muve Media & Marketing, "Five Ways Blockchain Will Change the Legal Profession", *LawDonut* (2 December 2020) <https://www.lawdonut.co.uk/business/blog/20/12/five-ways-blockchain-will-change-legal-profession>.

137 J M McCauley et al, "Is It Ethical for Lawyers to Accept Bitcoins and Other Cryptocurrencies?" (2018) 23(3) *North Carolina State Bar Journal* 36.

be navigated. An early market entrant in this space is Ethereum, the enterprise behind the world's second-largest value[138] cryptocurrency, the "ether" or ETH. An enterprise-focused version of the Ethereum system is marketed as "alleviat[ing] labor-intensive manual processes while providing increased accessibility, transparency, cost savings, speed, efficiency and data integrity to the legal industry".[139]

Those with clients in sectors farther along the blockchain adoption curve, such as finance and energy, will need to skill up more quickly in order provide competent, commercially appropriate advice. Initiatives such as the Singapore Intellectual Property Office's 2018 announcement that it would expedite the patent grant process for inventions using blockchain to facilitate banking payments[140] are aimed at spurring development in this field, and will have a corresponding impact on clients' expectations of their intellectual property lawyers. So too will national intellectual property offices shift to blockchain systems to manage internet protocol (IP) rights recordation. As with AI, what this means is that lawyers' professional obligations will increasingly demand not just familiarity with but competence in this technology.

The future internet

[8.130] Is today's internet up to the task of revolutionising the legal profession through AI, blockchain and other nascent technologies? Recent proposals envisioning a new internet from a group within the International Telecommunications Union (ITU), the specialised UN agency dealing with information and communication technologies, suggest not. The ITU-T Focus Group Technologies for Network 2030 (FG NET-2030) was established in July 2018 to explore the "capabilities of networks for the year 2030 and beyond".[141] The principal output of the group, which concluded its work in mid-2020, is a proposal called "New IP" developed by Chinese telecommunications company Huawei (and its subsidiary Futurewei[142]), which reportedly "sent

---

138 See R Browne, "The World's Second-Biggest Cryptocurrency Is Getting a Major Upgrade – Here's What You Need to Know", *CNBC* (1 December 2020) <https://www.cnbc.com/2020/12/01/ethereum-2point0-eth-cryptocurrencys-network-starts-a-major-upgrade.html>.

139 "Blockchain in the Legal Industry", *Consensys* <https://consensys.net/blockchain-use-cases/law/>.

140 "Acceleration Programmes", *Intellectual Property Office of Singapore* <https://www.ipos.gov.sg/protect-ip/apply-for-a-patent/accelerated-programmes>.

141 "Focus Group on Technologies for Network 2030", *ITU* <https://www.itu.int/en/ITU-T/focusgroups/net2030/Pages/default.aspx>.

142 A Durand, "New IP", *ICANN* (Report, 27 October 2020) <https://www.icann.org/en/system/files/files/octo-017-27oct20-en.pdf>.

the largest delegation of any company" to present the proposal behind closed doors at the ITU in September 2019.[143]

From the scant information publicly disclosed and accessible on the New IP proposal, it is clear that its creators are looking well beyond near-future technologies such as AI and blockchain, both of which already place quite significant demands on computing power and infrastructure. The future, says Huawei, will demand so much more than these nascent technologies already require.[144] "There's a new paradigm", explains Bilel Jamoussi, the head of the ITU's study groups; "it's not voice and text and video and people chatting, it's the real-time controlling of something remotely, or having telepresence, or holograms … . Those new applications are requiring new solutions. And now it's more feasible, it's no longer science fiction, it's close to being a reality".[145] Notably, the Network 2030 study appears to have begun from a pre-determined conclusion that the current internet is not capable of supporting this future reality. It set out "to answer specific questions on what kinds of network architecture and the enabling mechanisms are suitable for such novel scenarios"[146] and presupposed the need for "a new or refined network architecture to carry information in a manner that may evolve from, or is quite different from today's networks".[147] With this as a starting point, it should not come as a surprise that the "New IP presentation paints a picture of a digital world in 2030 where virtual reality, holographic communication and remote surgery are ubiquitous – and for which our current network is unfit."[148] The natural corollary of this is that what is proposed is a radical re-start from scratch rather than a more modest program of improvements.

This final section of the chapter offers a glimpse of New IP and the arguments made for and against it. This discussion is relatively limited, because so little about the proposal has been publicly disclosed. From the law's perspective, the most immediate questions arise around the governance of this proposed new internet. Huawei states that the New IP proposal is not about governance,[149]

143 See "Focus Group on Technologies for Network 2030", n 141.

144 M Murgia and A Gross, "Inside China's Controversial Mission to Reinvent the Internet", *Financial Times* (28 March 2020) <https://www.ft.com/content/ba94c2bc-6e27-11ea-9bca-bf503995cd6f>.

145 Murgia and Gross, n 144.

146 See "Focus Group on Technologies for Network 2030", n 141.

147 "Focus Group on Technologies for Network 2030", n 141.

148 See Murgia and Gross, n 144.

149 "A Brief Introduction about New IP Research Initiative", *Huawei* <https://www.huawei.com/au/industry-insights/innovation/new-ip>.

but numerous technology experts who have reviewed the documentation disagree.[150] The chapter thus ends with speculation about the future of internet governance, and the law and lawyers' place in that future.

New IP for lawyers

[8.140] The New IP (as in internet protocol) proposal itself remains mostly secret; "there appear to be no publicly available, specific design documents describing the New IP architecture".[151] Much of what was initially disclosed about New IP came to the public's attention through a *Financial Times* article that makes reference to "a simple PowerPoint"[152] that:

> didn't bother with much detail on how this new network would work, or what specific problem it was solving. Instead, it was peppered with images of futuristic technologies, from life-size holograms to self-driving cars. The idea was to illustrate that the current internet is a relic that has reached the limits of its technical prowess. It was time, Huawei proposed, for a new global network with a top-down design, and the Chinese should be the ones to build it.[153]

Subsequently published blogs and analyses by incumbent technical standardisation bodies still offer only a limited sense of why or how New IP proposes to provide an alternative to today's internet. Importantly, many of the most fundamental design principles of both AI and blockchain technology draw from those same fundamental design principles of today's internet, including the notion of distributed, decentralised control and interoperability. Leaving control to the next and final section of this chapter, as to interoperability, Huawei maintains that New IP preserves and improves this. A burgeoning view within the Internet Society, a non-profit organisation founded by many of the internet's early innovators, disagrees: "Developing a new protocol system is likely to create multiple non-interoperable networks, defeating one of the main purposes of developing the new protocol architecture."[154] Fundamentally, they question whether New IP is a solution in need of a problem, and whether that orphan solution creates new problems of stability and security.[155] Herein lies yet more circular logic, in that the New IP presentation purportedly

---

150 See, for example, H Sharp and O Kolkman, "Discussion Paper: An Analysis of the 'New IP' Proposal to the ITU-T", *Internet Society* (24 April 2020) <https://www.internetsociety.org/resources/doc/2020/discussion-paper-an-analysis-of-the-new-ip-proposal-to-the-itu-t/>.

151 See Durand, n 142, 11.

152 Murgia and Gross, n 144.

153 Murgia and Gross, n 144.

154 Sharp and Kolkman, n 150.

155 Sharp and Kolkman, n 150.

describes extant internet protocols as having "lots of security, reliability and configuration problems".[156]

So what, exactly, is New IP, and how does it differ from what we have today? We know that New IP offers a radically new internet architecture, and that this new architecture is intended to address the following three purportedly extant challenges:

- Firstly, due to historical reasons, the current network is designed for only two kinds of devices: telephones and computers. [...][The] development of [Internet of Things] and the industrial internet will introduce more types of devices into the future network.
- Secondly, the current network system risks becoming "islands", which should be avoided.
- Thirdly, security and trust still need to be enhanced.[157]

Taken together, these purported problems suggest that the current network cannot deliver data packets with sufficient speed, volume or accuracy required to, for example, populate a city's streets with driverless cars or have a conversation via hologram. Critically, where today's internet addressing system is fixed, New IP improves speed through a "dynamic address system" which "would allow for devices on the same network to communicate with each other without having to go through the internet".[158]

New IP also focuses on the concept of ManyNets to embrace the so-called Internet of Things, meaning the billions of "smart" devices around the world that are connected to the internet. "ManyNets refers to the myriad heterogeneous access networks with which the proposed new system needs to interconnect."[159] In this way, New IP is premised on impending disaster in the anticipated one trillion devices being connected to the internet in 2035.[160] While today's internet architects acknowledge that more than 60,000 of these independent network "islands" currently exist, "each making its

156 Murgia and Gross, n 144.

157 Sharp and Kolkman, n 150.

158 C Tonkin, "China and Huawei Want to Rebuild the Internet: Propose 'New IP' that Will Be Better Suited for Holograms", *ACS* (31 March 2020) <https://ia.acs.org.au/article/2020/china-and-huawei-want-to-rebuild-the-internet.html>. See also Sharp and Kolkman, n 150 (analysing the proposed "flexible length address space").

159 Sharp and Kolkman, n 150.

160 "A Brief Introduction about New IP Research Initiative", n 149, citing "Realizing 2030: Future of Connected Living", *Dell Technologies* <https://www.delltechnologies.com/en-us/perspectives/future-of-living.htm>.

own technology choices to serve its customers/users and interconnecting using interdomain routing protocols and bilateral agreements", they attribute interconnectivity problems to "non-technical business, accounting and policy reasons" that cannot be solved by a new technical protocol.[161]

In response, the Internet Society points to various efforts within existing internet standardisation bodies such as the Internet Engineering Task Force (IETF) and Institute of Electrical and Electronics Engineers (IEEE) to resolve the upscaling challenges of the existing internet. They argue that "[p]roposals for new protocol systems and architectures should definitively show why the existing work is not sufficient", and question why Network 2030's proponents have not engaged with these efforts.[162] It seems unlikely, despite Huawei's assertions,[163] that it will engage with these existing standards bodies and their longstanding consensus-based models; the timeline – which anticipated an initial rollout for testing in the second half of 2021[164] – leaves little room for traditional, time-consuming, iterative, consensus-based standards development.

Some ITU members have publicly expressed grave reservations.[165] If these grow, they may impede internal consensus within the ITU, which is "based loosely on majority agreement. If the delegates are unable to agree, the proposal will go to a closed-door vote in which only member countries can participate, cutting out the views of industry and civil society".[166] Therein lies what is for

---

161 Sharp and Kolkman, n 150.

162 Sharp and Kolkman, n 150. See also M Hogewoning, "Update on WTSA-20 Preparations and New IP", *RIPE Network Communication Centre* (10 November 2020) <https://labs.ripe.net/Members/marco_hogewoning/update-on-wtsa-20-preparations-and-new-ip>.

163 "A Brief Introduction about New IP Research Initiative", n 149 ("Hundreds of high-level researchers from academia and industry in dozens of regions, including China, Europe, Japan, South Korea, North America, South America, and Africa, proposed future-oriented business visions and requirements with a focus on driving the wider societal digitalization through Internet technologies. We believe that the New IP initiative follows this tradition to the point through engaging with key international research communities to explore the space of possibilities to evolve IP technologies, while engaging with standardization organization to derive the requirements driving the evolution and ultimately agreeing on common solutions. In this, work in bodies such as the ITU Network 2030 focus group addresses the requirements, while our existing as well as future engagement with SDOs, such as IETF, ITU, ETSI, and others on a number of New IP solutions shows the integration into the consensus process the Internet community has established over time.").

164 Murgia and Gross, n 144.

165 See, for example, Murgia and Gross, n 144; International Communication Union, "Comments on the Proposed Questions for New IP" (7 July 2020) <https://www.itu.int/md/T17-SG13-C-0915/en>.

166 Murgia and Gross, n 144.

many the most suspect aspect of New IP: its shift away from "the 'open and adaptable nature' of the internet – both its technical structure and how it is governed" – which takes us to the final topic of discussion in this chapter.

The future internet and lawyers' role in its governance

[8.150] The theoretical framework and governance of the internet is a mix of good will, such as domain name addressing, and jurisdictional regulation, and thus should be the starting point for evaluating the most radical and controversial aspect of the New IP proposal. Suffice it to say here that the internet's early architects saw the continued development and success of their creation contingent on keeping it in their own hands, unencumbered by slow, intergovernmental bodies. The story of the design of the internet's architecture is one in which the principal players were non-government actors, mainly university researchers and private corporations. When faced with the prospect of handing over the reins to a UN body that could make decisions without even consulting them or their being present in the room, quite understandably they actively worked to find another governance model.

Given that there is no single international internet regulator, arguably what we have is not so much a governance model but a confederation of standards bodies.[167] It is this that fuels popular media claims that control over the internet "is largely held by a handful of US corporations – Apple, Google, Amazon, Facebook".[168] Any model that involves civil society, of which in particular the technical innovators with the knowhow and vision to evolve the internet, will inevitably include these large corporate players with their correspondingly large budgets. Imagine, by contrast, a world in which the internet is run by non-technically skilled diplomats in Geneva. This must have been the internet's early architects' worst nightmare.

While they may not have had much greater faith in lawyers' ability to resist wrecking or slowing down their creation, the internet architects, with the backing of the US government, nevertheless supported the establishment of various private sector-led standards bodies in which lawyers have not only had access but actively participated and contributed. Far from being excluded, in the Internet Corporation for Assigned Names and Numbers (ICANN), for example,

167 There are many excellent comprehensive studies of internet governance, including M L Mueller, *Networks and States: The Global Politics of Internet Governance* (MIT Press, 2010); R Radu, J-M Chenou and R H Weber (eds), *The Evolution of Global Internet Governance: Principles and Policies in the Making* (Springer, 2014); L DeNardis, *Global Internet Governance* (Routledge, 2018).

168 Murgia and Gross, n 144.

lawyers sit alongside technologists in policy making and hold senior leadership roles.[169] Government representatives are invited to participate, but they are not the ultimate decision-makers in ICANN's bottom-up, multi-stakeholder, consensus-based model. This, not secret proposals offered behind closed doors in Geneva, is the essence of today's internet governance framework.

The internet functions without a centralised authority thanks to its most foundational concept, open architecture networking:

> In this approach, the choice of any individual network technology was not dictated by a particular network architecture but rather could be selected freely by a provider and made to interwork with the other networks through a meta-level "Internetworking Architecture". ... In an open-architecture network, the individual networks may be separately designed and developed and each may have its own unique interface which it may offer to users and/or other providers, including other internet providers. Each network can be designed in accordance with the specific environment and user requirements of that network. There are generally no constraints on the types of network that can be included or on their geographic scope, although certain pragmatic considerations will dictate what makes sense to offer.[170]

Some interpret New IP, which appears to propagate "a patchwork of national internets, each with its own rules"[171] ("Any country will be free to adopt it."[172]) as a radical course change from this foundational principle. They base this assessment on Project 2030's explicit reference to "top-to-bottom design" and its emphasis on "data-sharing schemes across governments".[173]

Consequently, it is reported that "[m]any experts fear that under New IP, internet service providers, usually state-owned, would have control and oversight of every device connected to the network and be able to monitor and gate individual access".[174] Such control and oversight unquestionably advances China's interest in "cyber sovereignty".[175] Content developers would

169 See, for example, T Little, "'Milestone' Election of IP Constituency Member to Lead ICANN's GNSO Council Announced", *World Trademark Review* (2 November 2017) <https://www.lexology.com/library/detail.aspx?g=dff6fc1a-3648-46b1-ba78-39b18ec1378c>.

170 Sharp and Kolkman, n 150.

171 Murgia and Gross, n 144.

172 Murgia and Gross, n 144.

173 Murgia and Gross, n 144.

174 Murgia and Gross, n 144.

175 Murgia and Gross, n 144.

also be brought into this new regulatory web by "mandating the reporting and tracking of all users' identities (in fact, the identities of all users browsing free content) and activities in order to get authorization to provide content and services".[176] Ironically, "the rise of online surveillance" is one of several justifications for a radically new internet and governance model.[177]

As noted above, Huawei vigorously rejects the suggestion that New IP deals with internet governance at all. Rather, its stated intention is to be a "technology study initiative".[178] Further, Huawei acknowledges the tradition of civil society's participation and claims to follow it by "engaging with key international research communities to explore the space of possibilities to evolve IP technologies, while engaging with standardization organization [sic] to derive the requirements driving the evolution and ultimately agreeing on common solutions".[179] These sentiments are difficult to square with assertions in early 2020 that "the blueprints" for New IP "have already been drawn up, and construction is under way".[180] Detailed technical analyses by internet standards bodies[181] likewise seem to review something far closer to a finished product than a work in progress.

Those who consider today's internet to be "deeply flawed, if not broken"[182] are welcome in the discussion rooms and threads of the IETF, IEEE and ICANN. Their active contributions to the internet's future development are encouraged by and in those bodies. The secretive origins of New IP and its behind closed doors publication do not bode well for the future of lawyers or indeed civil society in its version of the future internet.

Conclusion

[8.160] There is much that could be said about a possible global technocracy or whether the impacts of the last two years will have lasting change. It is

176 Durand, n 142, 26.

177 Murgia and Gross, n 144.

178 "A Brief Introduction about New IP Research Initiative", n 149.

179 "A Brief Introduction about New IP Research Initiative", n 149.

180 Murgia and Gross, n 144.

181 See, for example, Durand, n 142; IETF, "Liaison Statement on New IP, Shaping Future Network" (30 September 2019) <https://datatracker.ietf.org/liaison/1653/>.

182 Murgia and Gross, n 144, quoting J Griffiths, *The Great Firewall of China: How to Build and Control an Alternative Version of the Internet* (Zed Books, 2019).

clear that the disassociation aspects, where people are further distanced from in-person interactions, will have ongoing social influence.[183] Other changes are less certain: will working from home become a new norm? Will education move online? Will technology be required for simply day-to-day tasks such as shopping at the supermarket for cheese? These influences will be a fundamental change to how we live, certainly in developed nations.

183 "Overall, this Review suggests that the psychological impact of quarantine is wideranging, substantial, and can be long lasting." S K Brooks et al, "The Psychological Impact of Quarantine and How to Reduce It: Rapid Review of the Evidence" (2020) 395 *The Lancet* 912.

Table of Cases

S

T

V

W

Y

Z

Table of Statutes

Commonwealth

Australian Capital Territory

New South Wales

Northern Territory

Queensland

South Australia

Tasmania

Victoria

Western Australia

European Union

France

United Kingdom

United Nations

United States

Convention

Index

E

J

L